The Best of Benson

A Twenty-year Anthology of Sports Writing

By Lee Benson

SHADOW MOUNTAIN®

Photograph credits: Page xi—John Stockton and Karl Malone by *Deseret News*/Tom Smart. Page 5—Magic Johnson by *Deseret News*/O.Wallace Kasteler. Page 33—Jim McMahon by AP/John Swart. Page 67—Arnold Palmer by UPI/Ray Foli. Page 109—Gene Fullmer by *Deseret News*/Howard C. Moore. Page 133—Larry Bird by *Deseret News*/Garry Bryant. Page 157—Henry Marsh by *Deseret News*/Tom Smart. Page 189—BYU's, Mike Smith and U of U's Mitch Smith by *Deseret News*/Ravell Call. Page 241—Alma Richards by *Deseret News*. Page 261—Prince Charles and Lady Diana by AP. Page 273—Homeless in Pioneer Park by *Deseret News*/Garry Bryant. Page 285—Lee and Dee Benson by Don Blair.

Library of Congress Cataloging-in-Publication Data
Benson, Lee, 1948-
    The best of Benson : a 20-year anthology of sports writing / Lee Benson.
        p.   cm.
    Includes index.
    ISBN 1-57345-417-6 (pbk.)
    1. Sports.   2. Sports—United States.   3. Sports—Utah.
    4. Deseret News (Salt Lake City, Utah : 1964)   5. Benson, Lee, 1948-
    I. Title.
    GV707.B446   1998
    796'.0973—dc21   98-29420
                                                                            CIP

Printed in the United States of America

10   9   8   7   6   5   4   3   2   1   72082 - 6417

To Eric,
who made it all
a good time

I guess that's the kind
of place this is.

—THE MIGHTY QUINN

Contents

BIG NAMES

TRIBUTES

PEOPLE AND PLACES

HUMAN DRAMA

COMMENTARIES

MAGAZINE LENGTH ARTICLES

SIDE TRIPS

PERSONAL FAVORITES

LIFE AFTER SPORTS

Acknowledgments

First of all, I concede that unearthing a bunch of your old columns, compiling them, and calling that a book is a literary cheap shot.

I would also like to acknowledge the entire staff, from the board of directors to back shop to management to accounting (thanks Mary), at the *Deseret News,* circa the latter half of the twentieth century—especially the sports writers—who, besides greatly sharpening my "garbage-ball" skills, have had, and continue to have, a tremendous influence on me. I have nothing but respect and admiration for: Linda Hamilton, Mike Sorensen, Dave Blackwell, Steve Schowengerdt, Kurt Kragthorpe, Gary Blodgett, Brent Checketts, Bill Ewer, George Ferguson (my first mentor), Dan "The Man" Pattison, Lee Warnick, Dave Kadleck, John Robinson, Rich Evans, Loren Jorgensen, Dirk Facer, and, most especially, my close column compadres Brad Rock and Doug Robinson. And also Ray Grass, the glue who always has and always will hold it all together and a Ute who to this day refuses to overlook the fact I graduated from BYU . . .

. . . None of whom have to take any responsibility whatever for this book.

Introduction

I didn't set out to be a sports writer. I didn't set out to be much of anything, other than employed. But there I was, an undergraduate at BYU in the 1970s, the beginning of the Me Decade, running out of majors and, worse, running out of excuses to spend my dad's money. Journalism! I hadn't tried that yet. I walked into the office of *The Daily Universe* one day and asked if I could write a story. The sports editor was R. C. Roberg, the first of thousands of fascinating characters I have since met in and through journalism. R. C. used Scotch™ Tape to keep his hair behind his ears. BYU had its standards. R. C. Roberg had his.

I was dispatched to the Smith Fieldhouse that night to "do a story" on a wrestling meet between, appropriately, BYU and Utah. I say appropriately because nothing has given me more material, or more enjoyment, over the past twenty years than Utah vs. BYU. Nothing. I love that rivalry. May it never die or enter detente.

At any rate, I discovered something with that innocuous wrestling assignment: I liked to write. Whether anyone would want to read what I wrote, well, that would be up to them. But I liked to write. It felt almost like recreation to me. A light went on. *And they pay you to do this!* The rest, if not exactly literary history, is my history.

I chose to write about sports because I like sports. I like to play them, I like to watch them, I like to read about them. It's never been an obsession with me. I wasn't one of those kids who memorized everybody's batting average and slugging percentage. I was no budding Thomas Boswell. But I always liked sports, even if I wasn't encyclopedic about it, and to this day the only iron-clad rule I have for writing is this: be interested in your subject matter and write what you like. Writing without passion is like cooking without salt.

Okay, that's as heavy as this is going to get. These are mostly sports columns, after all. But as you might note, there's not necessarily a lot of sports in them. Sports is just an excuse to write about people. Basically, *everything* is just an excuse to write about people.

I've been lucky. Writing has been very good to me. I happened to latch onto the sports writing wave just as it was emerging from Red Smith and moving into Rick Reilly. It was a big improvement, if you want my opinion, lifting sports writing out of the realm of the serious, the solemn, and the profound into the arena of pure entertainment. What a concept. We all owe a great debt to Jim Murray.

I started out at the *Deseret News* writing high school sports—a period I still look back on as one of the most enjoyable times of my life, although it did wear me out. I started writing a regular column in 1979, the year the Final Four came to Utah. I got a stiff neck before I wrote my first column. I turned in the shower and something popped. It was the pressure. Fortunately it got better—the neck and the pressure—but to this day there remains a certain amount of trepidation about putting yourself out there on public view on a regular basis, trying to avoid, at the very least, outright embarrassment.

Sports writing has taken me around the world. I've traveled on assignment to Japan, Korea, Scandinavia, all over Western Europe, Hawaii, Saudi Arabia, even Budapest. I think it's amazing how much has happened in twenty years. I've seen Utah get a national football champion, win the bid for the 2002 Olympic Winter Games, send a team to play in the NBA Finals, while the deer hunt has become just another weekend in the fall.

They called the 1920s the Golden Age of Sports. Well, the last twenty years have been the Transition Age of Sports. We've seen the proliferation of women's sports, the revival of the Olympic Games, a sonic boom in salaries, metal woods, aluminum bats, plutonium rackets, luxury boxes, the Senior Tour, pro sports teams in North Carolina, talk-radio, constantly rising ticket prices, and, overall, an increased interest in sports that is unrivaled by anything leisure man has ever known. I saw a scalper sell Super Bowl tickets in Atlanta for $2,500. Each. He sold out in five minutes, and walked back to his Benz thinking he should have asked more.

What follows is a compilation of columns and stories that span the last twenty years and thus chronicles, in a loose kind of way, the Transition Age we've all been a part of. Where else are you going to read about the Trappers' streak and the Nancy Kerrigan–Tonya Harding affair; about the day Karl

Malone got drafted and the day the Dream Team won gold in Spain; about the Bonneville Salt Flats and Centre Court at Wimbledon?

In addition to columns from my "sports years," I have also included a few columns that show there is life after sports, chronicling my personal transition into a general interest *Metro* columnist.

These columns and stories cover a diversity of topics, events, opinions, and commentaries. For each one, I've provided some background as to why I wrote the column, or how, or some other detail you may or may not find interesting. In the interest of timeliness and quality control, there has been some editing. Out of about three thousand columns written these past two decades, these are the ninety or so that made the cut. Makes you wonder what the others were like.

Big Deals

Magic & Bird, 1979
BYU Football No. 1, 1985
Drafting the Mailman, 1985
Streak City, 1987
Breaking Ground, 1990
Stockton & Malone, 1993
Winning the Bid, 1995
Losing the Bid, 1995
NBA Finals Welcome, 1997

This somewhat prescient column features the two stars of Salt Lake City's one and only Final Four, held at the Special Events (now Huntsman) Center on the University of Utah campus. Did these two guys go on to live up to their press hype or what? This was written when I was heavily under the influence of Los Angeles Times columnist Jim Murray, the master of metaphor, simile, and hyperbole. Reading it almost two decades later is a lot like looking at an old photo of myself, wearing a white belt and a three-inch shirt collar—a '70s fashion statement that remains to haunt me forever. Some things go out of style . . . although Bird and Magic never did.

Magic
and Bird

In the midst of basketball's power era, the day of the in-yo-face stuff, of power forwards and enforcers, along comes the NCAA tournament with a whole new twist. These finals are a passing fancy.

The best two players in the Final Four—the best, hands down—are a couple of guys who would rather set up a dunk than score one.

Earvin Johnson of Michigan State—the Magician—and Larry Bird of Indiana State aren't players, they're passing artists. Calling them a guard and a forward is like calling Rembrandt a painter and Beethoven a piano player. These guys didn't get where they are by just playing ball; what they're working at is perfection. They're playing the game like it's non-contact.

Their approach to basketball is "just passing through." They need a new statistic—passes attempted, passes completed. More than a few pros are worried about losing their jobs to these two, and some of them are quarterbacks.

With Johnson and Bird in the lineup, Michigan State and Indiana State don't have forwards and guards, they have wide receivers. They don't run motion offenses, they work out of the I-formation—with the center eligible.

Of course, the pass has always been part of the game. You always could throw it forward or backward or underhanded if you wanted to, and you've never needed to have a huddle first. But what Bird and Johnson are doing is revolutionary. They're making the pass something other than what you do when you're covered. They're developing an art form. A lot of players are wondering why they didn't think of it first.

There have been passers before, true, but what sets the Bird and Erv apart is that they really don't have to pass. Larry Bird is the second-best scorer in the country and a 14.5 per game rebounder besides. Earvin Johnson is a 16.5 ppg scorer and a 6-foot-8 guard who is never bothered going one-on-one. They can both dunk but they'd rather pass. The result has both their teams in the NCAA Final Four.

Not that Johnson and Bird are part of a passing plot—a conspiracy. Fact is, they could have arrived at this stage of their careers much differently. Bird, speaking of passing through, started college that way. A quiet, down-home kid out of French Lick, Indiana, he first chose to attend the University of Indiana—a relationship that lasted two weeks. He didn't much care for crowds.

He laid off a year before taking up Indiana State on its scholarship offer. Ever since, he and the Sycamores have been raising other people's eyebrows.

Johnson, just a sophomore, had no such transition problems. He moved out of high school and into college stardom in his and MSU's hometown of Lansing, Michigan, and it wasn't long before he was quieting the town's streets on game nights—as MSU's Jenson Fieldhouse started selling out to bands of fans who knew a good pass when they saw one.

Both Johnson and Bird turned down lucrative pro offers after last season, and both are rumored to be on their professional way after this season (Bird, a senior, for sure)—to the tune of maybe $3 million each—and both have been on every first team All-America ballot this season.

Clearly, the pass is paying off for this most celebrated and publicized NCAA Final Four twosome since West and Robertson (1959), Lucas and Havlicek (1962), Alcindor and Hayes (1967), and Walton and Thompson (1974). Every so often the NCAA comes up with these dynamic duos. This year it's a guy named Johnson who goes by "Magic" and a guy named Bird who goes by "Larry."

It's uncanny the way these two diverse personalities—the only thing they couldn't pass for is twins—have arrived at the Final Four simultaneously. Two players who looked at the game and decided the best way to improve on it was to give it an assist.

When the Brigham Young Cougars won their storybook national football title following
the 1984 season, the polls were released late on Wednesday afternoon,
January 2, 1985. LaVell Edwards, BYU's head coach, heard the news while sitting in
his car in the parking lot outside the football offices in Provo,
listening to KSL Radio.

BYU Football
No. 1

January 3, 1985

I f the world will now indulge us, we will exercise our bragging rights and
lay claim to the national football championship, however mythical, and
the attendant privilege of being proud, excited, thankful, thrilled, ecstatic, cel-
ebratory, overwhelmed, and maybe a little bit haughty, cocky, and obnoxious.

Humble, we'll save for later.

Go ahead, take the day off.

Take the week off.

It isn't every day the absolute best college football team in the world
comes from your home state.

Or every year.

Or every century.

There have been Utahns who have worn Super Bowl rings and NBA
championship rings and who have held national ski jump championships for
decades, and there have been Utahns who have held every land speed record
created and Utahns who have caught the biggest brown trout. There was a
Utahn who won an Olympic gold medal, a Utahn who was heavyweight
champion of the world, a Utahn who was middleweight champion of the
world, and a Utahn who beat Bobby Jones for the U.S. Amateur golf championship in 1926. Utah teams have ruled the college basketball world, in the

NCAA and NIT, and teams from Utah have been the national champs at skiing and golf and gymnastics.

But there has never been a Utah team crowned national football champion, not until now, not until Brigham Young's Wednesday night dubbing when the UPI Coaches' Poll and the AP Writers' Poll finally got together and made it unanimous: "B.Y. It's You," "Only You, BYU," "B.Y.You."

The rush of the moment suggests it's the greatest athletic accomplishment in the history of the state.

Okay, *you* tell them it isn't.

The arguments about a weak schedule and a weak league don't cut it around here. This was a team that beat every team it had to play, and then it beat the system, winning the title via a cable network in a bowl game nowhere near New Year's Day. You weren't supposed to be able to get there from here. The football establishment may never recover. For four months they laid traps for the Cougars, only to be foiled at the end, when Barry Switzer couldn't ruin anything, neither with his team, his mouth, or his vote.

BYU.

National Champion.

By a landslide.

Tell the White House the area code is 801.

Thirteen wins and zero losses did it. Nobody else came close. This was the year the title went west to the Rockies, way out to Provo, Utah. Number 4,789 in TV markets, but No. 1 in the polls, and in your hearts.

The best part was that it was a local production. This wasn't some road troupe out of Poughkeepsie or a bunch of mercenaries from France or a group of The Best Talent Money Could Import.

The coach was a native of Orem with a name as Utahn as any old LaRae or LaRue or LaVere or LaVerne. He coached high school ball in Salt Lake City and spent a decade waiting his turn as an assistant at BYU, where losing season after losing season impressed upon his defensive mind the need for the pass to come to pass. It was the LaVell Edwards' system of football, born and bred out of necessity in the Beehive State, that ultimately won the national crown, appropriately ousting the power ground game of Michigan and the wishbone ground game of Oklahoma in the doing.

And it was a team that was representative of its own student body that won the national title. Of the 112 players on BYU's year-ending Holiday Bowl roster, there were more Utahns (33) than anything else, and almost as many

Californians (28), reflecting similar proportions on the campus at-large. And the vast majority of players were Mormons, fifty-two of them returned missionaries, which isn't to glorify any particular way of life but to illustrate that the church that named, sponsors, and runs the school didn't sell its birthright, or its scholarships, for a national title.

It's a crown with the common touch, as easy to identify with as Mount Timpanogos or Mirror Lake or the Salt Flats or the Great White Throne. This one was for us, Utah, thanks to a bunch of overachievers from BYU who not only knew where they were going but where they were coming from.

In the summer of 1984, the Jazz had drafted a no-name point guard from Gonzaga named John Stockton; now they'd followed that by drafting an obscure power forward who was leaving Louisiana Tech a year early. What were these knuckleheads thinking?! Note the half-price deal on season "ducats" in the fourth paragraph. Those were the days.

Drafting the Mailman

Ignoring for a moment that Karl Malone, a young 6-foot-9 man from rural "Looziana," thought Utah was a town, the NBA draft went off with flying colors Tuesday—re-proving that in this day and age of peace and prosperity and sports obsessionism, even non-contact events like drafting can draw good audiences and decent ratings.

Live from New York City, the 1985 NBA Summer Draft came at us Tuesday, either to our living rooms or to the big screen in the Salt Palace over the WTBS Network.

Scores of people came to the Salt Palace at midday for the big show. Basketball zealots numbering between 3,000 and 7,000—the estimates varied—showed up, getting free hot dogs and the chance to watch Jazz officials buzzing around on the stage. When you get to this level, it takes a committee to choose up sides.

Both owners were on hand, the car dealer and the entrepreneur, as well as the coach, the general manager, the special consultant, the president, the assistant coaches, the public relations director, the office staff, and the entire season ticket sales force, who were in the back of the room offering half-price deals on '85–86 season ducats if you act now.

Amid this circus atmosphere, NBA commissioner David Stern appeared on the bigger-than-life TV screens at 11:15 A.M., mountain daylight time, to announce the draft was under way and, to no one's astonishment, that the New York Knickerbockers would begin by selecting Patrick Ewing of Georgetown. All seven feet of him.

Rick Barry, WTBS's penetrating commentator, asked Patrick if he will play pro ball without the T-shirt he wore in college.

"I will if I have to," said Patrick.

Barry next probed as to whether Patrick anticipated any problems with his contract.

"Talk to my lawyer," said Patrick.

On the other channel, *As the World Turns* was eating its heart out.

The best interview, and this wasn't Barry's fault, came when Dallas selected West German Detlef Schrempf as the No. 8 pick, and Schrempf said he wasn't thrilled with the prospects of living and playing in Texas and eating barbecue for the next few years of his life.

The intrigue built in the Salt Palace as Utah's No. 13 pick approached. Picking No. 13 isn't exactly can't-miss territory, but it isn't just a field bet either, and when the Washington Bullets took forward Kenny Green of Wake Forest as the No. 12 selection, the floor was the Jazz's. The 3,000 to 7,000 began shouting out their suggestions to the brain trust on the stage.

The overwhelming consensus among the hard-core, opinionated fans (excuse the redundancy) was that the Jazz select one Karl Malone of Louisiana Tech, a 6-foot-9, 250-pounder nicknamed "The Mailman"—because he delivers.

"Deliver us The Mailman, Frank," they chanted at Jazz coach/general manager Frank Layden.

Layden—the same man who stunned previous draft-day audiences chanting for their favorites by ignoring the advice and drafting such mystery men as Danny Schayes, Thurl Bailey, and John Stockton—took the mike and said, in his best ring announcer's voice, "The Utah Jazz are very happy to announce, we're gonna bring a MAILMAN TO UTAH!"

He had obliged.

The place went bonkers.

Myself, I'd never heard of The Mailman.

And he hadn't heard of Utah. Or at least he gave that impression when he got on the amplified Salt Palace telephone moments later with Hot Rod Hundley and said, "I want to do everything I can for the people and the town of Utah."

One day on the job, and he's already delivering—to the wrong address.

But we'll be seeing more of him, not to mention his lawyer, and soon enough he'll know the difference between Salt Lake City, Utah, and Summerville, Louisiana, population 400, his hometown. By edict of the NBA draft, Karl Malone is now Utah's property, and vice versa, and to toast that marriage, 3,000 to 7,000 zealots have already given him a rousing ovation.

A rookie league team made up of players cut, discarded, and otherwise cast off by the baseball establishment, the 1987 Salt Lake Trappers set an all-time professional record with 29 straight wins in the summer of 1987. This column was written following the 28th consecutive win, which set the new mark that would be broken a game later. Throughout the streak, as Derks Field sold out for the first time in anyone's memory, the team's players and coaches consistently downplayed its significance, insisting that winning the Pioneer League championship was what really mattered. In September, the '87 Trappers did win the title at Derks Field. Less than 5,000 people attended.

Streak City

The Salt Lake Trappers had their date with destiny Saturday night and of course the world tagged along. It isn't every night at the ballpark you have the chance to be a part of history.

Derks Field was under siege. On a normal night, the park is as spacious as Canyonlands. On this night, it looked like a compromise between a rock concert and a civil war.

Only twice before in the history of the world—or baseball, whichever came first—had a professional baseball team tried to win a 28th consecutive game. And the fact that neither the 1902 Corsicana (Texas) Oilers nor the 1921 Baltimore Orioles managed to pull it off didn't dissuade the masses from coming to see if the third time would be a charm.

This was the first try in sixty-six years.

To miss it would be like missing Halley's comet.

The 10,000-seat stadium was sold out by mid-afternoon. More than sold out, actually, since the Trappers had sold a number of passes at the start of the season, good for the night of the purchaser's choice, and a lot of the purchasers chose last night.

This caused Trappers general manager, Steve Pearson, a huge pregame mathematical headache, and he loved every ache of it.

Away from the "closed" signs on the ticket windows, the resultant seller's market created a phenomenon rarely if ever seen in front of Derks: a gathering of scalpers.

Suddenly, history had a price. Seats were still available, depending on if you had enough Andrew Jacksons with you. One ticket-holder was observed giving up his date with history for $150—for four, $4 box seat tickets.

Some fans, effectively shut out from buying tickets, improvised. The occasion called for it. The roof on the office building beyond left center field was filled to capacity. One fan took a red blanket fifty feet up the pine tree located beyond the left field wall and set up camp for the evening. Fifty years from now, he can tell his grandkids he was there, in that tree.

From as far away as New York City they were trying to get into the park. Radio station WFAN, the 24-hour-a-day sports station in Manhatttan, phoned just before game time. They wanted to hook into Randy Kerdoon's broadcast on local station K-TALK. Jim Dubakis, a K-TALK executive, was called out of the stands. He talked to WFAN. The radio station from the East wanted to know how much he'd charge. "I'm the world's worst negotiator," Dubakis said afterward. "I told them $500, and if they'd said no, I'd have said they could have it for free."

But they said yes. The night had history written all over it.

The Hall of Fame in Cooperstown also placed a call. They wanted dibs on the official scorebook. Dan Pattison, the official scorer, sharpened seven No. 2 pencils for the occasion and had a ballpoint pen at the ready, just in case.

Such was the atmosphere emanating from Derks on a night loaded with expectation. And on a night, as it turned out, well worth the buildup.

It was historic all right.

The Trappers, who had gotten into this position by winning their twenty-seven previous games, knew a set stage when they saw one. They scored two runs in the first inning, six more in the second, and cruised from there. John Groennert pitched eight of the best relief innings this side of the big leagues. The only ingredient the game lacked was suspense.

Which seemed to be fine with everybody there.

They rocked and rolled in the stands all night. When they did the wave, those on the office building roof joined in.

When Groennert got Pocatello's Glenn Abraham to strike out to end the game some three and a half hours after it started, it was all over but the curtain calls. There were three of them as the scoreboard flashed, "TRAPPERS IN HISTORY!"

The team strolled from baseline to baseline as PA announcer Mike Runge said, "In the history of baseball, there has never been a streak like this one."

The standing ovation lasted ten minutes. No one left. No one wanted to leave. They were enjoying the view too much, just as back in New York, they were enjoying the audio.

Getting into Derks Field Saturday night had turned out to be a bargain, whatever the price. Nobody was asking for a refund. History had been advertised, and history had been made.

It was a big day for Salt Lake City when Larry Miller put his gamble where skid row
was and began to build what would become the Delta Center. Yes,
the building did come in on time and under budget (officially checking in fifteen months
and twenty-four days later). And, yes, I'm still trying to figure out why
Donny Osmond was there.

Breaking
Ground

It was your typical ground-breaking ceremony scene. The people who would be collecting the interest were smiling, and the people who would be paying the interest were crying.

"Times like this, I tend to get emotional," said Larry H. Miller as he flicked away a tear. This is the one man in Utah who has an idea how the national debt feels.

This is a man whose credit rating is so good he can buy a basketball franchise for $20 million and then buy a 21,000-seat multi-purpose arena for another, oh, $66 million, by the time they paint the lines on the floor.

He pays more in interest than guys in New York who make their payments in paper bags to people named Louie.

Miller was feeling no strain yesterday, however, at the official ground-breaking ceremony of the new Jazz arena at South Temple and Fourth West. For one thing, more than a thousand people—most of whom sweat out making mortgage payments of a whole lot less each month—interrupted their lunch hour to give him a standing ovation.

For another thing, the interest on the loan doesn't begin accruing until July 1—when the project will collect its first draw of the $66 million. The first draw will be around $3 million. The interest will be a mere $1,000 a day.

It won't be until the late summer of 1991 that the interest will hit its peak—at $17,000 a day.

Or $708.33 an hour.

Or $11.80 a minute.

Which is why the Japanese gentlemen seated on the dais yesterday looked so radiant.

A Japanese bank—Sumitomo Trust—agreed to loan Miller the $66 million. Their officials were on hand, making sure there really is a Fourth West & South Temple in Salt Lake City and that Larry H. Miller honest to goodness exists. Mr. Kaneaki Hori of Sumitomo Trust spoke, saying, "We realize the significance of this project to the city and state." He didn't specify which country.

For some reason, Miller couldn't find a lender in America. Only when he went to the land that made him his first fortune—by selling him their Toyotas—did he find someone who would lend him another fortune.

In case you missed yesterday's ceremonies, a collection of politicians stood up to speak and applaud the project, and entertainer Donny Osmond stood up to adjust his shades. Why Osmond was there, no one was quite sure, including the Soldier of Love himself, who said he'd heard "Larry Miller is a good man," explained that he doesn't live in Utah anymore, and added that he'd "like to be able to do a concert in this building."

As the festivities went on, there was a haunting presence from across the street, where the Triad Center sits, a shell of its original projection. In a similar ground-breaking ceremony not many years prior, Saudi Arabian billionaire Adnan Khashoggi, who recently spent some jail time in New York, talked of grandiose plans for the Triad Center—and then he sailed off in a yacht to sell arms to the Iranians and forgot he'd ever been in Utah.

This history was not lost on master of ceremonies/Jazz president Frank Layden—not a lot is lost on Layden—who interrupted the chain of politician's speeches to read a telegram.

"It says, 'Congratulations on the new arena. I've been detained in New York,'" Layden began, "'Please give my best to all my friends in Utah. If you need additional money please call.'" It's signed . . . Adnan Khashoggi."

Everyone laughed. Even Miller. Even the executives from Sumitomo Trust. No deal is a bad deal at the ground-breaking ceremonies.

After that, the politicians took up gold shovels to officially break the ground, and then looked like real city workers by leaning on the shovels to pose for photos.

And Donny Osmond said he might have his next album finished in time for the arena's completion date of October 1, 1991.

And Layden said, "You know, eleven years ago I walked into this valley and said, 'This is definitely not the place.'

"Well, I was wrong."

And Larry H. Miller said, "What we need to do now, is we need to come in on time and under budget."

*Being a cynical journalist, I of course had serious doubts that the MVP vote **really** ended*
in a tie between the Jazz teammates. But it was poetic—after playing on
their own court in front of their own fans, the two best players in Jazz history sharing
the trophy. If I'd been in charge, I'd have rigged the voting too.

Stockton and Malone

First, there's the problem of the trophy. Who gets it? Will they cut it in half? Will Stockton pass it to Malone? Will Malone pass it back or take the assist?

An hour after becoming the first NBA All-Star Game co-MVPs since 1959, and the first-ever co-MVPs from the same franchise, Utah Jazz teammates John Stockton and Karl Malone had answered all the questions but that one.

"I've got one already," said Malone, "so I'll let Stock take this one home."

"I really think he should keep it in his truck," said Stockton.

"Anybody have a coin?" said Malone.

The NBA didn't bring two MVP trophies to its 43rd annual All-Star Game Sunday because normally they don't need two. But then they don't normally come to Salt Lake City, either, where Malone and Stockton don't do anything or go anywhere alone. They work you over as a team. Stockton hits you low and Malone hits you high. If they'd lived in Dodge City, they both would have been the marshal.

People in Utah have known for years that Stockton and Malone are joined at the hip, by an outlet pass. That they never met a player they couldn't post up. You'd cast a big shadow too if you were 13-feet-10 inches tall, weighed 431 pounds, and averaged about 20 assists and 45 points a game.

So it came as no surprise locally when the first-ever NBA All-Star Game to be played in the shadow of the Wasatch Mountains was over Sunday and they counted the Most Valuable Player ballots and the result was a tie. As sure as they knew they'd spent $75 a seat, at least, to watch this moment, the residents in the stands knew that among the mysteries of life is who came first, Stockton or Malone?

Malone had 28 points and 10 rebounds and Stockton 15 assists and 9 points to lead the West to a 135–132 overtime win over the East. As the All-Star circus now moves on to Minneapolis in 1994, they made sure they kept a souvenir for Utah. If the inaugural NBA Jam Session in the Salt Palace wasn't enough to permanently log Utah's All-Star Weekend as unforgettable; if guest appearances by Paula Abdul, Boyz II Men, and Nadia Comaneci; if Hugo the Hornet winning the mascot competition with his backflip off the backboard; if Dr. J regally judging the slamdunk contest; if Magic Johnson at courtside analyzing the game for NBC; and if Michael Jordan's putting problems didn't pull it off—then there was the sight of Stockton and Malone getting called on the red carpet together after the game, where NBA commissioner, David Stern, cleared his throat and, sounding like a ring announcer delivering the verdict, said, "Thank you Utah Jazz for the co-MVPs of the 43rd All-Star Game."

The Delta Center roared its approval. You couldn't have heard a pin drop . . . in the Tabernacle. Larry Miller sold another years' worth of season tickets, at least, and also got an earthquake-survival test for his new building. Some weekends, everything that could go right, does.

"I guess if you were writing a storybook, this is just about how you'd write it," said Malone, who added that winning this MVP trophy means more to him than the first one he won at the 1989 All-Star Game in Houston.

"Because I got to walk out there with Stock," he said.

Stockton was equally magnanimous. "I'm grateful and everything," he said, "but I have to share the credit. The kind of player I am, you need guys, and you need them bad."

Together they made the postgame rounds. An interview with NBC here, with CNN there, with ESPN in the locker room. Then a final bow to hundreds of fans lingering in the arena. Only when they walked outside to the parking lot did they go their separate ways—Malone in his Hummer, a four-by-four car roughly the size of Rhode Island, and Stockton in his family van. One thing about them, they're not hard to tell apart on the highway.

Which is of course what has always made their story even better. One is a short, white, private school graduate from Washington. The other is a tall, black, public school graduate from Louisiana. They met in the middle in Utah on a basketball franchise that hadn't flourished since Pete Maravich ruined his knee throwing a between-the-legs pass.

The rest has been a clinic in teamwork. For going on eight years now, working together, they have won hundreds of games, taken the Utah Jazz to heights they used to be afraid of, and, in their off-hours, helped the United States reclaim its position as Olympic basketball despot.

All winter long, as Utahns anticipated the influx of All-Star Game visitors, both live and via telecasts, they knew the world was in for a show if Malone and Stockton were on their games.

They were on their games, and the end result was Connie Hawkins, representing the Hall of Fame, coming in and taking their jerseys off their backs and putting them on a Federal Express plane bound for the All-Star Wing in Springfield—where they'll be placed alongside the jerseys of all the MVPs from the forty-two games that preceded Utah's. Side-by-side, of course.

They lost their shirts and got half a trophy. All in all, pretty much a perfect weekend.

*I was sitting in the Budapest Convention Hall the night Salt Lake City joined the
Olympic family. Being an objective and neutral journalist, I moved to
the stage toward the Utah delegation—where I hugged the Mayor and high-fived the
Governor. I like to think I'd have done the same to the Swedish
prime minister if Ostersund had won.*

*The column below is the one that ran that night on the front page of the Deseret News.
Because of an extremely tight deadline (the bid announcement was
scheduled the same time as our press run), it had been written earlier and was ready to
go, with the exception of the two instructional lines at the top, which
differentiated it from the LOSE * LOSE * LOSE * LOSE column, which follows.*

Winning the Bid

`June 16, 1995`

BENSON COLUMN TO RUN FRIDAY, JUNE 16, IF SALT LAKE WINS BID

WIN * WIN * WIN * WIN * WIN * WIN * WIN * WIN * WIN

BUDAPEST—His timing perfect for the Rocky Mountain time zone, Juan Antonio Samaranch signalled the start of a wild and raucous celebration weekend today by saying three words:

"Salt Lake City."

The Olympics will be coming here soon.

This really *is* the place.

Finally. After four tries covering more than three decades, the Greatest Snow on Earth will host the greatest show on earth.

Pretty, great news.

Go ahead. Live it up. Let off steam. Gloat. Bask. Indulge. Carouse. Dance in the streets. Set off the sparklers. Paint the town red, black, yellow, green, and blue, the official colors of the official Olympic Games. Whitewash a big block O on Mount Olympus. Have a burger on the deck at Park City. Call La Quaille and make a reservation. Leave the biggest tip you've ever left. Go to Snelgroves, and make it a double.

Run into the yard and high-five your neighbor. Brush up on your French. Make a fireworks run to Evanston. Stay up late. Give your snowblower a hug. Look up at the mountains and say thanks. Go to Alta and do a barrel roll down High Rustler. Hike the interconnect. Climb Ecker Hill. Call Alf Engen and tell him *tusen takk*. Call Alexis Kelner and tell him too bad. Make a toast with the Greatest Snow on Earth, liquid version. Mow five interlocking rings in your lawn. Any babies born today, name them Citius, Altius, or Fortius. Well, middle name. Call the boss and ask for February off—in 2002.

The Olympic Games are coming. We couldn't have a more universal gathering unless we invited Jupiter. Just like that, Salt Lake City is Athens West. Where Oslo and Innsbruck and Lake Placid have gone, we're going. What Zeus got started, we're continuing. The Wasatch Front is about to become a household name.

The world will be welcome . . . here.

Lugers included.

Within another eight hours Salt Lake City will be in headlines in every newspaper around the world. Newscasts from Berlin and Beijing will be showing footage of our famous ski runs. They'll be saying "Bear Hollow" and "Park City" in 173 different languages. President Clinton will invite Salt Lake City to the White House.

For the next seven years budding ice skaters and bobsledders and slalom specialists will fantasize about Salt Lake ice and Salt Lake mountains. Ice dancers will dream of nailing dreamy routines in the Delta Center. Hockey players will dream of nailing opponents in the Delta Center. Foreign luge teams will plan pilgrimages to the spectacular Olympic run at the spectacular Olympic Winter Sports Park. Nordic skiers will come here to get high. NBC Sports will produce a series called "The Road to Salt Lake."

They're going to light a torch in the sacred grove of Olympia and send it here, to Olympic Plaza.

Gold will be mined here again, and silver, and bronze.

There's a certain symmetry that makes it all the more satisfying. A place that began as a melting pot will now be the ultimate melting pot. It was a

European immigrant, Alf Engen, who first told us there was more to be done with the mountains in the winter than wait for them to melt.

Now the whole world will be able to see what he meant.

Salt Lake City, the official city of the 2002 Olympic Winter Games. *Salt Lake City, letat officiel de les jeux Olympiques d'hiver.* It has a nice ring to it. Five nice rings.

All things come to mountains that lie in wait.

Take the weekend off. Let the gardening go. The verdict is in. There will be no recount. There will be no protests. The IOC came, the IOC saw, and the IOC said OK. The Games of Winter and the youth of the world are on their way.

This doesn't happen every generation. Observe a moment of silence for the Lake Effect. Put on your "Salt Lake City 2002" polo shirt and throw your "Salt Lake City 2002" hat in the air. Write "Olympic City" on the city limits sign. This is "We Got It" weekend. Revel in it. There are a lot worse things to be than chosen.

Losing the Bid

BENSON COLUMN TO RUN FRIDAY, JUNE 16 IF SALT LAKE LOSES BID

LOSE * LOSE * LOSE * LOSE * LOSE * LOSE * LOSE * LOSE

BUDAPEST—His timing awful for the Rocky Mountain time zone, Juan Antonio Samaranch, president of the International Olympic Committee, dashed what might have been a wild and raucous Salt Lake City celebration weekend today by refusing to say the three magic words:

"Salt Lake City."

The Olympics will not be coming here soon.

This is *not* the place.

Again.

For the fourth time in more than thirty years of trying, Salt Lake City did not win the approval of the IOC voters. What the IOC said to SLC in 1966 and 1971 and 1991, they said yet again in 1995.

No.

But this was the worst. This was real rejection. In none of the other votes was Salt Lake City considered the clear favorite, the soon-to-be king. Salt Lake had come to Budapest the way Forest Gump came to last spring's Academy Awards. The convention would be a mere formality. There was no stopping us now. It was all over but delivering the acceptance speech. All we packed were our sunglasses.

This time we hadn't just prepared, we had overprepared. We built every facility imaginable, even a luge run—to accommodate the fifty-five people in the world who luge (and half of them come from one family in Italy). We built ice sheets. We flew in an Austrian to design a world-class downhill course at Snowbasin. We spent $56 million in tax money. We bought land. We built roads. We built ski jumps. We moved mountains.

If we did it, we would win.

We treated the IOC voters as if they were more than royalty. We spoiled them like grandkids. We kept an open tab for them at the Red Lion Inn. We let them order cashews from room service. We flew them around the Wasatch Front in choppers. We gave them better seats at Jazz games than the players' wives. We fed them entire cows at a farmhouse in Norway during the '94 Lillehammer Games. We told them they looked handsome or beautiful. We let them shake hands with Steve Young.

We did cartwheels to not offend anyone. We downplayed our liquor laws. We downplayed our religious roots. To Europeans we were European. To Asians we were Asian. To the Aussies we had no worries.

We never stopped smiling. When they said jump through hoops, we said which one.

We watched as the IOC voted Atlanta over Athens for the Centennial Olympic Games of 1996 and congratulated the committee on its wisdom. We didn't take our hat out of the ring despite this latest reminder that fairness and tradition often has little to do with how the IOC votes.

Now we've become the next Athens. The latest IOC casualty. The city that should have won but didn't.

Who knows why? Somehow, someway, during a week of conventioneering halfway around the world, the tide turned. Maybe our gifts weren't good enough. Maybe our unspoken promises didn't cut it. They say Japan helped grease the wheels for its successful bid for the 1998 Winter Games by making a sizeable donation to help build the Olympic museum in Lausanne. Maybe we didn't support a big enough museum.

So that's it and that's that and there's no sense in being bad losers on top of being bad bidders. That would only make it worse. No one can say they didn't know up front that there were no guarantees. No one ever said this was like AYSO soccer where everybody plays—eventually.

But it does put a damper on the planned revelry this weekend. Forget the Evanston fireworks run. Cancel the reservations at La Caille. Terminate those plans to mow the five interlocking rings in your front lawn.

President Clinton won't be calling from the White House. Newscasts from Berlin to Beijing won't be showing footage of our Rocky Mountain ski runs. Nine-year-old ice-skaters won't be dreaming of Salt Lake City at five in the morning.

Gold won't be mined here again, or silver, or bronze.

Forget whitewashing that big block O on Mount Olympus. Maybe next year. Maybe next generation.

The Olympic Games aren't coming. The world won't be welcome here. Not in 2002.

The curse has continued.

Pretty, rotten news.

Writing a sports column is actually just an excuse to write about stuff you always wanted to write about. For the first NBA Finals game ever played in Salt Lake, I was able to, among other things, write about Utah powder, fry sauce, and the origin of the word "fetch."

NBA Finals
Welcome

On the auspicious occasion of the first NBA Finals game ever to be played here in Salt Lake City, I would like to take this opportunity to welcome all members of the Chicago Bulls, their bodyguards, accountants, body piercing artists, hairdressers, manicurists, podiatrists, managers, book agents, and, of course, both their fans.

I realize introductions aren't completely necessary since some members of the Bulls have enjoyed extended stays here before. Michael Jordan, of course, came here for the '93 NBA All-Star Game and played golf in Las Vegas, a suburb to the south. We like to go there for the 99-cent shrimp cocktail.

Aside: it might be interesting for you to know that besides settling the Salt Lake Valley, Brigham Young—Steve Young's great-great-great grandfather, no relation to Jim McMahon—also sent the first settlers to Las Vegas. He told them to plant soy beans; they thought he said slot machines.

Here in Salt Lake a hundred and fifty years ago, it wasn't easy, building a city from scratch on a valley floor that even the indigent group Columbus politically incorrectly called "Indians" didn't want any part of. Unlike the vibrant, thriving valley you see now, back then there were no trees, no conveniences of any kind, no Denny's restaurants on every corner. Nothing was named. It wouldn't be "The Great Salt Lake" until after a citywide name-the-lake contest.

Anyway, to make a long story short, they built the city, built the Delta Center and, voila! Exactly a century and a half later, here they are—the NBA Finals.

The appropriateness of The Finals descending on the valley in the year of the Sesquicentennial commemorating the first settler's footsteps to arrive here in 1847 has not been lost on the natives. Nor does anyone here think it's just coincidence that the Salt Lake Valley and Karl Malone were born on the same day—July 24th. Although the Valley is slightly older.

You should know that this area is justly proud of its many innovations, including but not limited to: irrigation, salt water taffy, the first Kentucky Fried Chicken franchise, caffeine-free beverages, fry sauce, Merlin Olsen, Tom Chambers, and a version of basketball called Church Ball, a particularly spirited, brawling version of the game in which Dennis Rodman would retire the sportsmanship trophy, and where, incidentally, the word "fetch" was coined.

Rodman got technicals in thirteen games in a row? Fetch, there are Church Ball guys who are working on a string of thirteen *years!*

The Jazz, of course, follow in the transitory, refugee-fleeing traditions of the area. Like those original pioneers of a hundred and fifty years ago, they came from someplace else where they felt unwanted, persecuted, and the rent was too high. Also, when they got here they refused to change their name or their standards—although they did trade Pistol Pete Maravich.

It was a Mormon convert, Sam Battistone, originally from Santa Barbara, California, who first owned the Jazz and moved them here after five turbulent years in New Orleans, bringing everything, including Hot Rod Hundley, Pistol Pete's two BMWs, and the franchise nickname, because, not that he was mad about the way he'd been treated or anything, but Sam wanted to be sure that when the Jazz made it to the top, THE PEOPLE BACK IN NEW ORLEANS WOULD KNOW ABOUT IT!

Battistone, who later sold the team to local car dealer Larry H. Miller, now deals in sports collectibles but still has season tickets on the front row of the Delta Center. Check him out. He's the one with the "I Told You So!" signs.

Critics around the country were skeptical when the Jazz first came here in 1979 that they could make it in a city where the only tattoo parlor adjoined a car wash and Gas-and-Go. But they knew nothing of the sporting nuances of an area where basketball has always been as big as it is in Indiana and North Carolina. But who would know with Idaho buffering out all the noise?

Powder skiing and the forward pass may have been invented here, by Alf

Engen and LaVell Edwards, respectively, but basketball has always been the most popular game in town. And if you don't believe that, consider this: Why are there no Mormon churches without a gym?

In the meantime, enjoy your stay. Before you know it, it will be back to the Loop, the Miracle Mile, and your visit to the Beehive State will be reduced to a pleasant memory of a deafening Finals din in the Delta Center. Hey, cut us some slack. It's our first time.

Been There, Seen That

Seve at the Masters, 1980
Miracle Bowl, 1980
Celebration, Detroit Style, 1984
Villanova Wins! 1985
Jim McMahon, 1986
Bill Buckner and the Curse, 1986
End of an Era, 1988
Denise Claims Bronze, 1988
Detmer's Dad, 1990
Dream Team Gold, 1992
Bulls in Six, 1997

For three consecutive years I stayed in the same house as Severiano Ballesteros during Masters Week. Ballesteros's agent at the time was Ed Barner, a friend of mine and a fellow BYU graduate. Ed was in charge of arranging for the house, and he held a room for me, which was great, not only because Seve was in his prime, but because of Lucy, our maid. Lucy did your laundry, cleaned your room and, if you wanted a grilled ham and cheese sandwich at 11 o'clock at night, after you'd finished your column, she'd make it for you.

Seve at the Masters

April 14, 1980

AUGUSTA—An eyewitness account of Seve Ballesteros's Masters victory celebration party that started Sunday night and extended into Monday morning at the rented home on Brookwood Drive in East Augusta. I couldn't get to sleep until it was over.

At last count, a total of fifty-seven dinner guests had filtered past the buffet spread.

Included were full delegations from the Spanish and Mexican Professional Golf Associations, personal friends and family of the victor, assorted groupies, members of the British and Spanish press, and the chauffeur of the Cadillac Fleetwood that brought the 1980 Masters champion home wearing his new size 42 green jacket.

Starting time was approximately 7:15 P.M. Cutoff, or pass-out point, was 2:45 A.M. The predominant language spoken was Spanish. Loud Spanish. The din had an accent. The predominant word, shouted over and over, was "Olé!" (try saying "Olé" without shouting), and the highlight of the evening came when the Masters recap was shown on television between 11:00 P.M. and midnight, met by an hourlong chorus of Olé's.

As a sort of postscript, the King of Spain, Juan Carlos, called the house

Monday with a congratulatory telephone message along with another Olé or two. This also served as a general wakeup call for the house, although no one had requested or needed one.

The whole world loves a winner, especially when it's a European who has just won America's own snobbish invitational golf tournament. Only once before in Masters history had a foreigner—known locally as a "durn furriner"—won, and that was an English-speaking, Americanized, South African named Gary Player, so it almost didn't count.

And not only did Severiano Ballesteros strike a blow for the foreigners, he struck one for youth. At twenty-three years, four days, he is the youngest Masters champion in history, outdoing even Jack Nicklaus, who was twenty-three years, three months, when he won his first Masters in 1963.

Too, Ballesteros won by a whopping four strokes, and he did it by subduing Augusta National's famous and sometimes infamous back nine.

He had lost six strokes to the field on the first four holes of the back side, but then, after rounding "Amen Corner," instead of saying Amen, he reeled off three of the prettiest iron shots this side of the Mediterranean to birdie holes 14, 15, and 16. With two holes to play he had a three-shot lead, and back at Brookwood Drive, they were stoking up the barbecue.

This conquistador had reason to celebrate. By the time he was fitted for his green jacket and made the drive home, Neil Sedaka, Linda Ronstadt, the Bee Gees, Barry Manilow, and Anne Murray—Seve's musical tastes run slightly west of his homeland—were blaring out of the stereo speakers, and they kept blaring well into Monday, by which time Seve's right hand was weary from so many handshakes, to say nothing of the state of his feet.

"I feel happy, very happy," he said, the Bee Gees wailing in the background. "I dream of winning Masters one day. Now dream come true."

It hadn't been easy, even if he had taken a seven stroke lead into the final round. There were some spirited charges mounted, and he did slide back for a time, but Ballesteros once said he believed that in his destiny there were many wins to come.

He had an inkling the '80 Masters was to be his. Late Saturday night, watching TV, to get his mind off the upcoming round, he was told the skies outside had cleared and the threat of rain on Sunday was gone.

"Maybe," he smiled, "tomorrow be good day."

Twenty-four hours later, surrounded by his friends, as he waited for the king to call, he could eliminate the "maybe."

All these years, and thousands of press box buffets, later, BYU's 46–45 miracle win in
the Holiday Bowl remains the most amazing sporting event I have
ever personally witnessed. I remember sitting in the open-air pressbox, gulping in the
heavy San Diego air and watching the stadium empty like
a fire drill even before the fourth quarter began. This game was beyond hope.

Then, by the time the masses were in their cars on Friar's Road, headed out fast,
I watched as the brake lights came on. Some cars actually pulled
off to the side, reduced to "seeing" this miracle on the radio. When it was over, what I
remember most is walking into the BYU locker room, which was
curiously subdued, and, while interviewing the master of the comeback, quarterback Jim
McMahon, noticing his hands were shaking. Adrenalin withdrawal. Big time.

Miracle Bowl

December 20, 1980

S AN DIEGO—About halfway through the movie *The Empire Strikes Back,* while piloting the Millennium Falcon through a sea of asteroids in hopes of eluding the Empire's starships, Han Solo delivers a gem of a one-liner. The strategy is frowned on by C3PO, a robot, who analytically explains that the chances of making it through an asteroid field alive are roughly 22,000 to one.

"Never," says Han Solo, "tell me the odds."

If BYU had sat down and analyzed the situation with less than four minutes left to play in Holiday Bowl 3 on Friday night in San Diego Stadium, the prognosis would have been about the same as making it through an asteroid field. For one thing, the Cougars were trailing 45–25. For another, their opponents, the Southern Methodist University Mustangs, had this annoying habit of doing one of two things every time they got the football: 1) hanging onto it for quite a while, and 2) scoring.

Then the human element entered in. It must have. Otherwise, there's no explaining how a college football team could score twenty-one points in three minutes, fifty-eight seconds, limit SMU to a grand total of four offensive plays, and escape certain defeat in the process. Computers couldn't have come close to pulling this off.

Nobody told BYU the odds. And BYU didn't ask. The team just reached back to see how much was left and found there was quite a bit. "When everything else was gone," explained wide receiver Lloyd Jones, who caught three passes for thirty-one yards in the crucial four-minute countdown, "we went to pride and heart. If we were going to win, it had to come from there."

Thus began one of the great comebacks in the history of college football. Big Mo, as in Momentum, has never changed sides so quickly. This wasn't a rally, it was a revolution.

In a few days, the players and coaches who made it happen are going to think back on everything that fell into place—that *had* to fall into place—and break out in a cold sweat. What they pulled off was perfection. *Everything* went right. Maybe, as was intimated later, they had a few good breaks coming. They certainly came.

All BYU had to do to beat SMU in that final 3:58 was drive 72 yards in 1:27 for a score; recover an onside kick; drive another 50 yards in 34 seconds for another score; make good on a two-point conversion; hold SMU on downs; block the ensuing punt; and then score from 41 yards out on an alley-oop pass when no time remained on the clock—and make the PAT. That's all.

Help came from everywhere. Human-type help.

Lloyd Jones, Eric Lane, Scott Phillips, Clay Brown, Matt Braga, and Scott Pettis all caught crucial passes (they were *all* crucial passes) from Jim McMahon, and that was just for starters. The game was a goner if freshman kicker Lee Johnson hadn't executed a perfect knuckleball onside kick when the score was 45–31, and if freshman Todd Shell hadn't pounced immediately on the free ball.

It was a goner, too, if the offensive line hadn't finally decided to keep Michael Carter and Harvey Armstrong out of McMahon's pocket—allowing him to complete eight of his final thirteen throws, many for long yardage—and even after all of the above it was still a sure loss if Bill Schoepflin hadn't blitzed in to block a punt after the Cougar defense had held SMU to a minus-one yard rushing in three futile plays. These were the same Mustangs who had rushed for 394 yards on sixty-three previous carries.

Then it was down to just one more miracle—a touchdown in thirteen seconds from the 41. It took three tries to get it—stretching the odds to the limit. Finally, McMahon launched one that circled Jupiter before it came down in the hands of Brown, who had no business catching the ball since he was outnumbered four to one.

It ended that way. SMU falling by one, the odds by plenty more than that. And as BYU moseyed out to its buses parked in front of the stadium tunnel, the players and coaches were greeted by thousands of fans who wanted to get a closer look at these guys who would spit into the wind like that.

Among the throng was Hall of Fame golfer Billy Casper, a converted BYU backer who catches a game whenever he can. Casper knows about bucking the odds. Back in 1966 at the Olympic Club in San Francisco, he entered the back nine of the fourth round of the U.S. Open trailing the great Arnold Palmer by seven shots. Casper unbelievably made them up to tie Palmer and then beat Arnie in an 18-hole playoff the next day for the title.

"Hey, Casper!" shouted out a BYU fan. "This was a comeback to rival yours."

"There's no comparison," Casper shouted back. "In this one, there really was no chance."

It was after I'd written this column, and after I'd eaten Tom Monoghan's free pizza,
that I walked up Michigan Avenue to my downtown hotel and
realized I'd grossly underestimated Detroit's ability to dig up lawns, pull down street
lights, and set police cars on fire. I still wonder what they'd
have done if they had lost.

Celebration, Detroit-style

DETROIT—In tribute to the newfound world championship status of their baseball team, the Tigers, the citizens of Detroit launched into a postgame party/celebration/mugging Sunday night that, by press time, was still going on. When it will end, who's to say? By Wednesday is a good guess. If they run out of police cars to trash.

Enraptured by the Tigers' 8–4 World Series–clinching victory over the San Diego Padres, the fans spilled out onto Michigan Avenue shortly after 8:00 P.M., their time, and started hollering and honking horns and shouting "Dee-troit!" and letting off enough firecrackers to wake up their Canadian neighbors across the river in Windsor, who must have thought it curious getting so worked up when it wasn't hockey season.

Detroit's cup runneth over. It was something to see, if only through your fingers, and preferably from a safe distance. The part where four police cars parked in front of the stadium were bashed and clubbed and kicked in, and another was set on fire, wasn't exactly heart-warming. Nor were the occasional fistfights. Nor were the several thousand fans who broke through a phalanx of about 200 policemen after the game to steal away with the bases, home plate, and huge chunks of what Sparky Anderson calls the finest turf in baseball.

It was a scene that "makes Yankee Stadium look civil," according to a New York writer hunkered down in the press box.

Whoever said it was just a game?

It was a "celebration" that knew no bounds, some of them even legal. One reveler saw fit to jump out of his car, get a can of gold spray paint from his trunk, and proceed to do a "Just Married" routine on his own auto. Only he wrote "Detroit No. 1" and "Tigers No. 1" and "Awwwwwright," which, considering his general physical condition, was excellent spelling.

There was high-fiving all around, low-fiving too. Soul was everywhere. Like the sign in the stands that said, "No Jive, I'm Alive." It was right next to one saying, "It's a Cinch, We're Gonna Clinch," which of course the Tigers did, providing enough of an excuse for the thousands who decided to hang around downtown until it was time to go to work Monday morning or get a headache, whichever came first.

Included in the throng, or at least above it, was the new owner of the Tigers, Tom Monaghan, the Domino's Pizza founder who's worth as much as some Arabs and who paid $53 million for the Detroit franchise last spring. "The only encore I can think of is to run for president," he joked. Presumably.

But Monaghan didn't spray paint his car in his delirium, or burn it either. Rather, he phoned up the nearest Domino's and said, "Get a couple hundred over here, fast!" And then, to make sure his delivery men would make the 30-minute limit, he gave them the OK to use his private helicopter.

And so it was that a helicopter with a Domino's banner waving from its rotor and loaded with 200 pizzas arrived in a Detroit Stadium centerfield completely devoid of grass.

The pizzas were distributed to both clubhouses and also to the press box, where approximately 400 sports writers established a new World Series record: fastest pizza consumption in a five-game series while on deadline and waiting out a riot.

The game that sparked all the commotion wasn't much to see. This was a great World Series, if you don't care about close, exciting, down-to-the-wire, white-knuckle games. Nobody fainted during the five bores that made up the Fastfood Series of '84, unless maybe it was the TV executives at CBS.

Even as Detroit revels, the rest of the country is no doubt taping Monday Night Football over whatever videotape might have been devoted to the Series.

But in the Motor City, they'll save their tapes, and take all spoils coming to the victors, which includes the town's biggest bash, a new championship banner for Tiger Stadium, and a green car with gold spray paint that proclaims "Awwwwwright"—whether its owner wanted it that way the next morning or not.

I finished this column about three in the morning in a hotel room in Lexington, a humbled man. Prior to what was supposed to be a slaughter along the order of In Cold Blood, I had already written my championship game column some twelve hours earlier, well before the game began. I had an early plane to catch the next morning, and since Georgetown—with two regular season blowouts over Villanova already to its credit—was such a huge favorite, as well as the defending national champion, I wrote a glowing column about the college career of Hoya center Patrick Ewing. The column ended with Ewing walking off the court holding remnants of the championship net in one hand and the tournament MVP trophy in the other. It was in that frame of mind that I watched Villanova's methodic, assassin-like dismantling of the Hoyas . . . and of that column. It took me hours to recover.

Villanova Wins!

April 2, 1985

LEXINGTON, Ky.—About an hour after the deed was done, somebody asked Villanova head coach Rollie Massimino if he could explain his team's 90-percent shooting on nine of ten field goals in the second half.

"Yeah," he said, the Italian wiseguy in him coming out, "we missed once."

Other than that, the new national champion Villanova Wildcats—your Monday night prime-time conquerors of, gasp, Georgetown—were perfecto.

Pass the fingernail file, please.

A couple of days earlier, somebody had asked another Italian coach, Louie Carnesecca of St. John's, what you had to do to beat Georgetown. "Play a perfect game," answered Louie.

In losing to the Hoyas by eighteen in the semifinals, Carnesecca's St. John's team hadn't come close.

But in Monday's final, Villanova did.

The Wildcats, on the strength of 22-of-28 shooting, capped by their 9-of-10 audacity in the second half—shot 79 percent from from the field overall and 83 percent from the free throw line.

So Carnesecca was wrong. *Near* perfection was enough to do in the Hoyas.

By two points.

"Five people in the 23,000 here tonight thought we could win," said Villanova reserve guard Harold Jensen.

But how were the rest of us supposed to know that Jensen was going to replace starter Dwight Wilbur just five minutes into the contest and never come back out because he could not miss?

A 41-percent shooter all season long, Jensen took five jumpers against Georgetown and hit nothing but nylon every time.

For that matter, how were all those people who made Georgetown a nine-point favorite supposed to know Dwayne McClain and Ed Pinckney would each go 5-of-7 from the field and Gary McLain would go 3-of-3, and that Harold Pressley's 4-of-6 would qualify as the coldest of Villanova's hot hands?

Wilbur, for the record, did not score, mainly because he did not shoot. He thought Jensen was spelling him for a quick breather, and the next thing he knew it was Villanova 66, Hoyas 64, and he and Jensen were rolling around on the court, hugging each other.

All's well that ends well, and if Jensen had fought to find himself and his shooting touch all year, and if Villanova as a team had struggled through ten losses during the season, including two to this very Georgetown team it had to face in the finals, that meant all the more reason to celebrate an ending that *was* perfect.

Not that they realized they were being perfect when they were.

"I knew we knocked down some shots, especially in the second half," said Jensen. "But I had no idea we made 9 of 10."

No team in the forty-seven-year history of the national tournament had ever shot 90 percent for a half, or 79 percent for a game. Somebody named Northeastern shot 75 percent once against a matador defense from Virginia Commonwealth in a 1984 first-round, throwaway game. That had been the tournament record. And the championship game record was a mere 67.4 percent by Ohio State in 1960 against California.

This 79 percenter came against the strongest defense this side of Alcatraz.

During its previous thirty-seven games, Georgetown had held opponents to shooting 39.8 percent—just half of what it allowed Villanova.

This was the same Georgetown defense against which Kentucky connected on just 3-of-33 field goals in the second half of last year's NCAA semifinal game in Seattle—the game that set the stage for the Hoya's first of what was supposed to be a two-championship run.

Now here was Villanova, in the biggest game of all, forgetting about Georgetown's D and about steel elbows and about, apparently, everything, en route to a shooting accuracy that would be hard to pull off if there weren't any defense at all.

How do you explain that kind of shooting?

Other than Massimino's quip, "We missed once."

Monday night, that was easy for him to say; but sometime when the cloud they've chartered lets all the Villanovans back to planet Earth, where there are taxes and heartburn and no free lunches and where jumpers sometimes spin out, the coach is going to sit down and take a long look at the stat sheet.

Then he will break out in a cold sweat.

"How on earth," he will gasp, "*did* we shoot 90 percent!"

When Jim McMahon went from BYU to the Chicago Bears in 1982, he promised the
Bears he'd win them a Super Bowl. Three seasons later, he did.
McMahon remains the greatest competitor I have personally ever watched. The higher
the stakes, the more he thrived. If he'd been a stock, I'd have bought some.
But his greatest strength—his fearlessness—was also what brought him down. In high
school he once refused to stop playing after separating his shoulder. He
simply popped it back into place and kept going. Big macho points, but a stupid move. It
was that shoulder that would mar his senior year at BYU and keep him
in the hospital as much as on the field in the NFL. I believe a healthy Jim McMahon
could have made them forget Unitas and Starr and would have
won more Super Bowls than Joe Montana. An unhealthy Jim McMahon won just the
one Super Bowl (if you don't count his non-playing, backup role with
the Packers in '96). This was the one.

Jim McMahon

NEW ORLEANS—Just like in the good old days at college, Jim McMahon sat out the fourth quarter.

He didn't need to. He had a slight sprain on his left wrist, but he doesn't throw with that one anyway. He wasn't playing because the Chicago Bears were ahead of the New England Patriots 44–3 in Super Bowl XX. Some things never change. One year it's Colorado State, New Mexico, and UTEP getting thrashed, the next it's the Los Angeles Rams and the New England Patriots. Jim McMahon—the first of the BYU quarterbacks to go on and conquer the world just like he conquered the WAC—never met a team he didn't like to beat.

Well, at least not since Salt Lake City's West High School. The West High Panthers were the last team to beat McMahon in anything worthy of being called a big game. That was in the 1976 Utah State Class 4-A quarter-finals. West beat Roy High, McMahon's team, 13–6.

That was the last time.

McMahon moved on to BYU, and in his starting career there, he lost just three times. None of the losses meant much. He lost once to New Mexico in a season-opener, and didn't lose again that season; he lost once to Wyoming in a midseason game that didn't affect the team's conference championship, and he lost once to Utah after the Cougars had already clinched the 1979 WAC title and were Holiday Bowl-bound.

In all, he won 26 of 29 starts for BYU.

And now, counting Sunday's Super Bowl, he has won 26 of the 30 games he has started for the Chicago Bears the past three years, including this year's 3-for-3 playoff run.

You can't win them all, but if you're Jim McMahon you can make it seem like it. He was 2-for-2 in bowl games in college, and now he's perfect in the NFL playoffs.

Against the Patriots, before he took his early exit, McMahon completed 12 of 20 passes for 256 yards. Paltry stats compared to college, when he routinely hit those numbers by halftime. But the Bears don't throw on every down. Two times, McMahon rushed for touchdowns, tying a Super Bowl record. And, of course, there were all those points—more than any team had ever before poured on in a Super Bowl.

"We were going for 60," McMahon said postgame. "But we ran out of time."

McMahon showed his penchant for winning early in the game when he responded to an early 3–0 New England lead by dropping back on the first play from scrimmage and hitting Willie Gault for a 43-yard gain. The Bears were never headed thereafter.

It was deja vu of the BYU-Utah game in 1981, McMahon's senior season. The game was for the WAC title and a trip to the Holiday Bowl, and Utah's Del Rodgers scored on the Utes' first play. Just like that, it was Utah 7, BYU 0.

Forty-five thousand people were crowded into the old BYU Stadium, which was quite a gathering considering capacity was 36,000.

Undaunted, McMahon responded by taking BYU on a picture-perfect 80-yard touchdown drive that sent the Cougars on to a 56–28 win.

He won every game in college he ever had to—including the 1980 and 1981 Holiday Bowls, the 1980 classic being the legendary 46–45 comeback over SMU. In that game, BYU was prepared to punt during the middle of what would prove to be the winning rally in the final four minutes. McMahon called time out and ran to the sidelines. "What are we doing, giving up?" he screamed at Coach LaVell Edwards. Edwards relented, the Cougars went for it—and won the game.

Graduating to the NFL didn't change a thing.

Only West High could stop him, way back in 1976, on an afternoon in early November at Rice Stadium.

West scored 13 points in that game, McMahon scored 6—when he got loose on a sprintout and scored a touchdown.

"We knew he could do that," remembered West High coach Gean Plaga when contacted at his Salt Lake home Sunday after watching the Super Bowl game on television. Plaga recalled losing considerable sleep the week before the Roy game worrying about what McMahon might do to his defending state champion Panthers.

"We knew we had to contain him," said Plaga. "We wanted to force him to stay in the pocket. We were somewhat successful, but still, I think he threw for more than 200 yards against us.

"He was a good, hard-nosed football player. I thought he'd be a good one."

This good?

"Well, I don't know about that," said Plaga honestly. But what he does know is that he still has the game film from that 1976 West High win over Jim McMahon, and he doesn't plan on erasing it. The way things are going, it may turn out to be the only film of its kind.

It was a bad night to be a columnist; although not as bad as being a Red Sox fan. I was sitting high in the centerfield seats at Shea Stadium, in the auxiliary press box next to a chain-smoker, and this was when, if you asked someone to stop smoking, you were the jerk.

The game didn't start until after 9:00 P.M. on a Saturday night and was still going strong well past midnight. Back in Salt Lake, they wanted my column, and I was about to give them one. Word had spread that Bruce Hurst, the Utah-grown pitcher from St. George and one of the aces on the Red Sox staff, had been voted MVP of the World Series and would be presented the trophy at the conclusion of the game—the one condition being, of course, that Boston wins the game and clinches its first World Series in sixty-six years. I was just putting the finishing touches on my Hurst column when Boston's Bill Buckner, a consummate pro, inexplicably let Mookie Wilson's grounder slip through his legs and the Mets slip into Game 7 (which they would win). Just like that, Buckner ensured his place in the sordid lore of Boston sports, and both Hurst and I were done in by the Red Sox curse.

Back in Utah, the desk still wanted a column, and wanted it now! So I wrote this one, in about sixteen minutes, which begins with a sentence that includes the word "wracking." Since I don't think it exists, I've never looked it up.

Bill Buckner and the Curse

October 26, 1986

NEW YORK—As yet another example that all nerves have their wracking point—it just takes some longer to get there than others—there was the sixth game of the World Series, played here Saturday night in Shea Stadium. Or was it the Theatre of the Macabre? The game was decided in the bottom of the 10th inning when Boston Red Sox first baseman, Bill Buckner, allowed a weakly hit ground ball to roll between his legs. You could just hear Buckner's dad somewhere shouting, "Stay down on the ball. What did I tell you about staying down on the ball!"

Only this wasn't Little League, it was the Big Leagues, in the biggest series of all.

Sometimes it can be hard to tell the two apart.

Pressure giveth and pressure taketh away.

When Red Sox centerfielder Dave Henderson, the postseason path of terror himself, used the pressure to his advantage and hit a high fastball high and far out of a suddenly deadly quiet Shea Stadium in the top of the 10th inning, it appeared that Boston, leading three games to two entering this Biggest Game of the Year, would rack up its first World Series title since 1918.

But the Mets, being the home team, got their last at-bat. And in a game that had more weird plays and funny throws and tentativeness than, well, than a Little League game, you just knew this thing was far from over.

Things had started out shaky. Boston rightfielder, Dwight Evans, reputed to be the best in the business at that position, a man truly outstanding in his field, bobbled a routine ground ball that allowed the Mets' Ray Knight to go all the way from first to third, and then score.

Then Knight, the Mets' third baseman, returned the favor when he fielded a routine grounder at third and threw a ball that rose into the cold evening air until it was a good ten feet over the first-base bag. This led to a Red Sox run.

This kind of wild play was catching. In all, the official scorers recorded five errors. There should have been at least three more.

The players weren't the only ones succumbing to the pressure. Managers John McNamara of Boston and Davey Johnson of New York were white-knuckling the daylights out of this one.

Johnson got so conservative, he was calling bunts on practically every play. As for McNamara, he lifted his star pitcher, Roger Clemens, in the seventh inning, even though Clemens had allowed just four hits. Clemens's replacement, Calvin Schiradli, nervous as a June bride, loaded the bases in the eighth inning before the jubilant Mets fans could even come up for breath. Just like that, the game was tied, 3–3.

It might have been a Mets' lead had not Gary Carter, the New York catcher, swung on a 3-and-0 pitch when the bases were loaded and Schiraldi was having as much success throwing strikes as a weekend bowler. Carter managed to hit a sacrifice fly to left field and bring in one run, but there probably could have been more.

Allowing Carter to swing on 3 and 0 was a percentage move.

But it was not a percentage game. The tension was so thick you could carve a hit out of an out.

When the Red Sox had their lead going into the bottom of the 10th, they were in fine shape except for one thing—they had put too much pressure on themselves. Schiradli, by now calmed down enough to have found the plate, managed to get two fly-outs. But he never got the third. He gave up three singles, and McNamara signaled for another reliever, Bob Stanley, who was nervous too.

Stanley, trying to protect a 5–4 lead with runners at first and third, responded by throwing a wild pitch in the direction of Brooklyn that catcher Rich Gedman had to chase down. Enter one more Mets' run, for a 5–5 tie.

And now it's Buckner's turn.

Mookie Wilson hit a soft, enticing grounder down the first-base line—your routine groundout, even if the runner is Carl Lewis—and then Buckner decided to field it like your kid brother.

He shouldn't feel so bad. His was the last error, but not the first. And the way this game was played, it was a matter of who errored last.

The intriguing illustration seemed to be this: as long as human beings play these things, they're going to play like humans—even big leaguers who make a million dollars a year and probably never let one get through their legs while growing up. There comes a point when the event gets the best of you. It could happen to anybody. As a matter of fact, it just did.

It was a sad day when the Soviets finally brought down the Americans in Olympic basketball fair and square in the semifinals of the 1988 tournament in Seoul. But in the interview session afterward, it was hard not to enjoy Alexandre Gomelski's unbridled joy and his unabashed "thank-you's" to the American teams that got the USSR warmed up. His mood was in stark contrast to that of American coach, John Thompson, who asked with a totally straight face, "Do you think they'll allow us back in the country?"

End of an Era

SEOUL—You'd have been hard-pressed to find a happier man on earth Wednesday than Alexandre Gomelski, the head coach of the Soviet national basketball team. His was the look of a man who will never see the inside of a Siberian salt mine.

He had just finished coaching the Soviets to their 82–76 Olympic semifinal victory over the United States, and there were a few people he wanted to thank.

In the spirit of *glasnost*, he started with his friends/comrades in America. Let's see, there were the Milwaukee Bucks, the Atlanta Hawks, and the people who run the Atlanta summer league. And there were also the Portland Trail Blazers and any number of U.S. college teams, too numerous to mention.

If he missed anybody, well, they know who they are.

You had to give Gomelski credit; he was giving credit where credit was due.

He admitted that an Olympic victory over the Americans probably wouldn't have been possible if the Soviets had trained the past eight years only against the usual town teams in Leningrad and Omsk, and had only played in the Europa Cup championships against the Yugoslavs and Spaniards and other familiar stiffs from Europe. What the elite Russian players needed to get ready was In-Your-Faceski basketball.

"In America childen start dribbling, shooting . . . after talking," said Gromelski. "In Russia they don't start until fourteen. Big difference."

So the Soviets infiltrated our system. As Gromelski explained, they played exhibitions against colleges from Seton Hall to Cal-Santa Barbara. They played in the summer league in Atlanta with the best players greenbacks could buy. They came to Milwaukee and got blown out by the Bucks—but kept notes and made movies the whole time. They invited the Hawks over for a three-game series this summer to warm up for the Olympics.

And, just for good measure, they sent their 7-foot-4 center, Arvidas Sabonis, to Portland for the spring and early summer, where the Trail Blazers' doctors and trainers worked on his sore ankle in the hopes he'll one day repay them by playing the post as a Trail Blazer in the NBA.

John Thompson, the U.S. coach who went down with the ship Wednesday—the first coach to lose to Russia when the clock worked properly—said at the time of Sarbonis's treatment, "Lenin was right. The capitalists are selling the rope that they'll hang themselves with."

Showing no sign of injury, Sabonis scored 13 points and captured 13 rebounds Wednesday.

He was just the tip of the attack. This wasn't a Soviet team that had to be lucky to win, or, like in 1972, get a break from the officials. This was a Soviet team that looked very familiar. Close to home, even. They looked like, they played like, they ran the break like, they even talked jive like . . . like the guys they were beating.

Gomelski wanted to dedicate the win.

"I would like to thank America," he said. "I'm very happy to United States basketball. I know Coach Thompson critical when we play Milwaukee Bucks and go to summer league and play Atlanta Hawks. But after Atlanta visit everybody talks basketball. Basketball is now No. 2 in Soviet Union, only to soccer football.

"Not only is this friendship good for Russia-U.S.," he went on, "but it's very good preparation for me."

A more gracious winner you're not going to find.

"Mr. Thompson is a great coach but he's not foreign minister," said Gomelski, thankfully. "All people in Russia very happy with this (new) friendship. People sleep now, no problem. Maybe Coach Thompson not understand this."

What Coach Thompson did understand was that Arvidas Sabonis personally destroyed any notion America's Team had of playing pressure defense.

"His body and movement are such factors in pressure defense," said Thompson. "And he's improved a lot this summer. But he's been working hard —against America's finest—so he should have improved a lot."

Thompson said he didn't want to talk further about America's foreign aid. Not now, anyway. "It would not be appropriate," he said, biting his upper lip.

For his part, Gomelski said he just wanted to reiterate his thanks. And add this thought: "I think that maybe if Magic Johnson and Michael Jordan play," he said, "then we can't win."

But if they let the NBA players into the Olympics in the future (as they no doubt will following Wednesday's loss), that will be another Soviet coach's problem. By then, Gomelski will be enjoying his retirement in his villa overlooking the Volga River in Moscow, taking Sunday drives in his chauffeur-driven sedan, and dining on caviar—all of it courtesy of his capitalist friends in America.

With nerves of ice water, Denise Parker, the fourteen-year-old pride of South Jordan,
Utah, picked up the U.S. women's archery team, put it on her
ninety-pound back, and carried it to the bronze medal in Seoul. Denise's arrows were
clutch and dead-center. Still, my most enduring memory of a
late afternoon at the archery venue was of that arrow of Melanie Skillman's, sailing
completely over the bale, on its way to North Korea.
The only air arrow I've ever seen.

Denise Claims Bronze

October 2, 1988

S EOUL—Afterward—when she could finally relax; after they'd draped the bronze medal over her shoulders and the Korean girl in the ceremonial silk gown had given her a bouquet of flowers—Denise Parker talked about how pressure-packed it had gotten at the finish; how it was hard to breathe, let alone shoot an arrow. How it was so pressurized that it was . . . well, it was unimaginable.

"I mean, you can't sit back here and even think how much pressure there was," she was saying. "It was enormous. It was incredible. Nobody was secure. Anything could happen. It just all came down to that last end."

She breathed another sigh of relief. True enough, the United States women's archery team, of which Parker had been a member in good standing, had barely missed winning the silver medal at the Games of the 24th Olympiad—losing in a shootoff to Indonesia—but even truer enough, the U.S. had survived a Soviet scare to be able to still fly home as honest-to-goodness Olympic medalists.

Archery competitions are a lot like golf tournaments. They take all day to play, and they often come down to the final arrow. Saturday at the Olympics was like that.

Twelve teams qualified for the medal-round competition that began

Saturday morning at the Hwarang Archery Field. Four of those teams—Korea, the United States, the Soviet Union, and Indonesia—quickly asserted themselves as the strongest teams, moving, along with teams from Sweden, Great Britain, France, and West Germany, into the eight-team final round in the afternoon.

The morning scores were then wiped clean once the afternoon competition began, with each team shooting twenty-seven arrows (nine per team member) at distances of, in order, 30 meters, 50 meters, 60 meters, and 70 meters.

Indonesia started fast and actually took over first place from the Koreans—who boasted Kim Soo-Nyung, Wang Hee-Kyung, and Yun Young-Sook, the three medalists in the individual competition—after the 30-meter shoot. The homecourt Koreans soon retook the lead, however, and the competition settled rather comfortably into a match between Korea, Indonesia, the U.S., and Russia, in that order.

After a miserable 50-meter round, the USSR slipped well back into fourth place, twenty points behind the U.S. The halfway scores showed Korea on top at 498, followed by Indonesia at 496, the United States at 490, and Russia at 470.

After 60 meters, the Soviets had closed the gap, but only slightly. Korea still led, with 739 points, followed by Indonesia with 731, the U. S. with 724, and the Soviets with 711.

Now there were twenty-seven arrows left to shoot, at a distance of 70 meters, nine per end, three per archer.

After the first end, the positions stayed virtually the same: Korea 821, Indonesia 810, United States 803, Soviet Union 788.

Eighteen arrows to go.

"Now we're thinking bronze all the way," said Denise.

But the Russians were coming.

The Soviet archers quickly made up thirteen points on one end, the equivalent of, say, a 9–0 inning in baseball.

The scores going into the final end: Korea 901 (and uncatchable), Indonesia 879, the USA 873, the USSR 871.

This was the nerve-wracking, do-or-die moment Parker was talking about. Olympic medals were on the line, and the Soviets, of all people, had the momentum. Somehow, if you could, you had to forget all that and go out there and shoot bulls-eyes anyway.

Denise, who shoots fast anyway, stood on the line, thanked the Korean skies there wasn't much wind, and got her three shots out of the way in a hurry.

She scored a bulls-eye (10), a 9, and another 9.

Teammates Debra Ochs and Melanie Skillman added fifty-one points to Denise's twenty-eight—for a seventy-nine total. Skillman had a momentary flinch and scored only a six with one of her arrows. The three Americans quickly looked through their binoculars at the Soviets' target. It looked as good or better. In the stands, where he was watching through his telescope, Denise's dad, Earl, shook his head. "That six might have nailed us," he said.

The archers walked the looong 70 meters to the targets, where the judges scored their arrows.

The Russians had beaten the Americans by one point . . . on that end.

They'd scored eighty. They'd lost overall by one point.

In the meantime, the Indonesians had backed up to the field, shooting a poor seventy-three end. That gave them 952 points, identical to the U.S. total and one ahead of Russia's 951.

"We could have had a *three-way* shootoff really easily," said Denise. "Or we could have been out of it entirely."

Nerves were frayed for the shoot-off, another end of nine arrows. Skillman, who had gone further in the individual competition than either Parker or Ochs, took aim at the target—and missed everything.

The American team, to this point, had shot 216 arrows during the day, and had never come close to missing the bale. Neither had anyone else in the finals, or, for that, matter, throughout the competition.

But Skillman did. When last seen, her arrow was heading north, in the direction of the DMZ. And that, for all intents and purposes, was that. Denise, steady to the end, shot a 10–9–8 on her three arrows, but it wasn't enough to make up for Skillman missing that bale. The U.S. scored sixty-seven points—not nearly enough to match Indonesia's seventy-two, which, in itself, was no terrific end, either.

Still, as they walked back from pulling their arrows out for the last time in these Olympic Games, the Americans had only to look at the Russians to appreciate where they stood.

Moments later, the medals were presented. The capacity crowd cheered long and loud for the victorious home team Koreans. The Indonesians looked shaken and relieved as they received their silver medals.

When they announced the bronze medalists from the United States of America, they got the names backwards. "Parker Denise" was awarded her medal.

She didn't care. She smiled anyway, and waved to the crowd. When you're fourteen, and you've just won an Olympic medal, it's something to smile about. And when you've just shot two of the best pressure ends of your life to win it, it's a story that will only get better with age.

When BYU quarterback Ty Detmer was awarded the Heisman Trophy at the Marriott Marquis Hotel in New York City, flat nobody had more fun than his dad, Sonny Detmer, a Texas high school coach who had just flown first-class to football heaven.

Detmer's Dad

December 8, 1990

NEW YORK—The first time Sonny Detmer knew was in 1980, when his oldest son, Ty, went to Dallas with his San Antonio YMCA little league football team.

The opponent was a Dallas team that was undefeated and unscored-on all season. Undaunted, Ty's team scored thirty-five points on the way to a 35–zip road win. Ty threw five touchdown passes, and, as Sonny recalls, "he threw a total of eleven passes and completed nine of them, and the other two were dropped."

"Anyway," said Sonny, continuing, "on one of the touchdowns, he dropped the pass in over a defensive back who was right on top of the receiver. He just lobbed it over the top. I'm sitting in the stands watching, and I'm thinking, 'I've got high school quarterbacks who wouldn't even think to throw that pass.'

"So after the game I said to Ty, 'What about that pass?' And he said, 'Well, the defensive back was tight so I had to lay it in there.' He'd done it on purpose! I said right then, 'Wherever he plays, I'm coaching him.'"

Since they lived in the same house, that proved to be no problem. When Ty got to high school at San Antonio's Southwest High, he indeed played for his father/coach. They won more than 80 percent of their games as Ty dropped in passes all over Texas. That won him a full-ride scholarship to Brigham Young University, where he proceeded to drop in so many passes they gave him the Heisman Trophy.

And if that isn't storybook enough, on Thursday night, when they held the ceremony in a Times Square hotel to give Ty Detmer his Heisman Trophy, they drove Sonny to the banquet in a limo that he shared with football legends Jim Brown and Jim Taylor.

"I'm having a hard time believing all this," said the Texas coach. "I have a golf ball in my throat."

Even though he knew he had a natural on his hands almost a decade ago, he still couldn't quite believe it had come to this. All the perserverance, all the hard work, all the practice—all that had paid off. Had it ever.

There had been a time, and not long ago, when there was a question just how happy the endings were going to be. Ty had gone off to BYU, where he was redshirted his freshman year and was then slotted behind Sean Covey, the junior starter, on the quarterback depth chart.

And Sonny had been fired by Southwest High.

His teams had gone 12–1 and 7–3 during Ty's junior and senior seasons, and the Dragons had gone 7–3 the year after Ty left. But Southwest was upgrading from 4A to 5A status, and several members of the school board wanted a coaching change.

They came up with five reasons why Sonny Detmer should be relieved of his coaching duties.

"Four of them weren't true, and the fifth was because I played for him," remembers Ty.

Betty Detmer, Ty's mother and Sonny's wife, remembers, "They felt like Ty had gotten too much attention—and their kids hadn't. It was a political thing."

Sonny took a job offer in Arizona. After one season there he moved back to Texas, to the town of Mission, where he took over as coach of the Mission High School Eagles, a 5A school. He started his second son, Koy, at quarterback. Koy proceeded to throw for even more yards than his famous brother, and at last report, the Eagles were one of four teams left in the race for the 1990 Texas 5A state championship.

On Thursday, Sonny left his team long enough to fly to New York and take his limousine ride. It isn't every day your son wins the Heisman Trophy.

"He never says anything about what happened at Southwest," said Ty as he waited for his dad, flanked by Brown and Taylor, to drive in from the airport. "That's his way."

Nor is it Ty's way to dwell on the past or the negatives, either. But he does admit, "I got some congratulations from a lot of those people at Southwest. I don't accept those."

"Aw, you go through that kind of stuff every place," said Sonny. "I don't think anyone (at Southwest) doubted that he should have been our quarter-back; they just wanted more attention for their own kids."

Still, Southwest's firing is destined to take its place alongside the most ill-advised coaching changes in Texas football history. Hindsight ensures that. The coach they questioned has gone on to pound on the door of the Texas state championship, led by yet another gifted quarterback/son.

And the quarterback they questioned? He's one of fifty-six players to win the Heisman Memorial Trophy as the best college football player in America.

"I owe a lot to my dad," said Ty as he tucked his Heisman under his arm Thursday night. "He turned me loose when I was young and let me play. He didn't let me get burned out on football. I've heard all the war stories about parents who overdo it. With me, it was just the opposite. My dad couldn't have been better."

"I've always thought kids ought to be kids and play football as a game," said Sonny. "When it stops being a game, they should stop playing. Ty always played it as a game. He still does. He's just blessed that he can do it so well. He has something special."

The world knows it now. Sonny Detmer knew it a decade ago in Dallas.

Getting the secret recipe for Coca-Cola? Figuring out what Sigfried and Roy do with the Belgian tiger? Piece of cake compared to getting that game ball away from John Stockton.

Dream Team Gold

August 9, 1992

BARCELONA—For those skeptics—and I was one of them—who tended to believe that sending NBA pros to the Olympic Games would be like sending college deans to Fort Lauderdale for spring break; that they'd put a kind of corporate don't-ding-my-doors mood on the party; that they wouldn't know how to act like *Olympians,* well, they should have seen what I saw in the Palau d'Esports de Badalona late, late Saturday night after the best basketball players money could not buy brought the gold medal back to America.

After playing a game that won't add a dime to their bank accounts, Michael Jordan, Magic Johnson, Larry Bird, Karl Malone, John Stockton, and the rest of the Dream Team acted as if they'd just conquered the world *and* discovered it was round, all at the same time.

Bruce Jenner waving the American flag and lapping the track in Montreal? Mary Lou Retton leaping into Bela Karolyi's arms in Los Angeles? Jesse Owens standing at attention in front of Adolf Hitler in Berlin? Janet Evans sending a smile back to her L.A. high school all the way from Seoul? They had nothing on the Dream Team. Did the pros know how to celebrate a gold medal? Did they know how to destroy a zone?

"It's the most tremendous feeling I've ever had, anytime, anywhere," said Magic Johnson, whose previous accomplishments included an NCAA championship, several NBA championships, several more NBA MVP awards, and an NBA All-Star Game MVP trophy. Scottie Pippen said it beat the feeling of winning an NBA title, and he won his latest one only seven weeks ago.

They mounted the victory peristyle the way everyone would like to mount the victory platform, the way we all mount the victory platform in our dreams. They bounced up the steps. Happy to be there. Ecstatic to be there.

They led the crowd in a "USA" chant. Patrick Ewing flashed the V-for-victory sign. Charles Barkley hugged a referee. Chris Mullin hugged a Lithuanian. Jordan wore a flag. Magic waved a flag.

When the stars and stripes were raised and the national anthem was played—an anthem they'd all heard and endured at the start of thousands of games—they stood at strict attention. Buckingham Palace Guard attention. Bird put his hand on his heart. Stockton did something believed to be an NBA first: he sang the words. "I couldn't help it," he said. "It was spontaneous."

"Maybe we've been hearing the word 'dream' too much," Stockton said. "But I've been dreaming about standing on that stand and watching the flag go up all my life. When it did go up, it was just like I'd dreamed it. It was awesome."

He hadn't dreamed all his life about keeping the game ball as a memento. That was another spontaneous act. How much did it all mean to John Stockton, the most prolific assist-giver in the history of basketball? Enough that he wouldn't pass the ball at the end.

This one he gave to himself. He dribbled out the final 22.6 seconds and then grabbed the ball in a vise-like grip. When the buzzer sounded the referee first asked for the ball. Then he tried to physically take it away. Stockton said not over his gold medal.

"About a minute earlier, coach (Lenny) Wilkens hollered, 'get the ball, get the ball,'" said Stockton. "He meant to get it from them (Croatia) on a play, but I thought about it and I thought, 'That's not a bad idea.' They made a basket and I was bringing the ball down and I decided I'd just hang on to it—as long as I already had it.

"The guy from Croatia kept saying, 'Don't shoot it, don't shoot it.' I guess he didn't want us scoring any more. And I said to him, 'I don't intend to, pal.'"

Where is the gold-medal game ball now?

"Let's just say someone I trust has custody of it," Stockton said.

On and on they carried on, gift-wrapping an evening that had started in their locker room when they sat in their Team USA uniforms and got ready for the gold-medal game by watching a videotape of the 1972 Olympic final—

the one that featured three last-second reprieves for the eventually victorious Soviet Union.

"That gave us even more fire," said Malone. "We was robbed in that one."

But not in this one. Not with the best players in America playing their best for America, at absolutely no charge.

"Would I do it again?" said Malone. "In a heartbeat. In the beginning, I didn't know. It seemed like a lot of time and a lot of sacrifice. But to win the gold medal and hear our national anthem like that . . . yeah, in a heartbeat."

I think the Jazz-Bulls showdown of 1997 will go down in history as one of the best NBA Finals series of all-time. Not only did four of the six games come down to the final shot, but Michael Jordan, the best basketball player in history, was involved in every one of them. My advice is, don't record over those videotapes. They could be collector's items some day.

Bulls in Six

June 14, 1997

CHICAGO—So it wasn't meant to be. On the seventh game, they will rest.

After 102 games, 77 wins, a Midwest Division title, a Western Conference championship, and making even the Unbeatabulls begin to wonder, the Utah Jazz's karma ran into reality Friday night on the west side of Chicago, where the Chicago Bulls successfully defended their NBA title with a 90–86, Game 6 win.

The Jazz might have staged a successful comeback anywhere else, but not here, not the way the wind was blowing, not in the shadow of the Michael Jordan statue already erected in perpetuity outside the United Center, where the inscription reads: "The best there ever was, the best there ever will be." Hey, it's hard to beat people *after* the eulogy.

In the end, as in the beginning, it was Jordan who made the difference. At age thirty-four, he hoisted the Bulls on his back and carried them to their fifth NBA title in seven years. The Jazz's big mistake, their only sizable mistake, was being born in the Mike Era. If only he could have hit curve balls.

All series long, the Jazz handled and often manhandled the rest of the Bulls. Some of them may never recover. They could very realistically have sent Dennis Rodman into retirement, which, when you think about it, would take some of the emptiness out of taking second. They had players the calibre of Ron Harper and Luc Longley, who combined for two points last night, talking to themselves. They had Toni Kukoc, the best player ever to emigrate from Europe, longing for home.

But that still left Jordan, and he wasn't just interested in winning a ring for his thumb, he was *very* interested. He played hurt, he played sick, he played like he needed the money.

Without Jordan, the Jazz are pouring champagne on each other *before* Game 6. Think about it: coming into last night, there were three games that came down to Jordan's final shot. He made two, missed one. Reverse that, and the series is still alive. Make him 0-for-3 and Salt Lake is Championship City.

To seal their own fate, the Jazz finally did what they said they wouldn't do—double team him—and, sure as Lake Michigan is wet, when they did, he found the open man, Steve Kerr, who couldn't quite believe that, finally, for the first time of a very frustrating fortnight, John Stockton wasn't pestering him like a man with a flyswatter.

But not astonished enough not to nail the jump shot that now puts him in the Chicago Bulls annals with Bobby Hansen and John Paxson, who also hit title-deciding jump shots because Michael was so popular.

Kerr scores, Chicago goes delirious. Maybe the Jazz had led at least eighty percent of the game, just as they had led a vast majority of the series, and maybe they had five seconds to still make a case that they were Team Destiny, but with the United Center crowd finally turning off their cellulars at once and singing all the words to "Hey, Hey, Hey," the only chance for the Jazz was for another fire. And quick.

In the end, the Jazz could take consolation that for two weeks they'd kept all of Chicago on edge—as it became more and more apparent that they were ready to rumble.

You knew the series had reached an extremely high competitive pitch when Jordan told Rodman after Game 4 to cool it on trying to intimidate the likes of Karl Malone.

"This is skill versus skill," Jordan said, and that is as big a compliment as the reaction of the United Center crowd last night when the p.a. announcer, as the confetti was falling from the ceiling, said, "Congratulations to the Western Conference Champion Utah Jazz."

And the crowd booed.

It was over. And they were still worried.

Worried that John Stockton might pull through with another three to the heart. Worried that Karl Malone might again get the ball down low. Worried that maybe this celebration was all a mirage, because, man, it seemed like the Jazz *always* had the lead.

When it was all over but the traditional barricading of the downtown streets, it remained for Jordan to celebrate his title—which he did exuberantly, thrusting his hand to the adoring crowd as if to give them all five, which in fact he just had.

And it remained for Jordan to write the Jazz's epitaph. He'd done everything else.

He got that right too. He praised the team from Utah. Said they "showed a lot of heart," and took time to single out the series-long longshoremanlike defensive effort of Bryon Russell.

"Bryon, not Byron," he said.

The Jazz didn't get the Bulls' title, but they sure did get their attention. Sometime, later this summer, when even the great Jordan looks at the films, he'll realize just how close the team from Utah came.

Big Names

Duke Snider, 1980

Arnold Palmer, 1982

Jack Nicklaus, 1982

Bronko Nagurski, 1984

Bob Hope, 1986

Johnny Miller, 1990

Ron Abegglen, 1991

Danny Ainge, 1991

Edwards and Paterno, 1992

Rick Majerus, 1993

Larry Miller, 1993

Steve Young, 1994

David Stern, 1994

Frank Layden, 1997

I had just begun writing a regular column when I seized the opportunity to write about my boyhood idol, Duke Snider, and his chances of getting into the Hall of Fame. Actually, I just wanted the excuse to call him at his avocado ranch in California. Two days after this column ran, Duke Snider was announced as a 1980 Cooperstown inductee. It turned out he finally had his "good year" in 1979.

Duke Snider

January 8, 1980

Even if I hadn't grown up painting No. 4 on every T-shirt I owned; even if, heaven forbid, I'd been a Yankee lover; I'd still agree with Edwin Donald "Duke" Snider.

On the eve of yet another baseball Hall of Fame ballot—the 1980 inductees will be announced Wednesday in New York—the most famous No. 4 in history (in Brooklyn and Los Angeles, anyway) asks:

"How come every year I become a better player?"

What's got the Duke perplexed is that every year since he became eligible for Hall of Fame balloting in 1970, he has perpetually come closer to the needed three-fourths majority. He insists he has not swung at a good pitch, bad pitch, or any pitch since he retired in 1964.

"You can't help but wonder after a while," he said Monday from his home in California. "It's a fact I've become a better player—I've gotten more votes—every year since I became eligible."

Now he's wondering what kind of year he had in 1979.

If it was a good one, he'll finally be drafted into the Hall of Fame on his eleventh try. "I hope I became that much better in a few minds," he says, "and didn't become worse in the minds of voters who already had me up there."

Last year Snider finished second in the balloting, which is open to members of the Baseball Writers of America who have at least ten years' good-standing in the association. He had 308 points, just sixteen short of the 324 needed for induction. Only Willie Mays made the grade, being ushered in on his first year of eligibility. Enos "Country" Slaughter was a distant third, failing on his fifteenth and final try.

Duke admits that has him sort of worried.

"There's a theory that sooner or later you level off," he explains. "Slaughter leveled off about five years early and then started dropping votes."

Of course, Slaughter didn't help himself by leveling a few verbal blasts at the Baseball Writers in his declining years. The resulting animus doubtless contributed to his downfall.

Snider is neither lobbying or lamenting. He admits getting into the Hall would top out his illustrious career, but when they don't give you a bat, how are you going to swing or otherwise generate any offense?

He believes his biggest downfall—as far as getting votes—lies with his "numbers." He says many of his peers have better statistics. Like Mays and Mickey Mantle, for instance, the two men who played centerfield for the New York Giants and New York Yankees when the Duke was in his prime in centerfield for the Dodgers.

But if their numbers were better, they weren't by much, and Duke Snider's eighteen-year statistics still glaringly stand out.

He had a career .295 batting average, 407 home runs, 2,116 hits, 1,333 RBI, played on six pennant-winning teams and one World Series winner, and finished with a slugging percentage of .540, the eleventh best in history.

He has never lobbied on his own behalf. "I'm not voting," he says. "If the voters want to look up what I did, that's fine."

Apparently they have been looking it up and with increasing enthusiasm. Back in 1975 the Duke fared no better than ninth, while ex-Brooklyn teammates Gil Hodges and Pee Wee Reese, neither of whom has yet made the Hall, either, were respectively fourth and seventh in the balloting.

"I don't think it ought to be easy to get in," he stresses. "I've always thought you better have had some kind of career to make it into the Hall."

Few can argue that Snider's was some kind of career. Baseball people from coast to coast have said things such as, "There are some players in the Hall of Fame who couldn't carry his glove" (Buzzie Bavasi), and already he's been named to *Sports Illustrated's* All-Time-Non-Hall-of-Fame team.

And if he had a good season in '79, he's headed for the real thing.

I wrote this memoir from the U.S. Open in 1979, three years prior to the date Arnold
Palmer played in an event at Jeremy Ranch. Was it shameless cheerleading
for a lifelong idol? Pretty much; although I never did name a dog after Arnold Palmer,
like my friend Claudia Nielsen did. Ivy Baker Priest, by the way, was
the treasurer of the United States and the one who signed all the dollar bills of that time.

Arnold Palmer

The day was warm, sunny, and somewhat humid—one of those days that tend to run together in the summer in Ohio. Kind of like the landscape seems to run together, without any mountains to break it up.

The date was June 16, 1979. A Saturday. I had the day off.

And Arnold Palmer didn't.

The scene was the U.S. Open at the Inverness Golf Club in Toledo. I was there to cover the tournament; Arnie was there to play in it. When the third round came along on Saturday I was able, for a day, to forget about deadlines. The *Deseret News* didn't publish on Sundays back then, and I had time on my hands. Arnie, on the other hand, had made the 36-hole cut. His two-day total of 149 had him just ten shots back of the lead, and so what if his fiftieth birthday was less than three months away?

Such were the circumstances that Saturday when I meandered onto the grounds of the stately Inverness Club after sleeping in at the Toledo Holiday Inn.

I checked in at the press tent, ate a sweet roll, read the paper, and then walked out on the course. On the sixth hole I saw Arnie leaving the tee.

I pulled my press armband out of my pocket—a fringe benefit, to be sure, since a red armband that says PRESS is all you need to walk inside the gallery ropes of a U.S. Open. Even if you hate to watch golf, you'd still probably watch it if you had the advantage over 22,000 other spectators—people who are using trees and ladders and periscopes just to catch an occasional glimpse of a real live player. I slipped out onto the fairway.

I decided I'd watch Arnie for a few holes.

He got to his ball, took out an iron, and slashed a shot. Then we headed for the green.

The gallery response was deafening.

I don't know what it was like when Lindbergh came back from Paris and rode down Fifth Avenue, but this, I can tell you, was no slouch cheer. The fans in the stands surrounding the green all rose as Arnie approached and gave him a standing ovation; and the thing was, he wasn't even on the green, in regulation.

It was like that on every hole thereafter.

The pattern was the same. Arnie would approach the green and somebody would yell, "Go get 'em Arnie!" or "Attaway Arnie!" and everybody would applaud and then they'd stand and soon there would be a full-scale ovation going on.

No matter what he did.

Caught up in the parade, I followed Arnie through thirteen holes, finishing at Inverness's two-tiered 18th green, which sits at the base of a large amphitheater and comfortably handles two to three thousand people. It is one of golf's great finishing holes.

When Arnie got to the 18th tee, he was twelve-over-par for the tournament and five-over for the day—not blistering numbers—but he reached back for a big drive and a wedge to the green that was just a little long. It landed on the upper tier, a good thirty feet above the cup, which was cut on the lower of the two tiers.

The burgeoning ovation as Arnie approached the 18th green was biggest of the day, due to sheer numbers alone, but it quieted when he crouched over his putt. Then he ran the 30-footer dead in the back of the cup.

As soon as the ball disappeared, a roar went up that must have been heard in Columbus. Hale Irwin, who was leading the tournament, must have wondered what had happened, and if someone had overtaken him.

Arnie signed his scorecard—a 75—and aimed himself in the general direction of the locker room. Nearly an hour later he made it to his locker, having signed his name more often than Ivy Baker Priest.

I was waiting there—the armband came through again—and asked Arnie the question paramount on my mind.

"Does the adoration ever get old?"

He answered matter-of-factly. He said he was nearly fifty years old, and he was in good enough financial shape that he didn't need to play in golf tournaments anymore, and he was well aware of that fact.

But no, the adoration had never gotten old, not even close. He liked to hear people cheer and holler, "Attaway Arnie!" and it was his opinion that the birdie putt on 18, the curling 30-footer, had gone in chiefly because there were around 3,001 people, including himself, all wishing it would go in.

"You have no idea what a help that is," he said, "to have so many people on your side."

So there it was. A tribute to the Army from the general. In so many words, he said that nobody wins 61 PGA tournaments, and a couple of British Opens, without outside help. Not even Arnold Palmer. *Especially* not Arnold Palmer.

He said he appreciated it; he appreciated it a lot. And that makes it even clearer why wherever Arnie goes—to the U.S. Open in Toledo or to the Jeremy Shootout this week in Utah—he travels by Army. The society is of the mutual admiration kind. To the old challenge, "Oh, yeah? You and whose army?" Arnold Palmer can always answer, "Mine. That's whose."

We were standing on the putting green at the Jack Nicklaus–designed Park Meadows Golf Course, where Nicklaus had just played the inaugural round with Johnny Miller, when I asked Nicklaus if he ever thought much about where he stood in golf history. I expected the obligatory, "Aw shucks" answer. I didn't get it. Instead, for the next half-hour, the greatest golfer ever to play the game talked—he wanted to talk—about how many majors he'd won, about just where he ranked in the pantheon of great players, and about his knowing that someone would come along one day, some phenom, and take a legitimate shot at what he'd done. As he hoped, Jack still had one more major in him—the 1986 Masters, which he won four years later. It was his eighteenth major as a professional and twentieth overall, counting his two U.S. Amateur titles. At the time of this conversation, Tiger Woods was seven years old, but I swear Jack knew he was out there.

Jack Nicklaus

September 17, 1982

PARK CITY—Jack Nicklaus, the one and the only, was on the double green of his new Park Meadows Country Club golf course Thursday, laboriously fielding questions about his newest architectural creation, when somebody asked him about his putting.

Twenty minutes later, after rolling in three straight short putts to demonstrate the new stroke he discovered just a couple of weeks ago at the World Series of Golf, he asked if anybody had another question.

Rest assured that Jack Nicklaus's favorite subject is still golf—how it's played, not the design of its courses—and he's every bit as interested as the rest of the world as to just how far he can stretch the game's statistical fences before his spikes wear out.

"I sure haven't lost my nerve," he said Thursday as the subject turned from Nicklaus the Architect to Nicklaus the Golfer. He said that—that he still had his nerve—as a post script to his mini-lecture on putting, during which he explained how he was having trouble not following through and then, Voila! At the World Series of Golf he discovered that if he tucked in his right arm he was able to follow through exactly in the direction of the hole . . .

. . . And on goes the beat. In the past three years, Nicklaus, entering his third decade as a professional golfer and continents ahead of the field, has completely overhauled his game. He's not getting older, just (gasp) better.

It's true that Park Meadows, a $6 million development, is the twenty-sixth course he's designed, but architecture still remains a moonlighting venture for Jack, who is absolutely aware of where he fits into the history of golf and is still keen on improving his standing.

He is not quite so obnoxious about it as a Pete Rose—who knows exactly where he stands in the stat books as he chases the marks of Ty Cobb—or so deliberate and methodical as a Walter Payton—who knows he needs only to play X more seasons to surpass Jim Brown's rushing records. Nor is he given to fits of bragging, like a Muhammad Ali, who may not have been the best of all time but is constantly willing to give seminars on his belief that he was.

Jack Nicklaus is simply aware. And that's enough to keep him swinging, running, and punching. He's aware his name will be etched in the record books, in the all-time section, and he's aware he's at the stage of his career when it's up to his own intensity and motivation as to just when the final chapter will be written.

He's also aware that his situation differs by one key element from that of a Pete Rose or a Walter Payton. Whereas those stars in other sports are pursuing legends of another time, the only legend Jack Nicklaus has left to pursue is himself.

He's passed up all the rest. Vardon, Hagen, Jones, Hogan, Nelson, Snead, Palmer. You name them, he's shot by them. There may be occasional debates among golf historians as to the greatest golfer of all time—based on swings and temperaments and career lengths—but such debates are founded on philosophy and what-ifs, certainly not the facts.

Statistically, nobody stacks up to Nicklaus. He's won sixty-eight PGA titles, been the top money winner a record eight times, been the Player of the Year a record five times, and had the best scoring average on the tour eight times. And then, in the realm of the really big leagues, consider his record of nineteen major championships (five Masters, five PGAs, four U.S. Opens, three British Opens, and two U.S. Amateurs). In second place is Bobby Jones with a mere thirteen.

In the stretch run of his career, it's that number—19—that plays on Nicklaus's mind.

He said he'd like to extend his majors list to twenty and beyond. That is why he keeps tinkering with his game, why he keeps looking for new putting strokes, and why he prepares with such fervor for the four major tournaments every year.

"I think somebody someday will break my records," he said at Park City Thursday. This comment produced the expected snickers from the crowd— no doubt the same kind of snickers that emerged from listeners when Babe Ruth said somebody would hit more home runs than his 714.

But Nicklaus persisted. "I think, with time, somebody will break them all," he said. "And I know for a fact I'll have to quit sometime. But when I do, I want to make sure I retire with more than nineteen."

Then he got sort of a gleam in his eye and said, "Hogan was what, forty-three, when he had his best year?"

Jack William Nicklaus is 42 going on 43 . . . going on 20.

My favorite writer of fiction is novelist William Goldman, whose specialty is superlatives. In books such as The Princess Bride, Magic, Marathon Man, Brothers, Heat, *and others, Goldman's characters tend to be the biggest, the fastest, the slowest, the best, the worst, the ugliest, the prettiest. Another penchant of Goldman's is to slip into almost all of his make-believe books a cameo appearance by Bronko Nagurski, a football player and a walking, talking superlative himself. But unlike Goldman's other characters, Nagurski is the absolute truth. After reading bits and pieces about the Nagurski legend in Goldman's books, I looked up his record in the NFL history books to see if the stories—like the eighty-four yards he gained in the fourth quarter against the Chicago Cardinals as described in this column, and like the fact that when they tried to cast a ring for him at the football Hall of Fame they had to wait a year and a half before they could build a mold that was big enough—were true. They all checked out.*

You can imagine my surprise when Bronko Nagurski himself was ushered into an NFL press conference prior to Super Bowl XIII in Tampa. They had flown him down specially from International Falls, Minnesota—the coldest place in the United States—so he could be that year's honoree for the ceremonial Super Bowl coin toss. After the interviews, I walked up to Bronko Nagurski and stuck out my hand. It was the biggest hand I ever shook.

Bronko
Nagurski

TAMPA, Fla.—They say that one time, in an age when both he and professional football were much younger, he cracked a brick wall in Chicago's Wrigley Field. He was the Bears fullback and nobody knew for sure if he could run through walls, but they knew for sure he'd try. And with the game to be won, he took the handoff from his quarterback, knocked one defender unconscious, broke another's shoulder, and then, bouncing off the goal post after he'd scored the game-winning touchdown, he careened into the wall, which, to its credit, didn't break but did crack a little.

"That last guy," said the football player as he picked himself up, "he hit pretty hard."

They also say he was recruited to college off a Minnesota farm when coach Doc Spears of the University of Minnesota football team drove by one day and saw him pulling the plow after the horse had gone lame. More fiction than fact? Maybe, although he did do a lot of plowing and he did wind up playing for Spears at Minnesota, where he was an All-American at two positions—tackle *and* fullback.

They haven't made one like Bronko Nagurski since.

Sports writer Grantland Rice said he'd take eleven Nagurskis over eleven Granges or eleven Thorpes any day. The Chicago Bears said they'd take Nagurski, too, at whatever the cost. They signed him out of college in 1929 for $5,000. They got their money's worth. They knew it, the rest of the league knew it. Clark Hinkle, a hard-nosed fullback-linebacker for Green Bay, had to have five stitches the first time he tried to tackle Nagurski. "My biggest thrill in football," said Hinkle, "was the day Bronko Nagurski announced his retirement."

Football isn't an easy sport to terrorize, but Nagurski struck fear into whole teams. When a train derailed while carrying the Steelers back to Pittsburgh after they'd been thrashed by the Bears, someone shouted, "Run for your lives, Nagurski's still after us!"

He played eight seasons for the Bears, from 1930 through 1938, powering them to two NFL championships. He was 6-foot-2 and 225 pounds, a huge man in those times. His ring size: 19–1/2, his neck size: 19.

He was only twenty-nine when he retired, hardly washed up. Only fed up. Even though he averaged 4.4 yards per carry, the Bears kept cutting his salary. Depressing times, the '30s, and when it got to the point Bronislau Nagurski thought he was worth more than he was getting, he up and quit. He moved back to his Minnesota hometown of International Falls, on the Canadian border, and bought a filling station.

"If you ever need me again," Nagurski told Bears owner George Halas as he left Chicago, "just holler."

Five years later, Halas did.

It was 1943, the war had drained the NFL of much of its manpower, and Chicago had a title it wanted to win. Nagurski was brought back to play, but at tackle only. They wanted his bulk on the line. At thirty-five, he would not be needed at his old glory position, fullback.

The Western Division title came down to the last game of the regular season—an all-Chicago showdown at Comiskey Park between the Bears and the Cardinals. The winner would meet the Washington Redskins for the league title.

After three quarters, the Cardinals led 24–14 and, as fate had it, the Bears' fullback became ill. Sensing the possibility, the crowd took up a chant—"The Bronko," "The Bronko,"—and Bears coach Hunk Anderson responded by sending the Bronko, a man who hadn't carried a football for five years, into the game.

On the first down, quarterback Sid Luckman gave the ball to Nagurski, and the Cards were ready to show this relic what he'd missed while pumping gas in International Falls. But Nagurski didn't go down until he'd fallen forward for four yards.

The next play he fell forward for eight.

The Bears were marching. From the twenty, Nagurski shook off Cardinal tackles all the way to the one. Then he plunged in for the score. On the next Bears' series, he got six yards when it was fourth-and-four, setting up a Luckman touchdown pass that put the Bears into the title game against the Redskins, which would be all Bears, 41–21, and would see Nagurski score yet again.

Against the Cardinals he gained eighty-four yards—all in the fourth quarter.

Bronko Nagurski is seventy-five now, and he needs bifocals and a little help to get around on account of the arthritis, which is slowing him down with considerable more success than the Cardinals ever did. But he still weighs in at a steady 225, and the hands like hams, they're still there. This Sunday in front of 73,000 fans in Tampa Stadium and a worldwide Super Bowl television audience of over 200 million, Bronko Nagurski will step to the middle of the field and toss the ceremonial coin.

After that he'll retire to the sidelines to watch the game. But if either Washington Redskins coach, Joe Gibbs, or Los Angeles Raiders coach, Tom Flores, is up on his football history, he'll know where Bronko Nagurski is sitting, just in case . . .

There was this one time, they say, that he cracked a brick wall at Wrigley Field . . .

What I remember most about this column is that I called Bob Hope in Hollywood the day after his eighty-third birthday, and his agent said Mr. Hope would call me back at noon. "Yeah, right," I thought, "but he didn't say which noon." An hour later, at high noon in Utah, the sports desk phone rang. "Hi, this is Bob Hope," said the voice on the other end. Within seconds he was telling jokes. All these years later, it still remains a highlight of my sportswriting career.

Bob Hope

June 1, 1986

It was 11:00 A.M., North Hollywood Time, and on the first morning of his eighty-fourth year, Bob Hope was already in fine form as he broached two of his favorite subjects: Jerry Ford and golf.

"Jerry Ford," Bob Hope said, "the man who turned golf into a contact sport . . .

" . . . he's a wonderful guy. It's just that every once in a while he loses his concentration and wipes out the gallery . . .

" . . . he's easy to find. Just follow the wounded . . .

" . . . there are fifty different golf courses in the Palm Springs area, and he doesn't know which one he's going to play until he hits his tee shot."

Hope listed his favorite foursome: "Myself, Jerry Ford, a faith healer, and a paramedic."

Bob Hope and The Honorable Gerald R. Ford play golf together fifteen or twenty times a year if they can help it—one such occasion will be Monday at Jeremy Ranch in conjunction with the Great American Indian Shootout—and the jokes never stop. And even if Ford, the younger of the famous twosome, has the lower handicap and doesn't hit many people on the head anymore now that he doesn't have to run the country and can work on his game, he wouldn't have it any other way.

As he says in the foreword he wrote in Hope's recent best-selling book, *Confessions of a Hooker,* "Golf with Bob Hope has given me as much enjoyment, relaxation, and laughter as anything in my life."

Then he adds, "After all, where would Bob Hope be today without old, out-of-work politicians who keep trying to master the game of golf under public scrutiny?"

As ambassadors for golf and goodwill, Ford and Hope are at the head of the class. That's evident by their one-day stop in Utah. Double-handedly, they've turned what might have been a modest little fund-raiser into one that is expected to raise $175,000 for BYU's American Indian Services program.

"But I'm playing lousy," Hope lamented via telephone from California. "There's not enough time to work on my game." At that moment, he was late for a TV taping session. Then he would be off to Alabama for the Charley Boswell Classic, a benefit golf tournament for the blind. Boswell, a champion blind golfer, has counted on, and gotten, Hope's help for the past thirteen years straight.

"Charley Boswell told me I've got the worst swing he ever heard," said Hope.

He's not only got a million of 'em, he tells a million of 'em—on himself as well as on ex-presidents. In his book he recounts how Arnold Palmer once told him how he could cut eight strokes off his score . . . "Skip one of the par 3's."

Lesser known is that Hope hasn't spent the past fifty-six years playing golf as a joke. His handicap was once as low as four. In 1951 he played in the British Amateur. Jetted over to Wales (to a course called Royal Porthcaw) and teed it up.

"I got beat in the first round by a man smoking a pipe, which of course delighted Crosby," writes Hope in his book.

Hope was forty-eight years old at the time. Now, as of last Thursday, if you can believe it, he's eighty-three.

He plays in dozens of golf benefits a year. In all, America's first man of comedy still does between two hundred and two hundred fifty personal appearances each year. "It keeps him young," says his agent, Ward Grant.

Writing in his book, Hope says, "Some consider it remarkable that I'm able to maintain such a busy pace. They ask me when I'm going to retire. Retire? This is work? Play golf, tell a few jokes, and have so many friends all over the world?"

Among his friends and golf buddies have been a lot of presidents. Before Ford, he played golf with Nixon, Johnson, Kennedy, and Eisenhower.

For the record, he says former Vice President Spiro Agnew was wilder than Ford.

"Now there was a real wild man. When Agnew yelled 'Fore!' you never knew whether he was telling someone to get out of the way or if he was predicting how many spectators he would hit . . . It was exciting playing with Agnew. You never had to wait for the group ahead. They were all hiding in the bushes."

But his old buddy, and tomorrow's partner, remains his favorite target.

Hope remembered a day he and Ford were playing in England.

"On the 18th tee, Ford put a ball through the clubhouse window. It wasn't easy. It was behind him. That's when I remembered that the Russians used to say if we were really serious about disarmament, we'd dismantle his golf clubs."

Ford, non-plussed, has said putting up with the White House press corps merely seasoned him for Hope.

And Hope, in that voice that could turn a grocery list into a successful monologue, says that when it comes to golf, at least he doesn't play politics.

"I play with Tip O'Neill, and I play with Jerry Ford," he said. "And they both treat me exactly the same. Neither one will let me keep score."

The most entertaining talkers I've ever interviewed are Frank Layden and Rick Majerus,
but the best talker I ever interviewed, period, is Johnny Miller. When
Miller is in the mood he can make anything, even a golf round, sound riveting.

Johnny Miller

I f you watch golf telecasts, you may have noticed that NBC has retained the services of Johnny Miller, now in semi-retirement as a player, to do color commentary. If you don't watch golf telecasts—because they're too dull, too staid, and you don't need a Cadillac—you might want to tune in anyway. Miller could talk a good game when he was playing. And he still can.

You'll quickly note that what distinguishes Miller from other golf commentators, apart from the fact he has no British accent, is that he is frank, honest, candid, and glib. At least he has been in his first few telecasts. A regular John Madden in the tower on 18. He's breaking the color barrier in golf.

Golf broadcasts have always resembled the play-by-play of a funeral service, which is perhaps understandable for a sport that has a weekly ritual of sending 140 players off the first tee on Thursday and then goes about the slow-death process of eliminating 139 of them by Sunday afternoon.

Since none of these 139 so-called "losers" is ever done in by anything human—Bill Laimbeer's defense, Joe Montana's arm, Jose Canseco's bat, or anything else so physically obvious or understandable—golf announcers have traditionally been a mix of empathy and apologies. They sugarcoat collapses. They whisper. They gloss over temper tantrums. And they invariably precede difficult shots with alibis in advance, such as, "He'll be lucky just to make contact. He's got almost no chance to hit the green."

Invariably, if the golfer then hits the green—and if you watch much golf, you know this often happens—the announcer will talk about the terrific talent out on the tour.

Now, along comes Miller, who talks about golf in terms that it is basically a mental pressure-cooker invented to torment man.

Take, for example, a moment at the Bob Hope Classic a couple of weeks ago, when Miller observed an approach shot to the final green that was facing Peter Jacobsen, the tournament leader.

Miller looked at the shot, a downhill lie fronted by a lake and said, "That's a perfect shot to choke on."

Right there on national TV, he said the "C" word.

There were gasps, of course. One came from fellow semi-retired commentator Jack Nicklaus, who said, "Why not say, 'what an opportunity to win,' not 'what an opportunity to choke?'"

Answered Miller, "Jack doesn't think in terms of normal people."

He continued, "Jack actually taught me something with that observation. That's why he's such a great champion. He always looked at tough situations as pure opportunity."

Jacobsen did likewise, at least he did on that particular 3-iron shot. He hit the shot close enough for a birdie putt, and won the tournament.

In retrospect, Miller's comments only added to the dramatics, and to Jacobsen's stature.

As for Miller himself, it's well documented that he seized enough opportunities during his playing career to win twenty-two PGA Tour titles and a pair of major championships—the U.S. and British Opens; and the torture he once inflicted on the desert courses in Arizona is legendary to this day.

"It could be that I'm the right guy to pull this off," Miller says of his fresh approach to golf-on-TV. "I have been there. I do have some credentials. And I'm sort of a loose cannon anyway. I haven't ever been Hollywood-ized."

Miller has already been the subject of a player's complaint. After he observed that Chicago Bears Coach Mike Ditka, distraught after a poor shot during the Bob Hope pro-am, looked like "Curtis Strange after a three-putt," Strange complained about Miller to PGA Commissioner Deane Beman.

"There was nothing malicious in that remark," says Miller. "Curtis should realize that."

"I'm sure I might alienate myself to pros with softer skin, but I just hope they'll realize I'm telling the truth," he says. "I want to be fair."

Preparing for this weekend's telecast from San Diego, he says, "I feel like it's something I can do and do well. Jack Benny said the secret to TV is to be sincere, and after a while you can fake that."

Johnny Miller thinks he can manage that. And if he can't? If he chokes? He'll be the first one to say so.

One of the nice things about sports writing is that it exposes you to people who love what they do and do what they love and who are amazingly good at it. I'm convinced there are all kinds of Ron Abegglens out there, who could be coaching the Chicago Bulls or the Duke Blue Devils just as well as they ever coached Morgan High, Snow College, and Weber State. But they probably wouldn't have as much fun.

Ron Abegglen

Maybe Ron Abegglen has been coaching basketball for twenty-nine seasons. Maybe he has coached 553 wins and averaged almost twenty victories a year for his entire career. Maybe he has won championships at the high school, junior college, and four-year college level; but when Weber State University's new head basketball coach walked through the 12,000 purple seats in the Dee Events Center on Friday, he got goose bumps anyway.

"Do people around here know how good they've got it?" he asked.

Abegglen comes to Weber from a background of winning, and a background of background. He's seen more rural roads than a drug smuggler and more obscure gyms than a keyhole painter. If you can name it, his teams didn't play there. He's made a career out of faraway places.

He started coaching at the age of twenty-three in Morgan, Utah, where the cow-to-people ratio is dead even. After twelve seasons and 232 wins at Morgan High School, he moved to Ephraim, Utah, where the turkeys outnumber the cows and the people. After ten seasons and 212 wins at Snow Junior College, he moved on to Anchorage, Alaska, where he had to negotiate, for the first time in his coaching career, traffic lights. Anchorage is not, like Morgan and Ephraim, a small town, but it is nonetheless largely off by itself, city-wise and basketball-wise.

Abegglen stayed through seven seasons and 109 wins at the University of Alaska-Anchorage, an NCAA Division II program. He won the Great Northwest Conference three times and almost won the Division II national championship in 1988, when his Seawolves finished as the runner-up.

Now, he's at Weber. Richard Hannan, Weber's athletic director, picked up Abegglen's resume two weeks ago and couldn't put it down. If this guy could average nineteen wins a year in Morgan, Ephraim, and Anchorage, what could he average in Ogden?

Abegglen told Weber to make him an offer he couldn't refuse. They did. They offered him the job. He told them not to bother with directions on how to find the school. He could read a map; and, besides, Ogden is only twenty minutes west of Morgan. Coaching can be a funny business. Work thirty years, and you can move back into your old neighborhood.

"There's a certain appeal to moving back to Morgan," says Abegglen, who hasn't decided yet where his family will take up residence. "I have some great memories there."

One of those memories—great now, although it wasn't at the time—is of the day he packed up his car in Provo, where he had just graduated from BYU, and drove to Morgan as the new head basketball coach and assistant baseball and football coach.

"I thought this big building by the high school was the gym," he says, remembering back to 1963. "But it turned out that it was the elementary school. The gym was this little building off to the side. It was so small it had two 10-second lines."

The coach didn't just learn to live with it; he succeeded in turning it into "one heck of a homecourt advantage."

When they built a bigger gym three years later, Abegglen didn't know if he was happy about it or not.

His relationship with Weber State started then, in the '60s, when Weber graduated from a junior college to a four-year college (in 1962–63) and hired Dick Motta away from Clearfield High School as its basketball coach. Abegglen's Morgan teams would sometimes play in preliminary games to Weber's varsity games, and he became a regular at Motta's practices.

That's when he "got purple," as he puts it, and kept it in the front of his mind that if Weber ever needed a coach, and he was available, he'd be interested.

He came in second when Weber hired Coach Denny Huston three seasons ago; now he's replacing Huston, who won more games than he lost (43–42) but got fired anyway. His sin was that he didn't draw a crowd. An average of 8,000 Dee Center seats were empty for every home game.

Abegglen's never had to fill 12,000 seats, so he isn't exactly sure how to go about it. But he knows where he'll start.

"I'm going to call all my friends in Morgan to come down and buy tickets," he says. "That ought to take care of the first two hundred."

Beyond that, he'll see about approaching the job at Weber the same as he's approached the job everywhere else he's been.

"I'm a determined recruiter," he says, "If a kid's going to tell me no, I want to make sure he feels bad when he tells me."

He won in Alaska with Utah players—some years, the Seawolves had more Utah recruits than Alaska recruits—and his plan is to go especially hard after the Utah recruits in the Ogden area. He doesn't want to lose the likes of Reid Newey (Utah State), Kendall Youngblood (Utah State), and Kurt Miller (New Mexico)—local players of late who were spirited out of Weber's grasp.

"I don't know what's happened before, but I want to get those kids here," he says. "I want them knocking on my door."

He adds, "This is a place to be proud of—this school, this area, this facility. When I walked through those seats to the press conference, I really did, I got goose bumps."

The coach who's been around knew he had arrived.

Danny Ainge wound up playing in the NBA Finals six times in his twelve-year pro career: four times with Boston and once each with Portland and Phoenix. Coincidence? I don't think so. Some guys have a knack.

Danny Ainge

May 11, 1991

Ask Danny Ainge which was better, the Celtics teams he played on with Bird, McHale, and Parish, or the Trail Blazers team he's playing on now with Drexler, Porter, and Kersey, and Ainge says slyly, "Let's put it this way: Boston had better starters. Portland has a better bench."

"Covers me both ways, right?"

He's thirty-two-can-you-believe-that years old and still looking for an edge; still looking for the call. It's been a decade since he broke Frank Arnold's heart and graduated from BYU. It's been a decade since he fielded his last ground ball for the Toronto Blue Jays. It's been nine years since Tree Rollins bit him. It's been five years since he won his last championship in Boston. And now here he is with Portland, looking to win another one.

Not that he looks older. Not that he doesn't still have the baby face that's always gotten him in trouble with referees and with guys like Rollins, the face his own mother said was "too facial." By all accounts, he is as competitive as he ever was. He says he'd like to play at least three more years and reassess after that, to see if he can beat the aging process, too.

"There's no question that fewer minutes is lengthening my career," he says.

Besides, why quit? Who would want to? Adversity came and went quickly enough, in the form of Sacramento. From the Celtics to the Kings to the Blazers. It doesn't get any more topsy-turvy-topsy than that. If nothing else, those two seasons and 148 games of banishment in Sacramento taught Ainge the value of teammates. Statistically he was the best he's ever been as a King, but the team went nowhere. "If I'm the best player here, then we're in trouble," he said at the time, screwing up his face as he said it. He was traded last August, first to Portland, ninety miles from his hometown of Eugene. Even for someone who signed a professional baseball contract as a teen-ager, who won the John Wooden Award as the best college basketball player in America, who dribbled through Notre Dame, who won a lawsuit in a New York federal court that got him out of a Blue Jays uniform and into a Celtics uniform, who played in four world championships with the Celtics, and won two of them, who was an NBA All-Star in 1988, this may have been the happiest day of all.

And not just because he was coming home to Oregon green; but because the Blazers, fresh off their appearance in the 1990 NBA Finals, were winners.

"That's the bottom line. Winning. I learned a long time ago, that's what brings happiness to a basketball player," says Ainge. "There are a lot of times here I'd like more minutes, sure, but the main thing is, I like to win."

He was more contented in Boston, where he started in the backcourt with Dennis Johnson, got all those minutes, and still won. "I'm not sure it gets any better than it got there," he says.

But with Portland, as captain of the bench, as ace of the bullpen, he has no complaints. He averages about 22 minutes and 11 points a game, has the green light for three-pointers, has finally been forgiven by his fellow Oregonians for once defecting to a college in Utah, and won't be at all surprised if by June he'll be sized for his third NBA title ring.

"I think, one through twelve, this is the best team I've been on," he says of the Blazers. "Is it better than Boston? That's a difficult question. In Boston, we were so dominant. Now, there seems to be so much parity. Nobody's dominant.

"But any team we match up with, I feel we can beat them. We don't have any one glaring weakness. And we have a great homecourt advantage. That's a big edge. No matter who we play (in the playoffs), we'll have one more game at home."

That's the Blazers' hole card in their current playoff battle with the Jazz as their second round series continues today in the Salt Palace. After two opening wins in Portland, the Blazers have the luxury of losing all three games in Utah, and still moving on to the third round.

As he thinks about this, about the prospects of more winning, Ainge can't quite suppress a grin. He always has been facial.

It's going to be a long haul before college football comes up with replacements for these two Happy Valley residents. A couple of years after writing this column, I asked Paterno if he would write the foreword for a book I'd talked Edwards into co-authoring, and he couldn't say "of course," fast enough. By the time the book came out, Paterno had won nearly 300 games and Edwards had shot well past 200. Only ten major college coaches have won over 230 games, and of those ten, only two have won them all at the same school—these two.

LaVell Edwards and Joe Paterno

October 31, 1992

In running, there is a saying that goes, "You can find a lot of runners who are old, but you can't find a lot of old runners"—a commentary on a sport that exacts a high toll from knees, hips, ankles, and other joints.

Well, the same can be said of college football coaches, although the tolls exacted are different. For a variety of reasons, most of them having something to do with winning, losing, and worn-out welcomes, you can't find a lot of old football coaches.

All of which makes today's meeting in Cougar Stadium between the football teams from Brigham Young and Penn State something of an aberration. Between LaVell Edwards, who coaches the Cougars, and Joe Paterno, who coaches Penn State, they have logged seventy-four college seasons, each one exclusively at the same school.

Both still have the same area code they started with. Not once has either one looked up "Moving vans" in the yellow pages.

In their business, Edwards and Paterno are not normal.

Despite the fact they are quite different in personality (Paterno talks, Edwards listens), coaching styles (Edwards is hands-off, Paterno is hands-on), hobbies (Edwards golfs, Paterno doesn't), and roots (Paterno is from Brooklyn,

Edwards is from Orem), they are naturally close friends—naturally because after a few years of going to summer coaches' conventions and on Nike cruises you soon realize that familiar faces aren't all that plentiful, and, like foreigners in a foreign land, you should stick together.

Also naturally because of their similarities, which include:

* They're about the same age (Paterno is 65, Edwards, 62).

* Both of their schools' campuses are located in the middle of surrounding areas nicknamed (complimentary and otherwise) "Happy Valley."

* They've both turned down offers from the pros (Edwards could have been a millionaire and CEO of the Detroit Lions, and Paterno could have become coach and part-owner of the New England Patriots).

* They're both uncommonly loyal to their coaching staffs (the average length of service for the nine assistant coaches serving under both Paterno and Edwards is thirteen seasons) and to their schools (Edwards has spent all of his thirty-one years as a college coach at BYU—ten as an assistant, twenty-one as a head coach; the same is true of Paterno at Penn State, where he was an assistant for sixteen years prior to his twenty-seven seasons, and counting, as head coach).

* Neither one has ever been on NCAA probation.

* And they're both devoid of ulcers, other stomach disorders, divorces, migraine headaches, nervous twitches, abnormal hair loss, high blood pressure, and, for the most part, enemies—conditions that, considering what they do, makes them actuarily impossible.

Speaking of statistics, their longevity has both of them solidly entrenched on virtually every Who's Who list of coaches. With his 246–64–3, .791 record, Paterno is No. 1 among active Division I coaches in wins and No. 2 in winning percentage; while Edwards, at 187–66–3, .736, is No. 4 and No. 5, respectively, on those same lists. On the all-time lists, Paterno is No. 4 in wins and No. 13 in winning percentage; while Edwards is No. 19 and No. 37, respectively. And both are climbing fast. In bowl game appearances, Paterno, with twenty-two, is second all-time; while Edwards, with sixteen, is seventh.

Add it all up, and their meeting today takes on historical proportions. Not since the last time Woody Hayes met Bo Schembechler have so many coaching triumphs been locked up on the same football field.

Not that either coach is likely to know that. Which is another un-typical coaching tendency Edwards and Paterno seem to share: a studied reluctance to dwell on, live in, or attach much importance to the past.

"Over the years we've become good friends and our wives have become good friends," said Edwards the other day in talking of his good friend and fellow survivor from the East. "He likes to talk, and I like to listen, so we get along fine.

"We don't coach the same, but I think we're alike in a lot of ways. I think our basic approach to what we do is the same, the importance we place on college football, the perspective we put it in, and the way we look at our jobs.

"We both like where we live, we like the people we're working with, and we like what we do."

There have been worse formulas for success.

He may be one of the most gifted basketball coaches ever, but where Rick Majerus really shines is in the art of conversation. Whenever I needed a column, all I had to do was get near Majerus and clear out of the way. I felt I should send him part of my check for all the columns he wrote for me, although I never did. This column, about a trip to Africa, resulted from an hour-long phone call that seemed like five minutes.

Rick Majerus

The college basketball season starts Saturday, and for University of Utah coach, Rick Majerus, it means one thing: he'll know where he'll be sleeping at night. Whereas a lot of basketball coaches spend the offseason holed up in a kind of anxious stupor, living for the day their copy of *Street & Smith's* comes to the mailbox, Majerus spends offseasons often not sure just where he'll be when the sun goes down—until the sun actually does go down. He marches to a different drumbeat. This year make that literal, since the coach's travels included a two week trip to Africa, where he had the unique experience of being both scout and scouted.

Majerus and Golden State Warriors head coach, Don Nelson, went to Nairobi, Kenya, to observe the Tournament of Africa, a basketball competition that includes the national teams from Senegal and Egypt. Both of those teams will be in the USA's bracket next year at the World Games in Toronto, where Nelson will be head coach of Dream Team II and Majerus will be one of his assistant coaches.

"Nellie wants to win in Toronto, and he wants to win convincingly," says Majerus. "He doesn't want to leave one stone unturned. That's why we went to Africa."

The basketball in Nairobi was interesting enough, but what really got Majerus's attention was the guard standing outside his tent one night after he and Nelson left Nairobi and took a photo safari sidetrip into the African bush. Majerus was returning to his tent after a late night stroll when the guard grabbed him from behind. "I thought, Geez, I'm getting robbed in camp," says Majerus. "But then he turned me around and showed me an elephant no more than ten feet away, right outside Nelson's tent. It was so dark I didn't even see him. From that point on I stayed inside my tent all night."

Majerus loves to talk basketball, but get him started about his trip to Africa, and the closest he gets to basketball is telling about the time he was in a small village and he took the University of Utah basketball shirt off his back to trade for "a knife they hunt with.

"Grossed Nellie out all the way back to town, me with no shirt," says Majerus. "But I really wanted that knife."

"We'd asked our driver to take us somewhere the tourists don't go," says Majerus. "He told us that would be very far, and we said fine, let's go. So we went. It took a while. *Road* is a term they use very loosely over there. They're almost unnavigable, and there are poachers and bandits. We had a guy in the front with an AK-47 and a guy in the back with an AK-47."

Getting to the village was worth it, says Majerus, and not just for the knife. "This village was in the forest primeval," he says. "Right outside their huts, maybe ten feet away, is where they've dug for their water. They drink the water, the goats drink the water. Can you imagine the antibodies these people have developed?"

Majerus saw a "spectacular" array of animal life in Africa. He and Nelson saw more zebras—the real kind—than they knew existed, plus an over-abundance of wildebeests, along with an incredible number of lions, elephants, hippopotamuses and monkeys. They saw just one leopard and not very many rhinoceroses, because these two species have fallen special victims to whole-sale killing by man.

They also witnessed animals killing animals. "Every day we'd see a lion kill a zebra," says Majerus. "These animals were so healthy. Only the strong survive. Comparing the animals at Hogle Zoo to these animals is like comparing the over-50 basketball tournament at the Senior Games to the NBA.

"They say that most people who die of wild animal attacks are killed by hippos and crocodiles. They're the most dangerous to humans," says Majerus. "If you get between a hippo and a crocodile in the water, that's the most dangerous place on earth."

A close second for dangerous places was in the small airplane that took Majerus and Nelson to one of their safari camps.

"We got to this little airfield," Majerus says, "and this guy came out of the hangar walking sideways. He was drunk. He walked up to the plane and said, 'Good thing we're not in America. American aviation laws require you to have a co-pilot. In Africa you don't need a co-pilot.'

"We climbed in, and he asked if I wanted to sit next to him. I said I'd prefer behind him. I wanted as much metal as possible between me and the crash."

Majerus's African trip was sandwiched into an offseason itinerary that included another scouting trip with Nelson to the Tournament of the Americas in Puerto Rico; a trip to Europe that included stops in Belgium, Spain, Germany, Holland, and Italy as an assistant coach to P.J. Carlessimo with the USA Select Team; fifty to sixty speaking engagements, many of them to aid flood victims in the Midwest; and uncounted recruiting trips of his own.

"I covered a lot of miles," says Majerus. "I'll tell you, if I had kids and could afford it, I'd pack them up and take them right back and show them what I saw. As much as anything, it makes me appreciate America more than ever. You know that adage, 'The kids in China would give anything for what we have'? They would. So would the kids in Africa. To have a toilet to flush, parks to run in, taps you can turn on and get water, universities to go to . . . America is the nicest place in the world.

"I'm glad the season's starting. I'll be able to stay in town for a few nights," says Majerus, who returned this week to the room he rents permanently at the University Park Hotel.

"The way this summer went," he says, "I should have paid by the night."

Some wealthy people inherit their millions, others come up with an amazing invention,
but not many start out working the parts counter at a Toyota dealership
the way Larry Miller did. Utah's very own "owner" is a state treasure, and he'll still
sell you an alternator if you need one.

Larry Miller

He was sitting in a doctor's office waiting room earlier this week when he started to thumb through a magazine with Joe Montana on the cover. One article—about pro sports owners and what they're worth—caught his attention. There he was. Big as life. Wearing his softball uniform. He found himself reading about himself the same as he'd read about people in *Sports Illustrated* since he started his subscription thirty years ago. He still has every issue, in boxes in his garage, to prove it.

He got to the part about how much he's worth. The magazine said "$120 million."

He nudged his wife, Gail.

"I wish," he said.

Then he read the part about franchise market values and saw "Utah Jazz: $50 million."

He nudged Gail again.

"I hope not," he said.

Larry H. Miller, the owner of the Utah Jazz and faithful *S.I.* subscriber, had another reason to not believe everything he reads. Another *two* reasons.

But at least he'd made it into *Sports Illustrated.* And so had his softball uniform. There was a time, eighteen years ago, that he thought—hoped would be more like it—that he might make it into America's foremost chronicler of sport as a softball chucker. That was after the 1975 International Softball Congress championships in Wisconsin, where Larry Miller, playing for Stevinson Toyota of Lakewood, Colorado, hit .400 while his team went 3–1 in the tournament. He hit a home run in the 11th inning of one of the games to break a 2–2 tie and give his team, and himself, the win. "I'm tired of waiting for you guys," Miller had said to his teammates just before he strode to the plate and hit a chin-high knuckleball out of the lights. If that wasn't a game story, what was? But, alas, *S.I.* was somewhere else that weekend.

He was fairly certain his photograph would make it into the article on the owners. Why else would *S.I.* send a photographer to Utah this past July and spend one whole afternoon at the Cottonwood softball complex shooting 152 frames of Miller throwing pitches? It was the same shot over and over—a memory that sticks with Miller because it was ninety degrees that day, he was wearing a black uniform, which made it even hotter, and after every pitch (he hadn't thrown any in at least five years), the photographer would say, "Okay, let's try another one."

"They wanted the light just right, and the mountains just right in the background," says Miller.

The photo was nice, even if it was eighteen years late. Miller, not quite as private of a man as he was eight years ago when he was the anonymous stranger who bought the Jazz to save them from going out of business or out of state, says he actually rather enjoyed the notoriety.

Although he does wonder why a magazine that would spend all day getting a photo just right, wouldn't bother to ask him, or his accountants, about his net worth. He wouldn't have told them, but they could have at least asked.

"I have no idea how they came up with their numbers," he says. "All I know is, they're way off."

The $50 million market price on the Jazz is only half the $100 million Miller says he's turned down twice. "To put any NBA franchise at $50 million is ludicrous," he says. "The last three franchises that have been sold, San Antonio, Miami, and Houston, have averaged $94 million each."

As to his net worth—figuring in assets of the Jazz, the Golden Eagles, the Delta Center, Pro Image stores, nineteen car dealerships, and a TV station—he says it's not only hard to fix a number because of debt and inventory, it's hard for the average person (i.e. *S.I.* reader) to understand his kind of business. "A lot of people don't understand that owning equity in a business is a lot different than being able to hand somebody cash," he says. "It's complicated. Our employees, our friends in the neighborhood, my mom and dad, they see numbers like that and they think, 'Holy Cow!'"

Hitting closer to home, it's hard for his kids to understand the difference between equity and cash. "They wonder why I get them out of bed to turn out the lights," Miller says. "They wonder why we try to shop frugally at Smith's."

Life continues to amuse Miller. And surprise him. He's been a high profile pro owner for eight years now, and he still regularly wonders how this happened.

"Purely right place at right time," he says. "It's kinda crazy.

"You know, I enjoyed reading about the owners," he says, referring specifically to the No. 1 man on the money list, Portland Trail Blazers owner, Paul Allen, the founder of Microsoft.

"I told Gail, 'Now there's a heavyweight,'" says Miller.

Allen's net worth is $3.2 billion.

Give or take a billion.

*I always thought Steve Young was just another guy until you gave him a ridiculously
difficult challenge, at which point he'd turn into either Indiana
Jones or Harry Houdini. Following in the footsteps of Jim McMahon at BYU and Joe
Montana with the 49ers might not have made for out-and-out tranquility,
but it did seem to bring out the best in Brigham Young's great-great-great-grandson . . .
Oh, and as of 1997, Young had moved past Montana—and McMahon—
as the highest-rated quarterback in NFL history.*

Steve Young

September 11, 1994

He is suave and articulate. He has you–play–opposite–Kim Basinger looks.
He could buy Costa Rica if he wanted to. Advertisers like him, charities
like him, his family likes him. Sometimes he jets to Europe just because he'd
like to watch the bobsled. Nobody's suing him, and if they did they'd find out
he has a law degree. And he's been the NFL's best quarterback for the last three
years. If you really wanted to find someone to envy, Steve Young would make
your short list.

But as is the case when much is given . . . a payment book is usually
attached.

In Young's case, fate said, "OK, you win the Roy Hobbs look-alike
contest, but you also have to be an Encore Act."

It's been as unavoidable as being Brigham Young's great-great-great-
grandson; as being lefthanded. Steve Young has been a leader but he's also been
a follower. He's had this habit of taking the stage in the midst of a standing
ovation—for the guy who's just left. The audience looks up, shrugs, and says,
Let's see you top that!

It's the only reason maybe you wouldn't want to be Steve Young. It's been
his personal ball and chain. Either he takes over from a legend, or he doesn't
take over.

It was that way at BYU, where Jim McMahon handed off to Young after
McMahon became the top-rated passer in the history of college football. And

in the NFL, it was that way at San Francisco where Joe Montana became the top-rated passer in the history of professional football—as well as a four-time Super Bowl winner—and then, albeit reluctantly, handed off to Young.

For most of his adult life, Young has been batting behind Babe Ruth. He's been the tape they put on the sound system after a Stones concert—who takes the stage when the lights are up and everybody's going home. He's been the next guy on Everest after Hilary; the next man on the moon after Neil Armstrong. He's made a career following the-best-there's-ever-been. A walking, talking sequel.

The amazing part isn't that he doesn't have a nervous twitch by now, or that he isn't being fitted for a straitjacket. The amazing part is that he's still playing; that he isn't a Who's He? By all rights, Steve Young should be coaching a secondary somewhere by now, talking about the perils of trying to replace legends, his hair either white or long gone, like Roger Maris's.

Instead, he's still chasing. In hot pursuit, as they say. Today in Kansas City he'll be one of the quarterbacks and Montana will be the other. If the plot has thickened it sure hasn't changed. Montana is still Joe Montana—and Steve Young is not.

Young's been here before—not much to win, most everything to lose. Montana holds all the cards. His immortalization came years ago. He's been there, done that. He and the Chiefs can beat Young and the 49ers today or they can lose. His orbit will not budge.

That coronations are not retractable was illustrated very well—if subtly—in this week's *San Francisco Chronicle,* a publication that has been treating the impending Young-Montana duel as nothing less than if the Bay Bridge and the Golden Gate Bridge were about to duke it out.

The *Chronicle's* Monday morning headline, after Montana opened the NFL season Sunday by completing 24 of 33 passes for 315 yards and two touchdowns in Kansas City's win over New Orleans:

"Just Like Old Times For Joe

. . . Montana Rips Saints—49ers Next"

That night, Young led a 49er rout of the Los Angeles Raiders by competing 19 of 32 passes for 308 yards and four touchdowns. The next day, Young wasn't part of the headlines, and in a report card analysis of the game, the *Chronicle* gave him an A-minus.

Still, if you have the stomach for it—and no one could argue that Young doesn't—this legend-chasing can bring the best out of you.

At BYU, instead of shying away from McMahon's superlatives, Young turned into the Second Coming of Jim McMahon, so to speak. By the time he was finished, McMahon was still the top-rated college quarterback of all-time—and Young was No. 2. (He has since moved to No. 3, with yet another BYU quarterback, Ty Detmer, in at No. 2.)

And as for the assault on Montana, it's the same story. Joe is still the NFL's all-time No. 1—and the guy who took his place in San Francisco is No. 2 (to take this 1–2 business even further, after one week of the '94 NFL season, the ratings are in and they show, you guessed it, Montana is No. 1 with a 122.7 rating and Young is No. 2 at 118.2).

It may end that way and it may not. There's football yet to be played—this afternoon, for starters. But if Steve Young doesn't surpass Joe Montana today in Kansas City (if the 49ers are, indeed, next), or if he never surpasses him, it's still obvious that Steve Young is the best there's ever been at knowing how to follow a good act.

Put him behind somebody with the initials J.M., who has just gone where no one's gone before, and get out of his way. It might not have made for a stress-free life, but then again it could have been a lot worse. In spite of all his blessings, if Steve Young had followed a bunch of no-names, he might be one, too.

Since David Stern took charge of the league in the early 1980s, the average player salary and average value of a franchise in the NBA has increased tenfold—and the players still grumble about him. I'm not just saying this because we're skiin' buddies.

David Stern

Whenever I see David Stern putting out another brushfire, I think back to when I first met him. It was at the Park City Ski Area nearly eleven years ago, only a matter of days after Stern had replaced Larry O'Brien as commissioner of the National Basketball Association.

We had spent the morning skiing and now we were in the resort cafeteria for lunch. As I went with Andrew, the commissioner's oldest son, to order our food, Stern glanced up from the table and said, "I have given Andy twenty dollars for lunch, please don't embarrass him by trying to pay."

Times were cheaper then.

But as the events of last week demonstrated, his style hasn't changed. David Stern is still the smartest man in professional sports. Either that or he always looks like he is. He keeps a step ahead of whoever or whatever he's dealing with. He is Bobby Fischer without the moods. It is his M.O. A decade ago it was making sure he bought lunch. Last week it was averting a winter without pro basketball.

Now I don't know all the subplots and subplanning that went into last week's negotiations between the NBA and the player's union. All I know is the result: that there will be no work, or play, stoppage during the 1994–95 season, despite the fact that the players and the league have yet to work out a labor contract.

In other words, the NBA found itself facing precisely the same situation as the National Hockey League and Major League Baseball. But whereas the NHL opted for a lockout and Major League Baseball opted for a player's strike, the NBA opted for the David Stern way. Business as usual. That full contact you heard this weekend? That was the NBA back in session.

This isn't to suggest that the current economic health of either pro hockey or pro baseball is comparable to pro basketball. Personally I find it refreshing that sanity is taking a turn at bat in both hockey and baseball, where I believe the owners really are losing money like they say they are. Choosing not to play the season can't be all that devastating when just opening the door means going in the hole.

After looking at basketball's salary cap with increasing envy over the past several seasons, the owners in both hockey and baseball decided they wanted one of those caps too. Maybe they could also turn a profit.

That was flattering news to the NBA owners, but also worrisome. Would the NBA players listen too long and too hard to the hockey and baseball players in their fight–to–the–golf course over a salary cap? Would the basketball players then conclude that they were schmucks for having one, and since they have yet to sign a new labor agreement, would they too hold out for the abolishment of the cap?

The answers are yes, and yes. The NBA players did, in fact, listen to what those other sports were saying and are, in fact, at odds over a salary cap (which is a lot like an Arab being at odds with gas-driven engines).

But the NBA is not on strike, or on lockout either, and that's because somebody thought of those eventualities before the players did, and the players' fears have been sufficiently soothed to usher in a season instead of a strike.

Thus creating a situation coated in irony: Hockey and baseball are out of business because they want to be like the NBA, which operates under a system that is deemed absolutely unacceptable by the work force . . . and the NBA is still in business.

All over, and behind, the scene are David Stern's fingerprints. He headed them off at the bounce pass. This looks like his kind of work all right. Everybody still has the potential to make a lot of money, even if they're not sure why.

Certainly there is nothing to suggest that basketball players and owners are appreciably different than their baseball or hockey counterparts, which is to say don't blame this healthy, uninterrupted season on them. Basketball's owners, like owners everywhere, are primarily successful businessmen with large egos and an affection for professional sports heroes. And basketball players, like players everywhere, are primarily talented young athletes with large egos and an affection for Ferraris. Neither greed nor groupy-ism stops at the NBA's borders.

The difference is a man at the front of the NBA who is smart enough to see what's coming well before it comes; a man hyperopic enough to save the owners and players from themselves, and also from the poorhouse. David Stern is the NBA's resident psychic. Whatever they're paying this man, it beats not paying him.

Frank Layden is not only capable of making Nietzsche sound interesting, he also almost single-handedly saved the Jazz in the early years. The humor is a nice cover. He is one of the smartest men I have ever met.

Frank Layden

F
rank Layden is keeping a low profile during the NBA Finals, and that isn't just a commentary on his recent dramatic one hundred pound weight loss. The man who built the Utah Jazz is casting a small shadow on purpose, out of deference to the current coach and the players. Nobody realizes like an old coach just how crowded the spotlight can get.

All this week, the best quote the Jazz ever owned has kept himself stowed away in his office in Jazz headquarters a floor above the arena floor and away too from the ongoing daily media sessions with the world. You want the ultimate commentary on just how far the Jazz have come? How about this: their No. 1 talker is out of sight, and nobody notices.

There was a time, and it wasn't that long ago, when Frank Layden was not just the franchise's coach and general manager, but also the person who positioned himself on the front lines and provided comic cover. For years, the Jazz rode Layden's sense of humor. He was always the master of deflection. They can't make jokes about you if you make them first.

He's still the funniest person in Utah this side of Brooklyn or Rick Majerus, take your pick, although in his new slimness he has had to retire some of his old standard self-deprecating fat lines. The one about "They'd worship this body in India" is gone, not to be replaced. "They'd worship this body at Jenny Craig" just doesn't cut it.

But Layden never had to rely on yesterday's jokes, anyway. His standard line this week, whenever anyone begins to wade into the subject of just how much he's responsible for the Jazz's success, is: "Are you kidding? It used to take me two years to do what Jerry's doing now in one."

Actually, that's no joke. In Layden's first two years of coaching the team—from 1981 to 1983—the Jazz won sixty-five regular season games. Under Sloan this past regular season, they won sixty-four.

But if Layden started low, he didn't stay there long. In 1984, after only his second full season as coach, he was named NBA Coach of the Year for guiding the Jazz to their first playoff berth and a 45–37 record, which doesn't seem like much in today's currency, but in 1984 it represented the first-ever above-.500 record for the Jazz and a fifteen-win jump from the year before.

The Jazz have not had a losing season since.

Five seasons later, after getting the team off to an 11–6 start in 1988, Layden, as team vice president, stepped down as coach, promoted himself to team president, and gave the car keys to Jerry Sloan, his assistant, with the gas tank on full. The Jazz haven't slowed down since.

All they have to worry about now, says Frank, is prosperity.

"Like my old friend Pete Carill said, 'if losing develops character, winning reveals it' . . . so now we'll see."

Layden has been with the Jazz long enough to develop plenty of character. He joined the franchise for the exodus out of New Orleans in 1979, just after Elgin Baylor had been fired as head coach. Then-owner, Sam Battistone, gave Layden, who came to the Jazz from the Atlanta Hawks, a choice. He could either be coach or general manager. He wanted to be coach, but out of sheer job-preservation, he chose general manager.

"They could get John Wooden and Amos Alonzo Stagg, and they couldn't coach this team," he remembers thinking. "This team stinks."

One of Layden's first player contract negotiations was with Gail Goodrich, a Hall of Fame guard, who had just observed his thirty-sixth birthday and finished his fourteenth pro season—and was now holding out for a big raise as a free agent.

"He wanted his salary doubled. He said he could be a big draw in Utah," remembers Frank. "I said, 'Gail, you're great, but we can lose without you.'"

A couple of seasons later, Layden made another money stand when the team's first star of the Utah era, Adrian Dantley, refused to report to training camp until the Jazz re-worked his contract.

"You know what's amazing about that?" asks Layden. "I got in a big showdown with Donald Dell and David Falk, Dantley's agents, and we fought over a hundred thousand dollars! Today, that's chump change! Biggest mistake of my life. I acted like it was my money."

For the last nine years, Layden hasn't had to hassle with anyone over money, or much of anything else. As team president, his duties are good-will ambassador, banquet speaker, and personnel consultant. With Sloan in place as head coach and Frank's son, Scott Layden, in place as director of basketball operations, mostly he just nods his approval. What's to argue with?

The Jazz have assured him he'll have a job with them forever or as long as he wants, although Layden, a Brooklyn native, prefers not to look that far ahead.

"I've always felt that the trick is to enjoy the moment," he says. "I'll never forget that in 1955 the Brooklyn Dodgers were world champions, and in 1957 they were headed for L.A." That left Frank with nothing but his sense of humor, which, it's turned out, was plenty.

Tributes

Wilbur Braithwaite, 1988

Rex Berry, 1989

Gene Fullmer, 1991

Karl Tucker, 1992

Bill Howard, 1994

Mark Eaton, 1994

Wendell Ashton, 1996

Alf Engen, 1997

I have a box full of letters sent to me by Wilbur Braithwaite. Over the years, he often wrote to compliment or congratulate me, but sometimes he only wanted to philosophize. He wrote poetry, and often would include a copy of his latest poem. I think I wrote him about one letter for every twenty he sent me. And he never stopped writing. That's the kind of man he is.

Wilbur Braithwaite

A t or around 4:00 P.M. this afternoon, depending on whether there's an overtime, Wilbur Braithwaite will conclude his high school basketball coaching career. The good die young. Wasn't it just the other day that it was 1951 and Wilbur was taking over his father's grocery store in downtown Manti—and teaching math and basketball at the high school across the street?

Manti isn't the biggest town in Utah, or even in Sanpete County, and there were those who warned Wilbur when he was twenty-five years old and a brand new basketball coach that coming back to work in his home town might not be such a good idea.

Just about everyone who had a charge account at his store—and that was virtually everyone in town—would also have an opinion as to how the basketball team ought to be run.

And in Manti, as in dozens of other towns in rural Utah where every barn has a rusted rim and basketball is as important as a good hay crop or gettin' a deer, those kind of opinions are not rendered without emotion.

But Wilbur went home anyway, and he never left, and thirty-seven years later, not only is the Associated Foods store on Main Street in downtown Manti still in business, but so is the coach—or he will be until 4:00 P.M. this afternoon when the outcome of the Manti vs. Millard, Class 2A state tournament consolation game is decided at the Dee Events Center in Ogden.

When the horn sounds, it will mark the end of a coaching era that covered more than 800 games and touched at least that many lives, times 1,000. It will also mark the end of Wilbur Braithwaite's 1987–88 Victory Tour. The Tour has been along the lines of the one Julius Erving took last year in the NBA, with down-home variations. As Coach Braithwaite and his Templars have traveled from familiar town to familiar town in Region 10, the fans threw things at him. Good things.

At Richfield, they paused at halftime to make a speech. "Wilbur Braithwaite, the coach we most love to beat," they said, and then they heaped a compliment on top of a compliment by making him an honorary member of the Wildcat Club. A first for anyone from Manti.

At North Sanpete in Mt. Pleasant, they gave him a tape recalling the memories of the Manti–North Sanpete rivalry over the years. At Juab High in Nephi, they tossed a bouquet at Jane Braithwaite, Wilbur's wife. And on and on it went.

At the Region 10 tournament they gave him an autographed basketball and sent him off to the state tournament—a March-time habit for Braithwaite.

Wilbur's teams have won over 530 games, while losing around 275, in a career that has spanned nearly four decades and included a state championship in 1955 and three runner-up state finishes as well as numerous region titles.

Still, as the vagueness over Wilbur's exact won-lost record suggests, winning was never the only thing. "I don't want my players to ever feel inferior because they lost if they gave it a big effort," were Braithwaite's words to live by. "Never confuse an honest effort in a losing cause with failure."

He didn't just say that, he meant it, and after a while even the skeptics had to agree. This was a coach of a different clinic. He didn't care about winning as much as he cared about character and discipline and above all about boys.

For his entire career he got two technical fouls, which has to be even more of an accomplishment than lasting thirty-seven years as the high school basketball coach in your home town.

He never worried more about the record than the boy.

Asked Friday, after Manti defeated Park City 61–45 to qualify to play in today's consolation championship game, what this year's won-lost record was, Braithwaite was stumped.

"Let's see," he said, "we're very close to thirteen wins . . . and whatever."

His players weren't sure, either.

"I don't know," said Richard Squire, the Templars' center, "I know we've won more than we've lost."

Squire, whose twin brother, Ralph, is also on the team, said he remembered going to the high school gym when he was a small boy, accompanying his older brothers to practice. "The coach would always take time with you, even when you were just a little kid," he said. "He didn't care if you were on his team or not . . . I don't know what it's going to be like without him . . . it will be empty, I guess. That's what it will be. Empty."

Squire said the team doesn't feel any added pressure today. They don't feel they have to go out and win the final game for the coach.

"It doesn't matter if you win," Squire said. "What matters is how you play."

To the end, the Manti Templars were molded in Coach Braithwaite's image.

I first met Rex Berry when he retired from pro football and moved to my hometown of Sandy when I was in the third grade. His son, Doug, walked into Sandy Elementary, and Doug and I have been best friends ever since. Rex Berry remains the most gifted natural athlete I have ever been around, although I did manage to beat him at golf once—two weeks after he had bypass heart surgery.

Rex Berry

September 23, 1989

HELPER—They went ahead and made Rex Berry's day here Thursday. Quite literally. By proclamation of the mayor, it was "Rex Berry Day," from city limit to city limit; from Castle Gate to the D&RG Railroad yard. And by further proclamation, the Helper Junior High School football field was renamed "Rex Berry Field."

Maybe it had been fifty years since Rex Berry, a.k.a. the "Carbon Comet," last played a down of football for coach Claude Cowley and the Helper Junior High Rams. But as Walter "Red" Borla, the instigator of this Day, explained to the recipient, "To tell you the truth, it's taken us this long to get a decent enough field to put your name on it."

It had taken a little time, too, to fly the idea past the Carbon County superintendent of schools, a relative newcomer to the area who wasn't initially acquainted with Berry's name, or his past.

Last spring, when Borla, a member of the school board, proposed naming school property after the only athlete in Carbon County history to make it to the big leagues, the superintendent hedged, reminding everyone that the people of Cincinnati named a street after Pete Rose, and now they had a problem on their hands.

So first they let the superintendent do his homework, to discover for himself that the only thing Rex Berry didn't make in his life was enemies.

Some legends wear well. This one, for instance. Berry may have recently retired from a full-time business career, but he still looks like he could cover Crazy Legs Hirsch, which is what he used to do when he was an All-Pro defensive back for the San Francisco 49ers. Among Berry's fondest NFL memories, he told those assembled for the Rex Berry Day luncheon Thursday, is the first interception he ever made, as a rookie in 1951, on a pass from Bob Waterfield of the Rams that was intended for Hirsch but wound up instead in his arms. He was thereupon tackled by Glen Davis, the Heisman Trophy winner from Army. Berry had hit the big time. And the big time had hit him.

But this day wasn't so much about football as it was about somebody from Helper who made them all proud, and who never forgot where he came from.

Well, almost never. Berry did admit that there was one time, when he was in San Francisco as a 49er, that a car pulled up alongside his car, and noticing Berry's Utah plates, the driver asked him where he was from.

Not thinking he'd have heard of Helper, Berry answered, "Salt Lake City."

To which the driver said, "I'm from Helper. Do you know where that is?"

Berry swore he'd never sell Helper short again, and by all accounts he never did. As the mayor's proclamation duly noted: "Whereas he always took pride in proclaiming Helper as his hometown . . ."

After playing at Helper Junior High and Carbon High School in Price—where he was All-State in football, basketball, and baseball, and second in the all-around at the BYU track invitational—Berry played a year of all-conference football at Carbon College (now CEU) before going on to BYU, where he distinguished himself on some undistinguished teams by (A) Scoring the touchdown in 1950 that tied the University of Utah and (B) Going in the thirteenth round of the '51 NFL draft to the 49ers.

He went to San Francisco expecting to be cut, but soon discovered that their playing field wasn't much different from the one in Helper. In due time he was elected team captain—making it a clean sweep on every team he'd been on since junior high—and, by his final season in 1956, was making $12,500 a year.

He retired with honors, not the least of which was a 49er franchise record for interceptions returned for touchdowns. A record that stood for nearly three decades, until Ronnie Lott, another All-Pro, broke it in 1981.

A lot of the Helper Junior High students who attended the ceremonies at halftime of the HJH–San Rafael football game Thursday afternoon had never heard of Rex Berry. But they proved to be quick learners. As soon as the REX BERRY FIELD sign had been unveiled, they knew he was outstanding in his field. In no time they had him surrounded, clamoring for autographs.

After all these years, the Carbon Comet was finally stopped in his tracks, and on the very turf that got him started. Not that he minded. He had all day.

They say the toughest men are those who don't have to act it. Gene Fullmer, who knocked out Sugar Ray Robinson, doesn't act it. My favorite story is the one Fullmer tells about his decision to retire: He walked into the house one day and saw his gloves hanging on the wall. "If you want them down, you're going to have to fight me first," his wife, who had put them there, told him. "They've been hanging there ever since," Fullmer said.

Gene Fullmer

It was a mild controversy as Hall of Fame controversies go—almost no controversy at all. It wasn't until Utah's Gene Fullmer was finally admitted this month to the International Boxing Hall of Fame in Canastota, N.Y., that anyone questioned why he didn't get in a year ago.

The IBHF was founded in 1990 with the intent of establishing a central location to honor the greatest boxers in world history. Several countries have national Halls of Fame, including the U.S. (to which Fullmer was admitted in 1974), but until 1990, there was no *world* Hall of Fame.

The IBHF's charter class of twenty boxers, inducted a year ago, included everyone you could think of, from Joe Louis to Muhammad Ali to Joe Frazier to Jose Napoles to Rocky Marciano to Archie Moore to Carlos Monzon to Sugar Ray Robinson to Carmen Basilio to Jersey Joe Walcott. Name a long-time world champion. If he was alive, he was in Canastota last summer to have his fist bronzed.

Except Gene Fullmer.

The phone never rang in his home in West Jordan until this year, when IBHF officials called to tell the former middleweight champion of the world that he would be inducted with a sophomore class of eleven that also included Floyd Patterson, Dick Tiger, Tony Zale, and Rocky Graziano.

"They asked me how I felt, if I was surprised, and I said I was honored but I wasn't surprised," Fullmer says. "They asked why, and I said, well, I'd beaten two of the guys they'd already inducted, twice each, and every time it was for the middleweight title."

He was referring to Robinson and Basilio, two of the greatest fighters of all time but a combined 1–4–1 against Fullmer in five middleweight title bouts from 1957 through 1961.

The plot begins to thicken when you learn that Basilio's hometown is Canastota, N.Y., the *same* Canastota, N.Y. that houses the International Boxing Hall of Fame.

Largely because of Basilio's success as a welterweight and middleweight champion in the '50s, Canastota, where Basilio was raised on his father's onion farm, became a boxing hotbed that's never cooled off. The town liked identifying itself with a fighter who had a reputation for never backing down, for taking on challenges bigger than himself—as was the case when Basilio, a welterweight at 150 pounds, successfully challenged the 160-pound Robinson for the middleweight title in 1957—and for almost never being knocked out.

In seventy-nine professional fights the "Canastota Clouter" was knocked out only twice—both times it was by the "West Jordan Mauler."

They met first in 1959 in San Francisco. The 15-round bout went 14 rounds, when Fullmer won by TKO. They met for a rematch in Salt Lake City, at Derks Field, in 1960. That fight lasted 12 rounds, when Fullmer won again by technical knockout.

At his Hall of Fame induction two weeks ago in Canastota, Fullmer's 55–6–3 career was the subject of much attention and adulation. His thirteen title fights in seven years were mentioned. They talked about the night in Madison Square Garden that he knocked Sugar Ray Robinson through the ropes and out of the ring.

But the Basilio fights went unmentioned.

"Nobody brought them up," says Fullmer.

"I don't blame them," he adds, rubbing his chin and smiling, "I don't like to talk about the night Robinson knocked me out, either."

While in Canastota, many of the Hall of Famers stepped in the ring for a series of three-round exhibitions. Fullmer and Basilio were paired together.

"It was just show and tell," says Fullmer, who will turn sixty in three weeks. "Nobody was trying to hit anybody. Nobody wanted to hit anybody. We just wanted to last three minutes."

He said getting older doesn't necessarily mean a fighter has lost his desire to box, however.

"Everybody thinks they can probably still do it," he says, "but they don't want to try just in case they can't."

Talking is a safer way to go.

"The more you talk the better you get," says Fullmer.

He says he got better and better during his four-day stand in Canastota, where the induction ceremonies were first-class and where more fight fans showed up than Fullmer thought existed. "I was really surprised by the turnout," he says. "We'd do these autograph sessions and there would be more people waiting in line at the end than at the start. I'm still getting letters from people asking for autographs who say they were there in Canastota and couldn't ever get to the front of the line."

As part of his induction spoils, they gave him a Hall of Fame diamond ring and they cast his right fist. They were surprised that, at 13-inches, it was the second biggest fist in the Hall (next to heavyweight Primo Carnera's 15-inches). Fullmer's fist wouldn't fit in the regular mold. They had to cast it in a bucket.

Two weeks ago in Carmen Basilio's hometown, they took some silent solace in that. At least the man who decked Basilio twice was no wimp. And better than that, when he and Basilio finally met for the third time, in the Hall of Fame ring in Canastota, both fighters were still standing at the finish.

That Karl Tucker managed to consistently compete with the top golf programs in America while operating out of a school where the first requirement is a "good warm pair of boots" remains a true sports phenomenon. For many years, if you said "Heber!" half the PGA Tour would look up.

Karl Tucker

June 7, 1992

He begins his retirement today, which may turn out to be an even more entertaining show than the one he's been putting on the last thirty-one years as BYU's golf coach. No one ever accused Karl Tucker of being the retiring type. Leading the Cougars to twenty-one NCAA championships, thirteen top-five finishes, the national title in 1981, and 168 tournament wins since 1961—while directing the BYU Ski School—was one thing. Riding off into the sunset will be another.

Probably the biggest reason he'd give for retiring is because that's what his brothers did before him. For one thing, it didn't seem to slow them down. For another, Karl has always followed in his brothers' footsteps. A lot of people thought his golf teams were simply an extension of the Tucker Brothers, whose philosophy was always *Don't Let Anything Get in the Way of Having a Good Time and Getting Good Results.*

Karl is the last of the five brothers who, along with two sisters, were born during the '20s to George Tucker, a fruit farmer in Orem, and his wife, Della. The first son was named George, after his father. Then came Wayne, Monroe (Toby), Ray, and Karl. The brothers were spaced roughly two years apart, just right for full-scale athletic competition whenever it wasn't harvesting season.

All of them found their own niche. George Jr., who died tragically in 1959 in a car accident, was an AAU boxing champion and professional boxer; Wayne played and managed for nearly twenty years in the New York Yankees organization and was named to the all-time Texas League team as an infielder; Toby and Ray, who died recently, excelled in tennis and golf; and then came Karl, who wanted to do everything his brothers had done—and then some.

He was the first of the five to go to college, enrolling at BYU just after World War II. He played shortstop on the baseball team and was also a member of the tennis team, the golf team, and the ski team. A man for all the seasons. No one at BYU before or since has taken the latter half of the role of "student-athlete" so seriously, or literally.

When BYU was looking for a golf coach to replace Buck Dixon in 1961, and Karl Tucker, then thirty-five and a veteran of eight years teaching junior high physical education in Salt Lake City, applied for the job, he was not an unknown quantity to the Cougars.

The story of how Tucker turned a cold-weather school with almost no golf tradition into one of the top two or three programs in the country has since become as well-known as the coach who made it happen. The most unique part of the story is how Tucker, still true to his multi-sport roots, added the BYU ski school, at nearby Sundance, to his duties. And then how he flew in the face of conventional wisdom by marrying the two sports, golf and skiing. He used ski breaks in the winter to rest and relax his golfers.

In time, he had his golfers looking as forward to the winter as the summer. He also had them adopted into a system that was more family than it was team. With BYU golf the Karl Tucker way, there was no such thing as "in-season" and "out-of-season." As Glen Tuckett, the former BYU baseball coach and current athletic director who once shared an office with Tucker says, "Karl inspired more loyalty with his players than any coach that I know. He provided for them some kind of a mix between a big brother figure and a father figure. If he were to phone today all the guys he's sent to the (PGA) Tour and say, 'I need you tomorrow morning at eight o'clock,' they'd all be there."

Karl's brothers followed and supported the program with similar loyalty. Wayne, Ray, and Toby were golf-cart fixtures at tournaments almost as much as their little brother, the head coach. They treated the team members like they treated each other, with heavy support and also heavy doses of irreverent reverence. Everyone was "Heber," and no one, from Johnny Miller on down, was ever exempt from their verbal attention.

Says Tuckett: "I'd pay money just to follow behind the Tucker brothers playing eighteen holes of golf and listen to what they had to say to each other."

To an outsider, the talk might be confusing; but not to an insider. "It isn't battling each other so much as it is battling together," Wayne Tucker once said.

Which is probably as good a phrase as any to sum up Karl Tucker's thirty-one-year run with the BYU golf team. It's possible that no coach has ever made golf look less like an individual sport. Under Tucker, the Cougars always battled together. Wherever he's going in his retirement, one thing is certain. He won't be going alone.

Whenever the journalists' image as just a bunch of vultures, parasites, freeloaders,
and malcontents would begin to look
warranted, we'd trot out Bill Howard for reputation control.

Bill Howard

In a way I have often found fascinating, the Siamese-twin occupations of sports writing and sportscasting share common pitfalls. Hard as it may seem for jobs that appear to consist of nothing more than "getting paid to watch a ballgame"—a mostly accurate appraisal, by the way—there are perils, and basically they are threefold:

One: A sportscaster or writer can become, or can continue to be, a huge fan, i.e. one who worships daily at the sports shrine; one who places his prayer rug in the direction of the jump circle or the pitcher's mound; one who is primarily a cheerleader but uses a word processor or a microphone instead of a pom-pom.

Two: A sportscaster or writer can become cynical. Usually, this is a pitfall of attrition, brought on by years and years of observing pampered, overpaid athletes, coaches, and owners—to say nothing of Little League parents.

Three: A sportscaster or writer can become a grumbler, constantly complaining about working conditions, about having to sit in the fifth row of the press box instead of the first, about an ESPN-delayed tipoff at midnight, about some bowl assistant not giving you a parking pass for the stalls five feet from the stadium entrance.

Personally, I have never had any trouble with number one. I do fight an ongoing battle with number two. And even now, as I write this, I find I am working myself into a heated state about what I *know* will go wrong with the bus system, the accommodations, and the starting times for hockey games next month in Lillehammer.

But I knew one in the profession who avoided all the occupational hazards. He died Friday. Bill Howard, the man with a voice so fine he should have had an ego the size of Dick Vitale (but didn't), was sixty-eight. Anyone who knew him always supposed that sixty-eight would be the year he would shoot his age. But Bill Howard was only human, which was the greatest thing about him. That and his ability to bring dignity to what he did.

Howard not only uplifted the profession, he uplifted the human race. He was handsome, he was articulate, he could write, he could pronounce, he was a war hero, he carried a single-digit handicap in golf. He had so many things going for him he might have been as unsufferable as Notre Dame. But he wasn't. There aren't a lot of sportscasters or sports writers who can walk freely over the boundaries, from the press room to the locker room to corporate headquarters, and receive the same warm reception in all three places. Bill Howard could. When I grew up I always wanted to be like him.

How he pulled it off no one knew exactly because he never expounded on the subject; probably it was for that very reason that he did pull it off. Bill Howard could coexist with the Ayatollah Khomeini and Sadam Hussein, at the same time, let alone Zelmo Beaty and Bill Marcroft.

Anyone inside the profession knows it is not light praise when both journalists and newsmakers alike are claiming you as their own. When Howard was the play-by-play announcer for the Utah Stars *everyone* thought he belonged to them. Owners, players, fellow members of the fourth estate, and most of all his listeners. He's by far the closest thing Utah has ever had to Walter Cronkite—another giant of journalism who seemed to avoid all the occupational hazards. Either that or Walter Cronkite is the closest thing America has ever had to Bill Howard.

His last few years were difficult ones because of the cancer that finally prevailed; proof positive that it is a disease that doesn't discriminate on the basis of character. The ultimate sucker punch. But as Bill Howard lost weight and didn't get around as much, he still got around as much as he could. His biggest problem was that when he did make his infrequent appearances in press boxes and locker rooms he couldn't get any work done—he had to work too hard getting through the press of people who wanted to talk to *him*.

People cared about Bill Howard because Bill Howard cared about people. During the moment of silence held in his honor prior to Friday night's Jazz-Kings game in the Delta Center, I found myself thinking about that. This was a man who was treated directly in proportion to the way he treated others—a living example that what goes around really *does* come around.

Mark Eaton is one of the nicest people around, although I did see him upset a crowd once. We went to a movie together in Park City, and we came in as the previews were showing. We took seats about a third of the way down, on the right-hand side. Hearing a commotion behind us, I turned around to see this huge V-shaped section of empty seats that suddenly had an obstructed view.

Mark Eaton

T rue story. Twelve years ago, just before Mark Eaton was to play his first season of professional basketball for the Utah Jazz, Jack Sikma, the veteran NBA center, was playing golf near Eaton's new home at Jeremy Ranch. Sikma said he'd like to meet the much-talked-about 7-foot-4, 290-pound rookie, so Eaton was dispatched to the course, where he proceeded to unfold out of the golf cart that had carried him.

"They were right!" said the 7-foot, 250-pound Sikma, looking up. "You ARE the world's biggest human."

As it turned out, in more ways than one.

The Jazz may be able to get by without Mark Eaton, whose retirement became official before the start of the new season, but how long can pro sports afford to keep trading in Mark Eatons for the deportment of Dream Team II?

They don't make them like Mark Eaton anymore. For that matter, they didn't make them like Mark Eaton before he came along, either. He was your basic one-of-a-kind—from being the only NBA player in history to survive eleven seasons without shooting a traditional jump shot—ever—to somehow managing to never get into a brawl, or even a borderline fight, despite the fact he was bigger than everybody in the arena.

If there is a book on how to act like a demanding NBA star, he never read it. He never pampered anybody, including himself, but he was sure no bully. He blocked more shots in history if you don't count Kareem Abdul-Jabbar, who blocked 125 more in five more seasons, but nobody ever accused

Eaton of throwing his weight around. He never did glare after one of his 3,064 rejects, or talk trash, or even smugly gloat.

He had all the tools to be at least as unsufferable as Bill Laimbeer. He wasn't just tall, he was big. His first couple of years in the league he changed a lot of shots and keyhole configurations all by himself—and he could have made a lot of enemies in the process. Established stars who were convinced they could out-maneuver this one-dimensional statue would come away incensed when they couldn't. They would shake their heads in disgust, like a golfer apoplectic over unfair greens or a jeweler looking at a fake Rolex. They didn't want a converted auto mechanic handing them their lunch.

If Eaton had smirked back in the early days, if he'd fueled their disdain, his eleven NBA seasons could have been as long as, say, Laimbeer's. But he did not smirk back. He never changed expressions, unless you count the beard he added in a vain attempt to look more stern out there.

He always acted as if he'd been lucky on that last one and it would probably be the final block of his career.

Instead of gaining enemies he gained respect. He tended to treat all aspects of the professional basketball business with similar aplomb. He was uncommonly accommodating of the media, a tendency that was readily apparent each time he eschewed the practice of making a quick retreat to the training room immediately after games to avoid the press. For a 290-pounder he was amazingly unobtrusive. He gave the media room to do its job. You want a tough assignment? Find one sports writer or sportscaster in this country who has a bad thing to say about Mark Eaton.

What set Eaton further apart was something he did that other well-known pros who have played in Salt Lake City didn't do. He did what Zelmo Beaty never did, and any number of others: He lived here.

He moved to Utah. He brought his wife, Marci, and his dog, Apollo, and his old Chevy, and he bought a house, got a mortgage, got a raise, bought another house, and paid property taxes.

He got involved in local charities, he joined a golf club, he bought property in the backwoods, he fished the local streams, he had a mountain bike custom made, he set up his own kids' summer camp. He didn't take up skiing, but Marci did. After home games he would go to his house in the mountains and soak in his own jacuzzi.

It was behavior completely out of step with normal and usual NBA behavior that says you don't live where you get paid.

Add it all up and it made for an uncommon NBA career that ended too soon. The refreshing thing about Mark Eaton's approach to playing pro basketball was he always gave off the unmistakable impression that he was glad to be here. That the condition wasn't very contagious only made it all the more obvious and refreshing.

*In lobbying hard to get the Jazz to Salt Lake, Wendell used to point out that just having
the name "Utah" listed every day in every sports section in America was
worth several million dollars in newspaper space alone. Wendell thought big. What I
liked about him best is that he lifted the door that got the* Deseret News
*to Super Bowls, World Series, Final Fours, and other major national sporting events,
just like other big-city dailies. Wendell was one of those
guys who didn't think you'd justified your travel budget until you'd gone over it.*

Wendell Ashton

January 29, 1996

When the Utah Jazz open their seventeenth season in Utah this Friday, it would be fitting to begin with a tribute to one of their Utah founders, Wendell Ashton, who passed away this past August 31st. Normally, a moment of silence is appropriate in honoring great persons for their great feats. But to truly honor Wendell, a moment of *action* would be more proper. Everyone in the Delta Center could turn to the person in the next seat and say something nice about them, and about Utah.

That was Wendell J. Ashton. Say something positive and say it fast. He lived life as if the 24-second clock was always on. He used to do his daily jog in combat boots, so he could get twice the workout in half the time. When he was seventy-six.

His life was a blur. He invented aerobics and never realized it. He ate Ben & Jerry's every night of his life and never put on a single pound.

Getting the Jazz to Utah was just one of the things he concerned himself with. He did that in 1979, squeezing it in between saving the Utah Symphony, serving as president of the Salt Lake Area Chamber of Commerce, and publishing the *Deseret News*. (As bosses go, Wendell was just about perfect. If you wanted to do something he'd say, "Do it," and he wasn't always hanging around the office.)

Former Jazz owner Sam Battistone remembers one of the first times he flew to Utah from New Orleans to discuss the potential move of the Jazz from the French Quarter to First South. He and his partner, Larry Hatfield, had arranged for a meeting with Wendell at a downtown hotel. At the hotel, Hatfield took a call from Wendell. "I'm running a little late," he said. "Tell Sam I'm doing my home teaching. He'll understand."

"It was the last day of the month," says Battistone, who was, like Ashton, a Mormon who knew a monthly home teaching deadline when he felt one.

Wendell Ashton was a religious man. But as Frank Layden says, "He was genuinely religious. He didn't wear it on his shoulder."

Layden was the Jazz's general manager in 1979. He not only credits Wendell for being the Jazz's biggest early supporter, but for being his mentor as well. "The confidence he placed in me had a lot to do with my success, with the reason I'm here," says Layden. "This may surprise you. But outside of my dad, Wendell Ashton is the greatest man I ever met. That's no smoke job. He was just a wonderful guy. I never knew a man so well-rounded, so patient, so fair. And he was a bulldog. If he had a task and he believed in it, watch out and get out of his way."

One of those tasks—and it was merely one of thousands—was to establish NBA basketball in Salt Lake City. The Jazz and Utah were a match first made in Wendell's mind. After that, he figured all he needed was to make the right converts.

His recent passing reminded Battistone of the NBA owner's meeting held in Chicago in 1979—where the vote was held to determine whether the Jazz would be allowed to leave New Orleans and move to Salt Lake City. The first order of business was a meeting of the advisory board, where separate presentations from New Orleans and Salt Lake delegations were heard.

First up was New Orleans. "The mayor was there and some other influential people," remembers Battistone. "They took kind of a cavalier attitude. They talked about why they didn't think the team should leave. Then they left, and Ted Wilson, who was the Salt Lake mayor, and Wendell Ashton came in.

"Before he sat down, Wendell walked around the room to meet the different owners there. He recognized every one of them and beyond just introducing himself, he had some little story or anecdote for each one. I remember the Washington owner was there and he talked about their coach, Dick Motta, being a Utah boy. To other owners he'd talk about a newspaper editor he knew in their city or something like that. Each guy on the advisory committee got the same treatment, something personal from Wendell. By the time he got to his seat, I looked over at David Stern—he wasn't commissioner then, but was a legal counsel for the league—and he looked at me as if to say, 'the decision has already been made.' I think that one action by Wendell Ashton got us the move. He'd really done his homework. Later that day, the board voted unanimously to let us go."

Battistone concluded, "I can't think of anybody in the state or the city who had any more to do with helping the Jazz get to Salt Lake and with making them a success."

It was no surprise to Battistone that when Wendell Ashton finally did stop, it was on the last day of the month. He was the kind of man who liked to make sure he'd first gotten his deadlines out of the way.

Alf Engen founded Alta, pretty much invented powder skiing, was a world record-holding ski jumper, had a great Norwegian accent and the best suntan I have ever seen, and was a friend to everyone, even those who couldn't ski High Rustler with their eyes closed like he could.

Alf Engen

July 28, 1997

A lot of people will remember Alf Engen for the way he skied. I'll remember him for the way he looked.

We were sitting in his office at the ski school. He was taking a break. Eating an apple. Giving the brownest face I have ever seen five minutes out of the sun. This was eight years ago. He was still young. Just turned eighty.

The subject was the first time he saw Alta.

His eyes, like they always did, lit up the leather face as he talked of the winter of '35, dead in the eye of the Depression, when he was scouting out "winter sports sites" for the United States Forest Service. A make-shift job for a make-shift time. He talked of gliding up Big Cottonwood Canyon on his skis, then climbing south at the top, over Catherine Pass, and having lunch with the Jacobsen brothers, miners who worked a claim in Albion Basin . . .

That's the day he saw her. Alta. She wasn't much to look at in 1935. Most of the trees had been cleared to build the mines, many of them long since abandoned; the surrounding slopes were pockmarked by mine shafts and crumbling, half-burned buildings. Didn't faze Alf. All he saw was beauty.

His smile grew as he remembered the way they assaulted the place the next summer: planting thousands of trees, filling in mine shafts, dismantling the ruins, running off the sheep . . .

"Little by little," he said, "Alta came to be the place God intended it to be."

Some people talk about the old days and you wonder how they ever managed. When Alf Engen talked about the old days, you wished you had been there.

A man's man, a skier's skier, a storyteller's storyteller, Alf Engen—a true Utah treasure who died last week at the age of eighty-eight—lived a life to be envied. You couldn't meet him without wanting to be him.

He emigrated from Norway to the United States at nineteen, beating the crash of the stock market by less than six months. After clearing customs and immigration, he took the train to Chicago on the Fourth of July, 1929. Starting out flat broke, and, worse than that, on flat ground, he would proceed, over the next half-century, to do as much or more for American skiing than any man, before or since.

He would aid in the development of more than thirty winter sports sites in the West, including Brighton, Snowbasin, and, of course, Alta, in Utah, as well as Sun Valley in Idaho. He would qualify to compete in the 1936 Olympics (although he wouldn't participate because his picture was on a Wheaties box and he was ruled a professional, which mattered back then), and he would help coach the U.S. team in the 1948 Olympics. He would win numerous U.S. national championships as a downhill racer, slalom racer, cross-country skier, and ski jumper. One year, at the height of his prime, he would win them all, the Grand Slam. He would set and re-set the world ski jumping record. He would teach the world how to ski powder.

It wouldn't become *The Greatest Snow on Earth* until *The Greatest Skier on Earth* came along.

But it wasn't so much that he *did* all of this, it was *how* he did it: with an enthusiasm, a joy, a gleam, that just naturally towed all those around him in his wake.

He was hardly the prototypical ski instructor—sleek, suave, in the constant company of movie stars and sunglasses, parking his Ferrari *wherever*. Where that image came from, it wasn't from him. He skied like a dream, he didn't look like one, indifferent that he packed around a few extra pounds; unconcerned whether neon was in, or out. He always looked, and acted, as if he'd just finished lunch with those miners, and now he was ready to go skiing again.

He told me once that his original goal was to come to America and make enough money so he could return to Norway and buy back his father's estate. He never made it. He skied over Catherine Pass instead.

People & Places

Paul Newman, et al, 1974

Wimbledon, 1980

Mike Malaska, 1982

Larry Bird, 1985

Notre Dame, 1992

Karl's Truck, 1993

Mickey Mantle, 1996

Jackie Robinson, 1997

This news story was written the second year I was a sports writer, back when the
Bonneville Salt Flats, and not some dried up lake bed in Nevada,
was the fastest place on earth. Luigi Chinetti Jr. was a rich Italian heir who brought two
Ferraris, two professional drivers, including Grand Prix world champion
Graham Hill, and the most famous movie star in the world, Butch Cassidy himself, to
the Utah desert to wipe out the world endurance records set back in
the '40s by a man named Ab Jenkins in a car named the Mormon Meteor. The big
plum was going to be the prestigious twenty-four-hour endurance mark. As
the story details, however, Team Chinetti and its two Ferraris didn't come close to doing
what Ab Jenkins did all by himself in one car. I still remember leaving
the Salt Flats at two in the morning, saluting Ab Jenkins as I floored my yellow
Camaro across the measured mile.

Paul Newman
and the
Ferraris

September 25, 1974

BONNEVILLE SALT FLATS—After a seemingly endless string of problems, the North American Racing Team—including drivers Paul
Newman, Graham Hill, Milt Minter, and Luigi Chinetti Jr.—cried uncle and
halted speed runs here Wednesday morning at 1:40 A.M.

The team, driving Ferraris, fell far short of the hoped-for goal of setting
fifty-six national and international speed records. They had to settle for just
ten, all in the smaller Class C division. None of the famous Ab Jenkins
endurance records, twenty in all, were exceeded.

But give the NART darters a D for determination. They struggled at
every obstacle Wednesday, not giving up until, as the baseball people would
put it, they were mathematically eliminated from the race.

After some good practice licks Saturday, Sunday, and Monday, along with four records set on Monday, the team had reason to be optimistic at the thoughts of having a go at some of the famed endurance records Thursday. But the fast—and fickle—salt had the last laugh.

In some semblance of chronological order, these problems came up:

* Tire and spark plug problems.
* Engine rod-throwing problems.
* Malfunctions with the lights.
* Brake failure.
* Surface problems.
* More tire problems.

The tire and spark plug woes necessitated a trip to Salt Lake early Tuesday, forcing an "early morning" starting time to be adjusted to early afternoon.

Then, when cars and drivers were finally ready for serious business, at 3:00 P.M., the engine of the more powerful Ferrari, a 512, blew just after Hill had begun a run.

Exit one car.

So the slower Ferrari, a Daytona Coupe, was wheeled out, given one practice lap, and sent out at 5:30 P.M. to get "as many records as possible."

The Daytona did right well for a few dozen laps, picking up Class C national and international records for 500 kilometers (171.3 mph), 500 miles (166.2), and 1,000 kilometers (166.4). Hill, Minter, and Chinetti alternated at the wheel.

But then troubles came back, first with the alternator, then with the lights, then with the brakes, and finally, with the right front tire.

The tire blew as Hill was rounding the far end of the oval in pitch blackness, just after 1:00 A.M. He limped all the way to the pits, entangling the rubber strands of what was once a tire around the axle and wheel.

That complication did the project in. Mechanics worked furiously to untangle the mess, but the pit stop measured twenty-six minutes, and even though Hill went back out, he was summoned in just a couple of laps later.

"We did some fast figuring, and it was obvious we weren't going to set any more records," said Dick Fritz, manager of the project. The Daytona had run just over eight hours.

Hill, the two-time world champ and former Indy victor, was quite calm about the unsuccessful finish.

"We've run out of cars, have we?" said the Englishman. "It's a shame, isn't it?"

And as Hill conferred with Newman, Chinetti, Minter, and Fritz about just what had been accomplished, another NART official summed up the feelings of the group.

"We had no idea what the salt could do to you," he said.

"It's spooky out there," said Minter. "I've never seen a race track where the straightaways get shorter and the curves longer, but it's happening out there.

"I went sideways on the curves twenty-five times. I counted them."

In the summer of 1980, the Deseret News budgeted a trip for its sports columnist to attend the Olympic Games in Moscow. Jimmy Carter and Russia's invasion of Afghanistan changed those plans, however, all of which brought about my summer trip to England, which began with a visit to Wimbledon for the tennis and then to Scotland and the British Open for the golf. The trip was terrific—Bjorn Borg won his record fifth title at Wimbledon, over John McEnroe, and Tom Watson won his third of four British Opens, over Lee Trevino—and, most important, the cardinal sin of newspapering was not broken: never, ever, underspend your travel budget.

Wimbledon

WIMBLEDON—He is a picture of an Englishman, with a full head of silver hair, gold-rimmed glasses, and a road map of broken blood vessels in his cheeks, hinting of harsh London winters and the pressures of his livelihood.

Almost age seventy, Roy McKelvie is hardly retired. He is a full-time journalist, writing "on sport" for the *London Sunday Express;* and for a fortnight (two weeks) each summer, he is press director for the Lawn Tennis Championships held upon the lawns of the All-England Lawn Tennis and Croquet Club—better known as Wimbledon.

In attempting to understand the phenomena of this ultimate world championship tennis tournament—considered as such according to both world acclaim and self-acclaim—Roy McKelvie is a good place to start.

He exhibits a reverence for Wimbledon that shows he places it well beyond a mere sporting event. He is himself a piece of tourney lore, even though he does not play tennis. His organization for the press is planned to the smallest detail. As a member in good standing of the 375-member All-England Club (after paying his dues by remaining on the waiting list for twenty years), he supervises the media each year as a labor of love. And honor. If he were asked to instead supervise, say, the coronation of a Queen, he would look upon the offer as a comedown.

Unfortunately, I arrived at Wimbledon halfway through the fortnight. Unfortunately, I met Roy McKelvie first thing.

I'd been warned I'd face his wrath, since he looks upon anyone entering the tournament one week late much as Shakespeare would look upon someone coming into *Hamlet* two acts into the play.

"From the *Deseret News!*" exclaimed McKelvie. "You're a week late. I've given your pass away. This isn't some meet in Wisconsin, you know. What do you mean, coming at the end of the tournament?"

It was at this juncture I made my only mistake. I opened my mouth. I told McKelvie that there was still a week to play and, for economic reasons, I came for the second week only, after which I planned to cover the British Open in Scotland.

He did not take kindly to a tennis writer also doing golf. Nor did he think much of a newspaper chopping the fortnight in half.

"These are the world championships, man," he bellowed.

Such is Wimbledon, a sporting event without equal. Even if it does say so itself. A happening—which means, by loose translation, an affair defying any otherwise conventional definitions.

There are many reasons why Wimbledon should not work.

First, it's played on grass, a substance treated generally archaic by tennis players.

Second, it's played in facilities that have hardly kept pace with the years—no lights for night play, no bubbles for when it rains, not enough seats, and tiny, crowded locker rooms.

Third, it's played for a full two weeks.

And fourth, it throws more rules and restrictions at its patrons than a customs agent.

Yet there isn't a name player who won't play or who hasn't played. And there is such an abundance of fans that even in the soggy conditions of 1980, with the first eight days plagued by rain (or so I heard), the spectators have been turned away in droves. And when the rains have come to Centre Court, no umbrellas have been opened until the shot in play has finished—as per instructions adorning the walls.

Wimbledon is a stage for all. Fans, players, press, officials. It transcends any individual. Perhaps more than any other sporting event, it is atmosphere.

It is atmosphere that has been on the build for 103 years. The first championship was staged back in 1877, when the original Centre Court was built on Worple Road. This was only eighteen years after Harry Gem, a solicitor and distance runner, no less, invented the game of lawn tennis by "experimenting on a croquet lawn in Edgbaston."

Even then the sport of lawn tennis did not take itself lightly. English royalty took an early interest and that association has rubbed off and stuck to this day. There have, for instance, been ten presidents since 1877 of the All-England Club, most all of them with royal blood. His royal highness, the Duke of Kent, is currently president.

The custom of Centre Court contestants bowing to the royal box—as Bjorn Borg and Gene Mayer did following their match Wednesday—began more than a century ago.

The tournament reached such popularity by 1922 that the All-England Club moved to new facilities on Church Road, where it still stands and yields to change slowly. While other tournaments have forsaken grass, and tradition too, Wimbledon remains locked to its past. While a stadium renovation would guarantee triple the fans on Centre Court (from 11,500 to over 30,000), it would also mean ripping the ivy off the walls.

That would be tantamount to an American journalist trying to crash the second week of the fortnight.

"Totally unfeeling and unprofessional," as McKelvie said just before he winked, imperceptively of course, gave me my pass, and let me in, revealing a clue to Wimbledon's other secret of success. Its humanness.

The ushers, ice-lolly vendors, even members of the All-England Club itself, are on the whole jolly and cooperative. They obviously enjoy their fortnight. Even this soggy one. It's rained and they've made jokes. Midway into the monsoons came a badge at a souvenir stand proclaiming, "I'm going to seed at Wimbledon."

On my first day here, a sports writer for the *Daily Mail*—one of London's biggest dailies—conducted me on a personal guided tour. When we got to a no-admittance sign he said, "This is the way to the player's team room and it's off limits to the press . . . but follow me."

He then showed me a back way into the room, winking and whispering, "only don't let on it was me that told you."

McKelvie likes to lump it all together, this fortnight called Wimbledon, and say, "I guess our secret is our class, and, I suppose, too, the way we attempt to think of everyone."

But then, he's biased.

This wasn't a column, but a news story after the opening round of the 1982 U.S. Golf Open at Pebble Beach in California. I included it in this anthology because of the impact Mike Malaska's remarkably upbeat disposition had on me. I ran into Malaska by chance later that night at the Adobe Inn, where not only did he freely talk about all his troubles that day at Pebble Beach, but joked about them as well. He'd just shot an 89! In the U.S. Open! If character is what we are after something bad happens, Mike Malaska retired the character trophy that day.

Mike Malaska

PEBBLE BEACH—It was late Thursday night, just after ten, when Mike Malaska, his wife, Charlene, and Dan Johnson, Malaska's caddy for the U.S. Open, made their way to a table in the Adobe Inn, smack in the heart of downtown Carmel. A late dinner to end a late day.

Malaska hadn't teed off until 3:33 P.M. at Pebble Beach for his first round ever in a national championship. He hadn't finished until after 8:00 P.M. In between, he had racked up 89 strokes, giving him a first-round score well behind the first-round leaders, which is putting it kindly.

"The thing of it was," sighed Malaska after ordering a cheeseburger and a salad, "I actually hit the ball pretty well."

But the wind was swirling in off the Pacific Ocean, and there were spike marks on the lightning-fast greens from the 150 players who preceded him, and there was tramped-down grass from the more than 12,000 fans who came to watch, and, of course, there was the unmistakable pressure that is part of a U.S. Open.

"It was a nightmare," said Malaska, an assistant pro at Hidden Valley Country Club in Draper, who came to the Open at the top of his game. He had fairly breezed through the qualifying rounds for the Open, beating out a talented field in local qualifying and then placing among the top finishers at sectional qualifying in San Francisco.

"I'd miss a fairway or a green and it was like automatic double bogey," Malaska said. "There was no relief. I only had one penalty stroke all day.

"I actually hit the ball 88 times," he said, still finding it hard to believe. "I've never shot that high."

The twenty-eight-year-old pro and former Utah Open champion admitted he became somewhat tentative as the round wore on and it was harder to keep his confidence up. Shots began to miss greens, and recoveries were tough to come by. But the Salt Lake native maintained his composure. He struggled up the 18th fairway with his sanity still intact and made a tricky three-footer to drive a stake in the round.

"Now that's pressure," grinned Malaska as a he did his best to unwind at the Adobe Inn, "having to make a three-footer to break 90."

"Dan tried to give me my bag back twice," quipped Malaska, gesturing toward his caddy, the son of Hidden Valley pro Don Johnson, "but I told him if I had to stay out there, he did too."

On Friday, Malaska had a midday starting time. He was looking forward to a more relaxed round and, he hoped, better results.

"Everybody's going to have a nightmare round sometime," he said. "You've just got to accept it when it comes."

More than anyone I ever watched, Larry Bird hated blowouts. Almost a decade after this game, I interviewed him following the gold medal ceremony in Barcelona after the U.S. Dream Team had finished its blitzkrieg through the Olympic basketball tournament. Amid the locker room celebrating, I asked Bird if he'd enjoyed himself. "It was all right . . . ," he said in that Hoosier twang of his, ". . . but I wish the games could have been closer."

The NBA still has never seen a points-rebounds-assists-steals quadruple double.

Larry Bird

O nly two things stopped Boston's Larry Bird from recording double figures in points, rebounds, assists, and steals and producing the first such
quadruple double in the history of the NBA Monday night: himself and the
fourth quarter.

With a decision that eschewed the pending historicalness of the evening,
Bird intentionally took the entire fourth quarter off, reasoning that 30 points,
12 rebounds, 10 assists and 9 steals were enough damage to wreak on anyone's
franchise, particularly since the Utah Jazz were down by 22 when the final
quarter began.

"I think I did enough in three quarters," he said.

Pete Rose record book mentality it was not. There Bird sat, on the end of
the Boston bench, just one steal away from being The First, and when coach
K.C. Jones, who had been given a statistical briefing by the scorer's table, asked
him if he wanted back in for a little more larceny, Bird said no thanks.

Like the Roman general Mark Antony said after botching his command
chasing Cleopatra in Egypt: "Only Antony can stop Antony."

Only Bird could stop Bird.

Unlike Antony, however, it could be argued that Bird was in complete
control of his destiny. Only by showing a measure of mercy, along with a dis-
interest in higher math, did he halt the cause.

If there had been a game to win, that would have been a different matter.

As it was, Bird looked on the situation like a college student having to take algebra—is this stuff ever useful?

Statistics aren't a top priority of his.

"When you first come in the league," he said, "you think of stats. But when you've got your contract, and especially after you've got a couple of championships, you don't think too much about things like quad*riple* doubles."

Heck, Bird didn't even know the title of what he'd forsaken.

"Ain't no question about it," he said. "When you've won a championship and you know that feeling, everything else sorta goes out the window."

To date, Bird has been on two NBA championship teams—in 1981 and again in 1984—and since the Celtics have the NBA's best regular season record to date, there's no reason not to think about a third in 1985.

As Bird and Boston pursue that goal, the quadruple double remains the NBA's statistical unreachable brass ring—at least insofar as points/rebounds/assists/steals are concerned. There has been one quadruple double recorded in points/rebounds/assists/blocked shots, that being accomplished by Nate Thurmond in 1974, when he was with Chicago and, on a particularly awesome night, blitzed the Atlanta Hawks for 22 points, 14 rebounds, 13 assists, and 12 blocks.

As far as NBA historians are concerned, that remains the only recorded quadruple double of any kind. It is possible that there might have been other quadruples in the earlier years of the NBA, particularly by the likes of Wilt Chamberlain and Bill Russell, but since blocked shots and steals weren't recorded until the 1973–74 season, no one will ever know.

As time goes on, Larry Bird's near-miss on a foggy night in Utah won't be remembered, either, in the official record book.

But as K.C. Jones said, what happened does say something about what Larry Bird thinks is important.

"Wins are important," said Jones. "Embarrassing somebody isn't."

Added teammate Danny Ainge: "He didn't want to take time away from some of the other guys on the team who got a chance to play (in the fourth quarter). I think it shows the kind of player Larry Bird is, and the kind of person he is. His attitude is contagious to the whole team."

Monday's episode prompted a recollection of last summer, when Bird flew to Salt Lake for the NBA awards banquet that honored him as the 1983–84 league Most Valuable Player. On the day of the banquet, a Salt Lake reporter, unable to locate Bird, called his mother's home in French Lick, Indiana, to see if he had left there.

"He left this morning," answered his mom, who then added: "By the way, what's he coming to Salt Lake for?"

Said Bird, "I told my mom what was important—when I'd be coming back."

Monday night, what was important took only three quarters to accomplish, after which Bird became an interested observer to make sure Boston had its 44th win in the bag. Then he took a shower and answered reporter's questions, and only then did he pick up a final stat sheet, which he studied with a curious look on his face.

"Oh, I don't know," he said finally. "Down the road I might wish I'd done it."

Then he shrugged, tossed the paper down, and walked out the locker room door.

The weekend I first laid eyes on the Notre Dame campus was in the late fall, with the leaves golden, the sky a deep blue, and a motion picture company on location, shooting crowd scenes. "What's the movie?" I asked one of the film people. "It's about a Notre Dame football player called 'Rudy,'" I was told. Next time you check out Rudy from the video store, notice the perfect weather, and all the BYU people on campus.

Notre Dame

S OUTH BEND, Ind.—When Brigham Young takes its turn, after all these years, on Notre Dame's football schedule this Saturday in Notre Dame Stadium, it won't necessarily be the 4–1–1, 1992 Irish team that the Cougars will have to worry about. The tough part about playing this program is what you can't see. Tackling Rick Mirer is a cinch compared to tackling a ghost.

Notre Dame isn't so much its present as it is its past. The Irish have nothing if not wakeup calls. Knute Rockne and The Gipper and the Four Horsemen, not to mention Joe Montana, aren't just names. They're alumni.

Sooner or later, the legends will come up this weekend. BYU can count on it. You can count on it. Hence, in advance of the kickoff, here's a short Fighting Irish primer, a kind of *Cliff Notes* of Notre Dame history (you could call it "Notre Dame *football* history," but that would be redundant). Put it by your TV and impress your friends in the Notre Dame sweats. Beat them to their punch.

Basically, there are four probably-true-but-probably-exaggerated Notre Dame legends that have shaped the Irish aura and turned people like Lou Holtz into insufferable gridiron monsters.

The four:

I. Nov. 1, 1913: The forward pass, and Knute Rockne, are born. It's hard to believe now, but in 1913 Notre Dame was a patsy and Army was a beast. Notre Dame accepted an invitation to play the Cadets at West Point for

$1,000 (a "money game," a la Utah State playing Nebraska). The Irish (although they weren't called the Irish back then, but rather "The Ramblers") sensed they didn't have much of a chance if they played conventional football, so they unearthed the forward pass, up until then a little-used novelty, and routed Army 35–13. The passes came primarily from quarterback Gus Dorias to a 5-foot-8, 145-pound Norwegian immigrant named Knute Rockne. Army grumbled about "wimp football," but the Irish laughed all the way to their bank.

II. Oct. 18, 1924: The Four Horsemen are born.

Army, again, was the fall guy. Notre Dame traveled to New York to play the Cadets in the Polo Grounds. After a 13–7 Irish victory, Grantland Rice, probably the most famous sports writer of all time, sat down at his typewriter at the *New York Herald-Tribune* and wrote probably the most famous sports lead of all time. To wit:

"Outlined against a blue, gray October sky the Four Horsemen rode again. In dramatic lore they are known as famine, pestilence, destruction, and death. These are only aliases. Their real names are Stuhldreher, Miller, Crowley, and Layden. They formed the crest of the South Bend cyclone before which another fighting Army football team was swept over the precipice of the Polo Grounds yesterday."

The most amazing part of the Four Horseman legend is that they actually used to write like that.

III. Nov. 10, 1928: "Win one for the Gipper" is born.

With his team an uncharacteristic 4–2 at the time, Rockne, by now Notre Dame's head coach, marched the Irish into New York again, this time to a sold-out Yankee Stadium, to play—you guessed it—Army. Rockne huddled his team around him in the locker room before the game and asked all the hangers-on to leave, with the notable exception of former heavyweight boxing champion Jack Dempsey, who was told he could stay, leave, whatever he wanted.

Rockne lowered his voice and told his maligned team that George Gipp, Notre Dame's first consensus All-American who died at the end of his senior season of 1920 with a strep throat, had, on his deathbed, asked Rockne the following:

"I've got to go, Rock. It's all right. I'm not afraid. Some time, Rock, when the team is up against it, when things are wrong and the breaks are beating the boys—

tell them to go in there with all they've got and win just one for the Gipper. I don't know where I'll be then, Rock. But I'll know it, and I'll be happy."

"This is the day," Rockne told his boys, "and you are the team."

Army fell, 12–6. Somewhere George Gipp (later to be played in the movie *Knute Rockne–All American* by Ronald Reagan) was smiling.

(Aside: Why Rockne waited eight years to win one for the Gipper has never been explained, or why the Gipper asked for only one win).

IV. Oct. 22, 1977: The green jerseys are born.

The occasion was a showdown in South Bend between Notre Dame and its "new" Army—now that the old Army couldn't even beat Holy Cross—namely USC. The year before, USC had won 17–13 in Los Angeles despite head coach Dan Devine's re-enactment of the "Win one for the Gipper" speech. Devine had asked actor Pat O'Brien, who played Rockne in *Knute Rockne–All American,* to drive over from his Beverly Hills home and deliver the famous speech just before the game. O'Brien did a terrific job, and the Notre Dame players had tears in their eyes as they hit the field. But the Hollywood "sequel whammy" hit them, and they couldn't quite win one for O'Brien.

So the next year Devine needed something different, something for the '70s. What he came up with was green jerseys. When the players got to their lockers that day in Notre Dame Stadium, their traditional blue jerseys were gone and kelly green ones—representing all that is good and strong and fightin' about the Irish—were in their place. USC got mauled that day by a bunch of inspired leprechauns, 49–19.

To be sure, there are more Notre Dame legends than these. You don't crown seven Heisman Trophy winners, 167 first-team All-Americans, and eleven national championship teams without there being plenty more to the story. The more than fifty books that have been written about Notre Dame football attest to that.

But these are the ones that wake up the echoes, that, when all else fails, keep Notre Dame thinking it is somehow destined to win even when the team is up against it. As BYU will no doubt discover Saturday, it's no small task when you've not only got to play the current team, but a bunch of boys who ran out of eligibility a long time ago but who are still hanging around.

My nephew Luke and I went to visit the Mailman and his truck at the bank in Provo. I have talked with Malone plenty of times after he has just scored 35 or 40 points in an NBA game, but I never had a more enjoyable talk with him than this day in Provo when the subject was his truck.

Karl's Truck

PROVO—The line stretched outside the bank door and spilled into the parking lot. The police were summoned to make sure there was no trouble. Anxious mothers tried to calm babies tired by the waiting as fathers craned their necks for a look inside the bank, assuring their sons not to worry, they'd get what they came for.

A bank run? Had Wall Street crashed? Another Black Friday?

Nope. The Karl Malone Truck Tour 1993 had arrived.

Or is it Karl MaLoan?

NBA ballplayers choose a variety of ways to spend their summers. Some go shopping for luxury automobiles. Some play golf. Some buy golf courses. Others fly to the Riviera and leave no forwarding address. Malone, he drives to banks and shows off his truck.

It's a custom-made 18-wheeler Freightliner with a C.M. Russell paint job on the outside and a cab you wouldn't mind living in if you could afford the rent. Karl drives it whenever he has a load to deliver or a reasonably good excuse, which is what brought about his summer-long bank tour. He was already a pitchman for Zions Bank, and the idea for a series of truck stop appearances was a natural. He didn't have an Olympics this summer, and banks have big parking lots.

For much of the summer now, Malone has been driving the byways and backways of Utah, hammering down the white lines in his big rig, listening to Dave Dudley songs, and stopping at banks. Once completed, his tour will have stretched from Logan in the north to St. George and Kanab in the south. Nobody in Utah can say they haven't been within a tankful of gas of Karl and his outfit. No need to go to the Delta Center. This time, Karl's come to your town.

Not a lot of professional athletes who make millions of dollars a year have gone into trucking. When they do, this is what it looks like. Neither the truck nor the trucker is easy to miss. Karl is, well, Karl; he has no visible gut hanging over his belt, he doesn't wear shirts with snaps on the pockets, and you just know he's never been behind in a log book in his life.

And the truck isn't at all like the basic model you'd generally see parked outside Rip Griffin's or some other place off an I-80 exit that sells mud flaps, radar detectors, chicken fried steak, and has tableside phone service reserved for professional drivers only.

Then again, you can just imagine what a professional driver would look like if he suddenly became an NBA player.

If Malone had any fears that people might not flock out to see him and his new truck on Truck Tour 1993, those fears vanished into his rearview mirror like a long lost heartache a long time ago. At every stop, the people have come, the people have gawked, the people have taken videos with their slimcams, and the people have bought T-shirts. Lots of T-shirts.

In Provo it was more of the same. The Mailman's truck store—an on-wheels version of the original Mailman's in Sugarhouse—did a nonstop business as the crowd continued at a slow pace toward the bank door. The store was conveniently located about halfway along the line, offering shirts, banners, posters, pins, caps, hats, and, of course, official Bank Tour 1993 paraphernalia.

These items were scooped up by the line-full of Karl Malone fans—who would give them to him to sign before they were another half-hour old—although anyone who thought they were in the world's longest teller line would have been genuinely confused once they got to the truck.

Inside the bank, Malone was at his gregarious best. He likes people in general, and he especially likes people who like trucks. He sat at a receptionist's table along with his teammate/sidekick Isaac Austin and signed anything thrust in front of him as long as it wasn't a loan application or a picture of George Karl. He looked up to talk whenever possible, or to respond to comments. One lady wanted to know if he'd ever seen so many white people gather in his behalf.

The Mailman laughed out loud.

"It's fine in the daytime," he said.

The banter continued on down the line. It isn't everyday the most famous athlete in your state parks in your parking lot and comes inside to sign his name. It's become the traveling event of the offseason. If that's Karl's truck outside, then this must be Zion.

*Mickey Mantle had it all: pals, power, and problems. I met him once,
when he gave a speech in Vernal at a Little League awards banquet. The entire
speech consisted of Billy Martin stories.*

Mickey Mantle

August 20, 1996

They buried Mickey Mantle this week and like a lot of people, I was made
to think back on other days and earlier places. Because that's what you
needed to do with Mickey Mantle. Return him to a time when he was who
he was, and you had no idea what "mint condition" meant.

The mere mention of Mickey Mantle brings back a time when kids collected baseball cards because they liked the players, not the price of their cards
in *Beckett's Weekly.* A Mickey Mantle was a primo card, the primo-est, but it
still went in your bike spokes on the way to baseball practice, alongside Marv
Throneberry and Felipe Alou and Wally Moon, turning your three-speed
Schwinn into a Harley Davidson.

Can you imagine a card-collector of the '90s being made to watch, without first being sedated, a mint condition Mickey Mantle being fanned by a set
of bicycle spokes?

Mickey Mantle's days were days when autographs were free and arthro-
scopic knee surgery was as hard to imagine as the Internet. For Mantle, that
meant dealing with a wrecked knee for seventeen of his eighteen big league
seasons. More innocent times all around.

It's why his funeral this past week was a lot more fun than his liver trans-
plant a few weeks earlier. The event that tried to give him life dealt with the
present, and was greeted by the criticism that the privileged live with, particularly those with self-inflicted injuries incurred because of a lifestyle made possible by those privileges. The event that brought Mickey Mantle's death, on
the other hand, dealt with the past and was greeted by tales of tape-measure
home runs, by grown men weeping, and by Roy Clark singing, fittingly,
"Yesterday, When We Were Young."

I liked the early Mickey best, of course, just as I liked the early Elvis best. I don't know about you, but the celebrity-turns-to-tragedy tune started to play thin for me a long time ago. Too many boyhood heroes have played it. Mantle's story would be sad enough if it were isolated, but it isn't. He was Babe Ruth all right, a generation later, right down to the dependency. And the Babe took the baton from Ty Cobb.

It makes you wonder. What price celebrity? One day you're on top of the world, the next you're either in rehab or in a lifetime bad mood, or, as in the case of Ali (in what may be the ultimate irony), unable to speak very well. Somebody needs to write a book for superstars on how to have a relationship with retirement. If you're Hank Aaron or Kareem Abdul-Jabbar, or Jim Brown or Pete Rose, or Wilt or Bill Russell, you spend the rest of your life wearing some kind of chip on your shoulder. And if you're O.J. Simpson, you just wear thin.

It's not a mandatory fate. Arnold Palmer, Gordie Howe, Julius Erving. There are three genuine sports idols who are yet to be indicted or rehabed. And what of Yogi Berra, Mickey Mantle's contemporary, who hasn't endured anything more traumatic than being fired once for winning a pennant.

But it is prevalent, and the point seems obvious: Life gives no free passes, not even to those who can run faster, slide better, and punch harder; and maybe *especially* not to those who can run faster, slide better, and punch harder. The evidence seems to show that being a contender in The-Best-There-Ever-Was sweepstakes carries with it a curious hole card of post-career adversity. Let's hope so. Then we have an explanation for the junkyard-dog mood that pervades the Senior Tour.

Not to mention an explanation for Mickey Mantle's life after pinstripes. The worst friend an ERA ever had, the first coming of Michael Jordan, the man who replaced DiMaggio, the man whom *everybody* wanted to buy a drink, could do it all, except retire. Well, and say no.

The way I choose to remember Mickey Mantle is precisely as he looked on that baseball card I finally took out from my bike spokes and put in a shoe box alongside my Duke Snider and Stan Musial—which my mother threw in the trash one spring after I'd left home. *A twelve-thousand dollar card!* From the stories I hear, she wasn't the only mother who did that. Mickey Mantle wasn't the only one who had trouble hanging onto his youth.

One of the most satisfying things that can happen to a journalist is uncovering some unknown fact about a well-known person. On the occasion of baseball's season-long celebration commemorating fifty years since Jackie Robinson broke the black-white barrier in baseball, I discovered that Robinson batted .097 at UCLA where baseball was his worst sport. I thought perhaps my "scoop" might be picked up nationwide, but I never saw it in print anywhere ever again, so I think it's safe to say this column remains an exclusive.

Jackie Robinson

March 2, 1997

I got a live voice on just the third voice-mail transfer, which was good news, but only to a point.

"We don't have very much on Jackie Robinson," said the staff person at UCLA sports information, "our records don't go back that far. There was this big fire . . ."

Bad news. A fire too late to help Jim Harrick and too early to preserve the college accomplishments of one Jackie Robinson, a UCLA student just before the war who would go on to become the first African American to integrate major league baseball. A man who, by the time the 1947 season was finished, would come in second in a nationwide opinion poll on the most popular people in America, placing behind only Bing Crosby, who had just finished recording "White Christmas." President Harry Truman finished fifth.

"But baseball is dedicating the entire season to him," I said. "Ted Koppel is doing a town meeting about him. Bill Clinton is giving a speech about him on opening day."

"Sorry," she said. "Wish I could help you."

But no more than an hour later she called back.

"Got a fax?" she said.

At the top of the three-page facsimile that soon arrived, someone at UCLA had written:

"This is the first time to our knowledge that this has been released, since it was lost in the files."

Outside of me, then, you are the first to know that:

* After enrolling at UCLA, in September of 1939, a transfer from Pasadena City College, Jackie Robinson became the first—and so far only—athlete in school history to letter in four sports: football, basketball, baseball, and track.

* He led the conference in scoring in basketball two straight seasons; he led the conference in rushing in football in 1939 with an average gain per carry of 12.24 yards! And as a long jumper in track, he not only won the conference meet, but the NCAA national championship meet, with a best jump of twenty-five feet (which, by the way, would have won the gold medal at the 1952 Olympic Games twelve years later!).

* In baseball, however, the story was different. As a Bruin on the 1940 baseball team, it's true that Robinson lettered, but just barely. He had sixty-two official at-bats that spring, got only six hits, accounted for exactly one RBI, committed ten errors, and batted a cool .097. He was so enthused about baseball that by the time the 1941 season came along, he dropped out of school and got a job.

So maybe it was Jackie who started the fire?

The irony, of course, is that if it hadn't been for the time and place, Jackie Robinson would have no doubt never played baseball again after college. Under today's conditions he might have gone to the NFL (he did, by point of fact, first pursue professional football, barnstorming in 1941 with an L.A. pro team—like all L.A. football teams, now defunct—called the Los Angeles Bulldogs). Or, as a two-time scoring champ from the Pacific Coast, he might have signed for about $120 million with the NBA (except for one problem, the NBA, which began in 1946–47, hadn't been born yet). Or, he might have pointed his track career toward the Olympics (which, due to Hitler, shut down after 1936 and didn't start up again until 1948).

But this was fifty years ago, when American sports had one king and that king was baseball. So when Jackie Robinson came home from the war—he served in the U.S. Army from 1942 through 1944—he turned to where they could show him the money.

He first played professionally for the Kansas City Monarchs of the Negro

National League in 1945, which is where Branch Rickey's scouts saw him. The next year he served his apprenticeship in the minors, at Montreal, and by April 15, 1947, there was Jackie, trotting out to second base on opening day, wearing the livery of the Brooklyn Dodgers.

To his old baseball teammates at UCLA, their biggest astonishment must not have been the witnessing of a black man playing in the majors, it was witnessing *that* black man.

But by then, UCLA was the old days. Jackie Robinson hit .297 that rookie season—a full 200 points above his UCLA average—and his twenty-nine stolen bases led the National League. He was hands-down winner of Rookie of the Year, setting up his MVP year two seasons later, in 1949, when he batted .342. He averaged .311 for his entire career, which ended in 1956, by which point everyone in baseball knew how to spell i-n-t-e-g-r-a-t-i-o-n, and by which point Jackie Robinson's was a name and a story worth preserving—everything that happened at UCLA included.

Human Drama

Henry Marsh, 1984
Henry Marsh, 1985
Jerry Chambers, 1986
Missy Marlow, 1988
San Francisco 'quake, 1989
Chris Yergensen, 1993
Nancy Kerrigan, 1994
Dan Jansen, 1994
Magic Johnson, 1996
Greg Norman, 1996

This is by far the most emotional column I ever wrote. When this race ended at mid-evening, Los Angeles time, on Friday night, I had exactly thirty-five minutes to make my deadline. During the course of the L.A. Olympic Games I had gotten to know Henry Marsh, and I liked him a lot. Henry had been hunted down by a virus not long after he won the U.S. Trials, and, privately, I was pulling hard for him to win a long-overdue gold medal. But not only did Marsh finish fourth—the cruelest Olympic finish of all—but he collapsed unconscious as soon as he crossed the finish line. Sitting in the Coliseum press box, thirty rows above where he lay stationary, I honestly did not know whether or not he was dead. But I had to start writing, so I wrote what follows, kind of a combination tribute and eulogy, just in case.

(For more on the Henry Marsh saga, see the next column.)

Henry Marsh

August 11, 1984

LOS ANGELES—The first time I met Henry Marsh was three years ago, in the summer of 1981, when he was running up City Creek Canyon and I couldn't catch him.

And I was on a bicycle.

We were going uphill, and if there's anything anybody on a bike is arrogant about, it's passing anybody who isn't. Yet here was this *machine* up in front, and he was pulling away. Before I ever knew his name, I knew he was strong and tough and fast.

In other words, a steeplechaser. Real men run steeplechases. As Bill Bowerman, the noted coach, says, "It's a race for *men*. Men who are talented, intelligent, and tough."

How tough? Friday night in the Olympic final, Henry Marsh showed just how tough by running perhaps the guttiest race of these Olympic Games. In the end it came for naught, insofar as medals are concerned, Marsh falling to fourth at the finish, spent of his strength as well as his consciousness. An ambulance rushed him from the arena, the crowd's sympathetic applause a far cry from the kind Marsh and most everyone else, his fellow runners included, had expected.

These were to be his Olympics, his retribution for suffering through the boycott and not holding up his training even one step. They don't come any tougher, or resolved, than Henry Marsh.

In the movies, he'd have found something at the finish when nothing was there, found that needed kick to stay with Korir, the Kenyan, who pulled away to take the gold. But the virus plaguing Marsh for the past seven weeks was no hallucination and on the final lap he proved it.

Over the final few meters, even Brian Diemer, Marsh's U.S. teammate, passed the man whose shadow he'd always been in. Marsh gave in to the virus, too, after that, admitting exhaustion but certainly not defeat.

Others wouldn't have even bothered to enter, or would have stopped when their body said to. Marsh didn't. With a lap to go he still had a shot, running on empty, and he went out sadly but in style.

He succumbed after he'd negotiated the twenty-eight barriers and seven water jumps and seven and a half laps as best he could under the circumstances.

That the steeplechase is not the world's most popular race is no wonder. Most runners, given their choice, prefer having nothing in front of them. In the steeplechase there's always something in front. It is nearly two miles of hassles; an outgrowth, in fact, of the original steeplechase run by horses. An Englishman invented the human version in 1850 in Oxford when, after a run aboard a horse he found disgustingly slow, said he could run the course faster by himself. Somebody bet him a pint he couldn't, and Henry Marsh's race was born.

Marsh accepted the steeplechase on its terms when, as a BYU freshman, he was looking for a challenge and found one. Ever since, they've gone at it, and in the process Marsh has found the steeplechase to be a worthy, and a slippery, foe.

In 1979, when he began to legitimately challenge the best there was, he overtrained and carried a bout of mononucleosis with him to a disappointing fourth-place finish in the World Cup in Montreal. In 1980 he was set to challenge for an Olympic medal, but was halted by Jimmy Carter's boycott. In the 1981 World Cup in Rome, he was penalized for running around a water jump and saw his first place finish fade to an official ninth. Then last year, in 1983, at the World Championships in Finland, he had the leader in sight on the final straightaway when he ran into the last hurdle and fell in a heap, getting up to finish eighth.

His knee was damaged in the tumble, but just five days later he ran an inspired 8:12.37 in Berlin, setting an American record and serving notice that maybe he wasn't world champion, but he wasn't quitting either.

All the times Marsh fell down he wouldn't back down. He'd just get tougher. Friday he was at his toughest.

Like with the Englishman in 1850, some people would call what he did crazy, others would call it just plain gutty. He was racing eleven of the best steeplechasers in the world in the biggest race in the world while battling a virus that for the past month had him feeling constantly like he was going to faint.

He finally did.

He didn't win the Olympic gold medal, or the silver or bronze, and that's as sad a story as you'll get from these Games. But shed no tears for Henry Marsh. If he'd wanted it easy, he'd have chosen another race, or no race at all, or found himself a horse. He'll always prove as tough as the going. Real men don't always win the gold, but they don't lose it, either.

Less than a year after the disappointment in the L.A. Olympic Games, Henry Marsh came back with a vengeance to reclaim his place as America's preeminent steeplechaser. His secret, he always maintained, was that he didn't compete against other people, but only against himself. He carried no remorse or regrets from his L.A. "collapse," where he had given it his all. After winning his eighth American national championship in 1985, he went on to set yet another American record of 8:09.17 in Koblenz, Germany, running what was, at the time, only the fifth steeplechase race ever run under 8:10. America has never had a more highly decorated—or more star-crossed—steeplechase runner.

Henry Marsh

June 12, 1985

The last time we checked in on Henry Marsh, he was face down on the track at the Los Angeles Memorial Coliseum. Although he'd been the pre-meet favorite to win the gold medal in the 3,000-meter steeplechase in the 1984 Olympic Games, he was dragged down by a virus on the final straightaway, where he was outsprinted by a Kenyan, caught by a Frenchman, and, horror of horrors, edged out, finally, by an American as the tape came into sight.

The Salt Lake lawyer finished fourth, one out of the medals, after he added agony to defeat and collapsed dead out, needing an ambulance to wheel him from the arena. Twenty minutes later he was coherent again, the only diagnosis for his passing out being that at the end, just when he needed it, he had nothing left.

Considering he was thirty years old and had been chasing an Olympic gold medal for nine full years, it was natural to assume he'd have nothing left forevermore, at least not for the fickle steeplechase, a race that, for Marsh, had a habit of giving and taking away.

Marsh came home to Salt Lake sick and tired and wondering himself if anything was left.

He didn't run a step for a month.

Then, when he finally did run a step, he found he had pulled a hamstring while running on empty down that Olympic straightaway. He had lost the gold medal to Julius Korir of Kenya, and watched Joseph Mahmoud of France slip in for the silver while Brian Diemer, a twenty-three-year-old American from Michigan, edged Marsh by three-quarters of a second for the bronze.

As a result, Diemer was hailed as the new king of American steeplechasing. His coach, Ron Warhurst, boasted in clinics that Diemer would have beaten Marsh even if Henry had been at full strength, and since he was the only American male to win a medal in the distances at L.A., Diemer's photo splashed across the cover of November's *Track & Field News*.

About the same time Marsh was testing out his pulled hamstring, he got his issue of *Track & Field News* and began hearing reports of what Warhurst was telling the running community.

In addition to that brand of motivation, there was something else, too, a kind of nagging feeling Marsh had that he couldn't stop now, not when he wasn't sure if he'd reached his peak. At the Olympics it had been the virus that had whipped him much more surely than the Kenyan, the Frenchman—or the American.

He'd felt this feeling before. When he began his sophomore year at BYU back in 1976, he watched as his friends went skiing and dated and in general enjoyed the good college life that doesn't include two-a-day track workouts. Since he was, at the time, a 9:25 steeplechaser—which isn't even fast enough for a free pair of Nikes—he decided what the heck, he'd quit, which he did, and that was when he first got the feeling—that it was okay to give up track, but only after you've given it your very best.

Realizing that wasn't the case, after two weeks he was back on the track. Three years later, he had become a two-time college All-American and the top-rated steeplechaser in the USA, a position he held every year for eight straight until Diemer passed him on that fateful August day in L.A.

Sometime late in 1984, when the Utah winter was at full rage, Henry Marsh decided he'd get healthy and fit again and give it at least one more shot.

He entered a warm-up meet at the University of Washington in the spring and won over a so-so field by five seconds; then he entered a favorite meet of his, at Modesto (California) and won by seven seconds, clocking an 8:34 that broke a meet record he had set back in 1977.

In all honesty, he was feeling very good again.

He met Diemer in late May in the Prefontaine Classic in Eugene, Oregon. More than nine months had passed since they'd run against each other in L.A., nine months during which Diemer was acknowledged as America's Best.

The Olympic bronze medalist and *Track & Field* coverboy took off on the last lap and held the lead until the final straightaway.

Then Marsh passed him, breaking free at the last barrier. His clocking, an 8:20.06, was the second-fastest time in the world this year.

Then came the national championships this past weekend in Indianapolis, where Diemer and Marsh would run their rubber race.

Marsh's 8:18.35 was the fastest time this year in the world.

He'd have hung it all up, Marsh said, if he'd lost, knowing he'd given it his very best.

Instead, he did the only thing he could do. He broke the tape, drafting Diemer behind him, and this time, instead of planting a face-first into the track, Henry Marsh did what he's always done—just kept on running.

When I set out to locate Jerry Chambers for an innocent "Where Are They Now?"
column that would coincide with the twenty-year anniversary of his
winning the MVP award as a Ute at the 1966 NCAA Final Four, I had no idea the
trouble he'd seen. At the conclusion of our telephone interview, I was
stunned to the point of not knowing how to write of his travails. Finally I just started at
the top and, like Jerry Chambers, went from there.

Jerry
Chambers

It's been twenty years now since it happened: since Jerry Chambers, a 6-foot-5 forward who wore the uniform of the University of Utah, be-bopped his way into the nation's basketball consciousness by scoring 143 points in four NCAA tournament games for a 35.8 per-game average. Nobody's ever done that, before or since. Even though Utah lost both games in the 1966 NCAA Final Four, Chambers was voted the Most Outstanding Player. Nobody's done that before or since, either.

Little did Jerry Chambers know, sitting there atop the world, that just because no one could guard him, life wouldn't stop trying to hold him down.

He had come to Utah for the 1964–65 season as an unheralded junior college transfer, and had then proceeded to take the nation by storm. By his second, and final, year, he was establishing a Western Athletic Conference scoring record for highest average in a season (28.8) that still stands. He scored 48 points against a BYU team that would go on to win the NIT. And he scored them in Provo. In the NCAA tournament that saw Utah score 318 points as a team, Chambers scored almost half of them. He had 40 against Pacific, 33 against Oregon State, 38 against Texas-Western in the national semifinal game, and 32 against Duke in the national third-place game.

After Texas-Western retired to El Paso to celebrate the NCAA title it had won with an upset over No. 1-rated Kentucky in the championship game, the Miners sat down to select the best player they faced all season. Jerry Chambers won on the first ballot.

He was drafted in the first round of the 1966 NBA draft by the Los Angeles Lakers, who were looking for an heir to Elgin Baylor. But transition to the pro game wasn't entirely easy, and after averaging 7.8 points his rookie season, Chambers was drafted again, this time by the U.S. Army. They made him an offer he couldn't refuse.

It was the height of the Vietnam conflict. He served for two years. Somebody told him he could do what Cassius Clay did, and refuse to fight, but he declined. He came back to basketball in 1970, finding he'd been traded twice, first to Philadelphia in a deal for Wilt Chamberlain, and then to the Phoenix Suns. He went to work for the Suns and was trying to whip himself back into playing shape, which wasn't easy, when Brenda died.

He and Brenda had met and gotten married in Los Angeles during his rookie year with the Lakers. They had a son, whom they named Jerome, after his father, and whom they planned to raise together. But Brenda had an asthmatic condition, which worsened while Jerry was off at war. She died of emphysema and heart failure.

Chambers continued to play ball, but emotionally he wasn't there. His career ended after eight years and almost as many stops: in Los Angeles, Phoenix, Atlanta, Buffalo, and, finally, in San Antonio with the ABA. As a pro, he never averaged in double figures, and he never played on a team with a winning record.

He raised Jerome alone. They settled in Los Angeles, where Jerry went to work in public relations and Jerome went to work following in his father's footsteps. He looked just like his dad, people said, and he had a jump shot too, like his dad.

On a hot L.A. day in July of 1983, Jerome, now thirteen years old, was playing in a youth summer league game in the suburb of Westchester. After a good first half, Jerome went to the side of the court to visit with his dad during intermission. Then the second half began. Jerome took one sprint down the floor and passed out. Paramedics were summoned, but they took an agonizing twenty minutes to arrive. CPR was administered, but at the hospital Jerome Chambers was dead on arrival—a victim of heat prostration.

Somehow, some way, Jerry Chambers regrouped. Today, although he admits he "isn't over it yet," he is pursuing an acting career that has been off-and-on for several years. He has had bit parts in a number of movies, most of them forgettable—*Cheech & Chong's Nice Dreams, New Year's Eve, The Fish That Saved Pittsburgh* (with Dr. J) and *Maurie.* He has had TV parts in *CHIPS, Fame,* and, most recently, in *Hill Street Blues.* In the past couple of months he has retained a new agent and says he sees a future as a character actor. "Pretty soon," he says, "I guess I'll be playing old geezers."

Jerry Chambers? An old geezer?

He reflects on the glory season of 1965–66 and speaks wistfully of "my finest hour," which seems so long ago. When the troubles began mounting, he lost touch with the people of his past, even those closest to him. Richard Tate, his best friend as a Ute, heard rumors about Jerome's death and tried to contact his old teammate, but was unsuccessful. Coach Jack Gardner, who tries to maintain phone numbers and addresses of his former players, lost complete touch. For years, and by choice, Chambers went it alone.

Now, at forty-two, and on the two-decade anniversary of being the best there was in the Final Four, he says he senses a light at the end of the tunnel and senses a need to renew relationships with things that are positive.

"If there's anything I've learned," he says, "it's that if there is anything good about life, don't push it aside . . . there are no guarantees it will be there tomorrow."

And then there was the night Salt Lake's Missy Marlowe and the United States women's gymnastics team ran into world politics. If it hadn't been for a questionable foul called by an East German judge who I can still see sitting there, as stoical—and unmovable—as a statue, Missy and her American teammates would have returned from the Seoul Olympics wearing bronze. If the Cold War had any good points, this wasn't one of them. Four years later, as a University of Utah senior, Missy would win the national individual collegiate championship with a new record score—probably because she was still ticked off.

Missy Marlowe

SEOUL—Melissa Marlowe was as incensed as her coach, Bela Karolyi. They just stated it a little differently.

Melissa: "What happened was totally ridiculous; it was an extremely cheap shot; a petty way for the East German judge to make certain her country got a medal."

Karolyi: "My reaction is that it's the same as if you're stopped on the highway, beaten, robbed, and you go home naked."

The United States women's gymnastics team may not have won the bronze medal Wednesday night in the Olympic Gymnastics Hall, but they didn't go away quietly, either.

Even as the East Germans—who did win the Olympic bronze medal— were in the arena mounting the peristyle alongside the Russians, who won the gold, and the Romanians, who won the silver, the Americans were in the hallway, crying injustice.

East Germany won the bronze by a bare three-hundredths of a point margin over the Americans—outscoring the U.S. 390.875 to 390.575.

The controversy that prompted Marlowe's and Karolyi's cries of foul centered around a five-hundredths of a point deduction from the U.S. score because of a platform infraction called on alternate Rhonda Faehn during Monday's compulsories. Faehn, who was assisting in moving the jump board on and off the runway at the uneven bars station, stayed on the platform during Kelly Garrison-Steves' performance because she couldn't get out of the way before the routine began.

Ellen Berger, the Jury President for the competition, jumped up after Garrison-Steves was finished and complained, calling for the penalty.

Ms. Berger is from East Germany.

She cited a rule prohibiting coaches from staying on the platform, and wanted it applied to Faehn, who she reasoned was acting as an assistant coach.

Four head judges—one from Russia, one from Romania, one from Czechoslovakia, and one from the United States—were consulted. Not surprisingly, they let the decision stand, and applied the penalty.

An official appeal from the U.S. Gymnastics Federation was denied, and when the team competition entered its optional stage Wednesday night, the U.S. found itself nearly a full point behind East Germany—195.425 to 194.450.

Making up a full point in top-level gymnastics competition isn't easy, but the Americans, buoyed by indignation, gave it their best shot. They actually passed the East Germans after the first optional rotation, scoring 49.075 on floor exercise to the East German's 47.900 on the beam.

The U.S. stayed ahead of East Germany through two more rotations, holding a narrow .125 lead going into the final rotation. That's when the East Germans managed a combined 49.325 on the uneven bars and the Americans couldn't quite keep pace by scoring a steady but hardly sensational 48.900 on the beam. The result was the loss by .300.

Forget the .500 deduction, and it would have been the Americans receiving the bronze medals.

"It's my fifth Olympic Games," said Karolyi, who coached the Romanian team before defecting and moving to America. "All the time I use my alternate to help with our routines. What Berger called was not even a rule. She cannot justify her action. It's impossible. She had to have a Soviet hold up the rule."

Marlowe said, "I really think the officials ought to consider who they're affecting. We're satisfied because we know we outscored the East Germans tonight, regardless of a silly deduction that had nothing to do with what happened [in the competition]. Talent-wise, we were the better team."

After a personally disappointing compulsory routine Monday—

lowlighted by a fall off the beam—Marlowe came back in style Wednesday. In the five-low-scores-count team scoring system, hers was counted every time.

She started with a 9.650 on floor exercise, followed that with a 9.725 vault, a 9.775 uneven bars routine, and a 9.725 beam.

Her uneven bars and beam performances came at pressurized times, when the East German-U.S. race was too close to call. On the uneven bars she had to go directly after Hope Spivey slipped and scored a low 9.225. And on the beam she had to follow Chelle Stack, who opened with a 9.625. In both instances, she responded with strong performances. "I was not happy with myself after Monday," she said. "On the beam, especially, I had a serious point to prove. This makes the Olympics much more worthwhile to me personally." Individually, Marlowe finished forty-sixth out of ninety gymnasts entered in the team competition, with a point total of 76.850.

Russia's Elena Chouchounova led all individuals with 79.675 points, followed by Daniela Silivas of Romania at 79.575. The top American was Phoebe Mills, tied for sixth overall at 78.675.

Mills will be joined by U. S. teammates Brandy Johnson, who was eleventh overall with 78.550 points, and Garrison-Steves, twenty-first at 77.825, in the individual all-around competition that starts Friday and features the top thirty-six scorers.

Marlowe's Olympic competition is over. Karolyi said she went out a champion. "What a super effort she gave tonight," he said. "I was thrilled to see such a powerful performance. I really think it was shocking to those other countries [from the Eastern Bloc] to see that we had that caliber of a gymnast to lead off our routines."

About midnight, seven hours or so after the earthquake, I sat my portable computer on top of a large marble-based ash tray in the lobby of the San Francisco Marriott to write this column. I dragged the heavy ash tray and one of the lobby's chairs over by the wall so I could plug in my computer. All set, I then sat down and turned on the computer. Nothing. "First an earthquake, now this!" I thought to myself—and then it dawned on me. I had just spent the past two hours walking around a pitch-black Union Square, dodging pieces of glass from all the broken windows, and then returned to a dimly-lit hotel whose only power source was emergency generators . . .

Hoping no one had noticed, I casually reached over and pulled the plug out of the wall, switched over to my batteries, and began to write.

San Francisco 'quake

October 18, 1989

S AN FRANCISCO—If ever there looked as if nothing was going to stop a sporting event, or anything else, from taking place, this was the time.

It was 5:04 in the afternoon, Pacific Perfect Time. The temperature was seventy-two degrees. There was no wind, there were no clouds in the sky, and there was no threat of foreign invasion.

On the field at Candlestick Park, the Gatlin Brothers were warming up to sing the national anthem as players for the Oakland Athletics and San Francisco Giants took their last grounders. More than 60,000 fans were in their seats, anticipating the first pitch of the third game of the 86th World Series in less than half an hour.

Then, at 5:05 P.M. the earth shook.

At first, I thought it was a massive organized cheer by the Giants' fans in the stadium. I thought they were all stomping their feet in unison, and my immediate thought was of that stadium at Memphis State, where the band was banned from playing "Louie, Louie" because when it does, the fans stomp so hard they actually make the stadium, which is not new, shake.

Well, that was what I thought was going on at Candlestick Park, which isn't so new either.

But then I looked around and saw that everyone else was also looking around, wearing that expression of, "Do you feel that shaking, or is it just me?"

A writer sitting next to me—we were in the upper auxiliary press box, high above the ground—stood up when the vibrations died down and said he was going out to get some air—even though we were already "out."

The odd thing was, after the shaking stopped, most everyone in the stadium still expected the game to proceed. There were shouts of "Play ball!" and "Go, Giants!" One fan yelled, "If we were just playing a team from back East, you know we'd win," meaning that if you don't want to be intimidated by an earthquake, it helps to be a Californian.

But it soon became obvious that now there was no power, that this had been no ordinary quake, and it might be a good idea if *everyone* went out to get some air.

Soon, reports from portable TVs and radios told of the collapse of part of the Bay Bridge and the I-880 freeway overpass in Oakland, and of a fire near Fisherman's Wharf, and of a collapsed building in downtown San Francisco.

Reports that there were cracks in the upper sections of Candlestick Park, and that the ballpark was unsafe, didn't come in until most of the baseball fans were in the parking lot.

In retrospect, that was fortunate. After the game was officially called off, the emptying of the stadium was orderly and without panic. There was thus no added stress on the structure. In days to come, as engineers examine the damage, and as the World Series moves elsewhere, we'll know further just how narrowly a major disaster was averted.

Not just at Candlestick Park, but throughout the Bay area. If Tuesday's earthquake—the strongest in San Francisco since the famous quake of 1906—had persisted another few seconds, who knows how much more damage it might have done? Who knows how close everyone at Game 3 of the World Series would have come to having a field-level seat?

As it was, returning by car to downtown San Francisco from Candlestick was no easy trick. The northbound freeways were closed, as was all mass transit, and power was out, effectively shutting down the traffic signals on sur-face roads.

Every intersection was a four-way stop. At many of them, people had taken it upon themselves to direct traffic. Earthquakes do seem to bring out many of mankind's more selfless virtues. In the traffic tie-ups, massive even by California standards, drivers were courteously letting each other in line.

To cover the fifteen miles from Candlestick Park to downtown took two and one half hours.

Perhaps the eeriest sight along the way was of the trolley buses, a main component of San Francisco's public transportation system, stopped in their tracks precisely where they happened to be at 5:04:50.

As nighttime descended, San Francisco turned black. No lights any-where, except those provided by portable auxiliary generators, and the fires.

At the San Francisco Marriott Hotel, where I had a totally inaccessible room on the twenty-first floor, portable generators were hooked up and a "Camp Marriott" was established in the convention ballrooms, one floor down from the lobby. The hotel staff distributed blankets and pillows—and mints—to all their guests. It was the best they could do. No one knew for sure what the rate was for a room for fifteen hundred.

Coincidentally, the Marriott had opened its doors for the first time that very morning, boasting, among other things, of a state-of-the-art earthquake-proof infrastructure. The newest and safest building in San Francisco, they said.

Little did they know how soon it would be put to the test.

Earthquakes are like that. One minute they're not there. The next minute they are. For me, that was the most revealing, and astonishing, part of Tuesday's earthquake in San Francisco. How suddenly it happened, how sud-denly it was over—and how suddenly and effectively it changed the day.

Few, if any, football games in the long and lopsided BYU-Utah rivalry have ended with more drama than when much-beleaguered placekicker Chris Yergensen connected on this 55-yarder to beat BYU in Provo. It was a particularly poetic field goal because of the heat Yergensen had taken for missing a short field goal in the Copper Bowl the year before. They really let Yergensen have it for that one. I can still remember Coach Ron McBride's postgame tirade. I thought it said a lot about Yergensen to come back the next year, period. But there's one thing you've got to say about sports. As much as they kick you when you miss one, they'll praise you when you nail one. Still, you've got to wonder why anyone would want to be a field goal kicker.

Chris
Yergensen

November 21, 1993

PROVO—Whether the University of Utah would win its first football game in Provo in twenty-two years came down to this: Either Chris Yergensen nails a 55-yard field goal or he doesn't. There are but twenty-five seconds left on the clock, the Utes are facing fourth and nowhere, and there's no other option. Either Yergensen kicks the 55-yarder in front of 65,894 fans, most of them hoping he doesn't, or it's back on the bus with tonight's lovely consolation prize—a 31–31 tie—and not much hope of the Utes going to a bowl game.

This isn't fair, of course, that the game and the season's outcome should come crushing down on the scaled-down shoulder pads of a field goal kicker. But nobody said football was fair, least of all to Yergensen, the goat of last year's Copper Bowl.

It was Yergensen who missed on a short 20-yard attempt with Washington State hanging onto a 31–28 lead late in the game. It was Yergensen who got the blame for that loss, from his coach, from his teammates, from the fans. A Ute defense that gave up 636 yards to Washington

State and couldn't get the ball back in the final 3:19 after Yergensen's miss wasn't vilified. Neither was a Ute offense that failed to score before Washington State already had a 21-point cushion.

It was Yergensen who spent the summer hearing about how easy it is to make a 20-yard field goal.

Now it's a different year, same scenario, and Yergensen, standing just past midfield in Provo, knows what time it is. It's time to either be the hero or the goat, one or the other, not much in between. It comes with the territory. So he takes a deep breath and tries to concentrate, feeling as vulnerable as you can feel in a madhouse.

He's worried, of course, and he's not about to admit otherwise. He's already missed two field goals in this game, one from thirty-five yards, the other from thirty-seven. Plus an extra point that hit the crossbar and bounced back harder toward him than when it left his foot. Even his kickoffs have been less than stellar, landing twenty to thirty yards short of the end zone. He's having trouble with BYU's uneven, muddy turf. He needs a good leg plant, and he's not getting it. He's always been a strong planter. It's the key to his power. But today he's having to back off because if he doesn't, he's afraid he'll slip.

Just a minute earlier he was standing on the sideline feeling a twinge of self-pity. Why him? Why today, in what could very well be his last football game ever? He had made one field goal, a 41-yarder, and two point-afters, but those misses hurt, and it didn't help after the second miss when a BYU fan stood up just behind the Ute bench and shouted, "Reminds me of the Copper Bowl."

One of Yergensen's teammates wheeled on the fan, told him to "Shut up!" and followed that with a wrong guess as to the fan's name.

Yergensen neither looked around or from side to side, just ahead to the next time, if there was to be a next time.

He watched as Utah got the ball with just over three minutes to play and eighty yards to cover. He watched as the scoreboard clock and his teammates continued on a collision course that inched slowly northward. He decided that if the drive were to stall, he hoped it would stall sooner rather than later. He'd rather kick a long one than a short one. A long one would mean he could throw out the finesse stuff, just plant hard, hope, and let it fly. Distance was never his nemesis anyway. He once kicked a 71-yarder in practice.

When the call finally came, he was glad it was from a distance most field goal kickers take one look at and feign a hamstring pull.

"I can go at least sixty," he thought as he set up. "Just aim it right and let it blow in."

Derek Whiddon's snap, although hurried slightly to beat the 25-second clock, was perfect. So was the hold by Justin Jones . . . and now, so too was Yergensen's kick. It came down a good ten yards beyond the crossbar, wiping out a twenty-two-year drought just like that.

Yergensen was mobbed. Yergensen was hugged. In the locker room, Yergensen was even kissed, by teammate Cedric Crawford, who shouted, "I love him when he makes kicks like that."

Yergensen looked around and took it all in. The TV stations wanted him as soon as he was ready. Everybody wanted to touch him. The lows can be low, but the highs can be high.

"One time," he sighed in satisfaction, to himself.

You could see it in Yergensen's face, the bemused realization of the inequity of it all. His kick—The Kick—had become the game's punch line and focal point all in one, overshadowing Jamal Anderson's 146 rushing yards, overshadowing Mike McCoy's 434 passing yards and three touchdown passes, overshadowing Harold Lusk's two interceptions, overshadowing Bryan Rowley's school record twenty-sixth touchdown pass reception.

"After the Copper Bowl I thought about giving it up," he said. "But I didn't."

"Good thing," smiled the man who once kicked the Utes out of a bowl and now, with one swipe of his leg, had not only beaten BYU, but had kicked them back into one.

I remember waiting for over three hours in the press lounge with about a hundred other American journalists to get a rinkside ticket for this event. Tempers were short in that room, I can tell you. Every American in Norway with a reporter's notebook was jammed in there, waiting until the seats allotted to other countries— who, hard as it is to believe, weren't as into the Nancy Kerrigan–Tonya Harding soap opera as we were in the States—were finally released. If the other countries had showed up, someone may have gone after their knees. The ticket I finally got had been reserved for Kazakhstan.

Nancy
Kerrigan

HAMAR, Norway—So at least this once, crime didn't pay. At least this once, adversity didn't medal. No matter what happens by the time the 1994 Olympic ladies figure skating title is decided Friday night, Nancy Kerrigan will know that her right knee, the one rendered useless by a club a month and a half ago at the U.S. Nationals, was just fine for Wednesday's technical skating program—and so was everything else.

With a performance bright enough to stretch all the way to Dan Jansen's smile, Kerrigan laid to rest all notions that she wouldn't be able to rebound, either physically or psychologically, from what had turned into the most well-known simple assault case in the world. It turned out that everyone was holding their breath but her. From start to finish of her two minute, thirty-six-second routine in the Hamar Olympic Amphitheatre, she skated as if her preparation had been as flawless as her performance.

She was back, playing offense. She knew it and, by the end, so did everyone else. She smiled, her parents smiled, her coaches smiled, the crowd that paid as high as $500 for tickets smiled. Anybody who liked happy endings, or at least happy halftimes, smiled. You could imagine prisoners behind bars smiling. Probably even Shane Stant, the man hired by her rival's husband to bash Kerrigan's knee, was smiling.

Even the judges had to fight to keep from smiling. They could give Kerrigan high marks, they could put her in first place—ahead of the defending world champion, ahead of the European champion and odds-on favorite— and not have to explain to anyone. No one would ask why. The sentimental favorite became the favorite, period.

Nobody said it had to happen like this. There was no new rule in place that said life now had to be fair. All the sympathy and all the million-dollar ProServ contracts in the world couldn't change that. When Kerrigan took the stage, the ice was still slippery. She could have cringed at the thought, she could have been like tennis player/assault victim Monica Seles, not sure if she wanted to play that hard anymore. She was going to get cheered no matter what she did, anyway.

But in what was perhaps figure skating's finest Olympic moment since Sonja Henie first showed it qualified as an athletic event, Kerrigan competed more like Emmitt Smith than Baryshnikov. She came through under pressure. Her knee had been attacked, she'd been scrutinized everywhere she'd gone for over a month, her chief rival and suspected conspirator in the assault had been on the same practice rink all week long—and she still did what she wanted to do when she needed to do it. She either blotted out the past or she used it to her advantage. Probably both.

Kerrigan's performance had nothing to do with Tonya Harding. Harding could have skated the routine of her life, too. She could have shaken off the last seven weeks and the pending criminal investigations and landed all her jumps and written her own overcoming-the-odds story. Whatever judgments await her in the future, she did not skate amid a negative atmosphere Wednesday night. There were almost as many "Go Tonyas" as there were "Go Nancy" admonitions from the stands.

When Harding finished her routine she scooped up as many bouquets as former Olympic champ Katarina Witt had three skaters before her. Norway is the country that brokered peace between Israel and the Palestinians; it wasn't having a hard time staying neutral on Harding vs. Kerrigan.

Whether Harding is guilty or not of conspiring to hurt Kerrigan, the fact remains Kerrigan was hurt. That's what she had to come back from Wednesday night. The least she could do was show up, the best she could do was prove what the assault had subtly (but forcefully) suggested—that she was a serious threat to anyone competing against her.

If they wanted her out of the way so badly, they must have had a very good reason. In that way, Kerrigan even made her attackers look good.

To win the gold medal, she'll have to keep it going through Friday's free program, but she's removed all doubt that she's a contender. Especially now that she's got the crowd with her. As strong as she was Wednesday night, she didn't make the Norwegians forget Sonja Henie. She succeeded in helping them remember her.

I wrote this story for inclusion in an Olympic history book series originally titled "Chamonix to Lillehammer." To me, the Olympics, in spite of their autocratic leadership, their political excess—even in spite of overly dramatic announcers like Jim McKay, Bob Costas, and don't forget John Tesch—by far produce our best sports stories. Dream Teamers aside, for the most part the Olympics are a sanctuary for the minor sports, a place where track & field, gymnastics, figure skating, downhill skiing, et al, can receive their due. The story of speedskater Dan Jansen personalizes and epitomizes all that is good and right about the Olympic Games, and it is not alone. There are thousands of such stories out there. So go out and buy the book.

Dan Jansen

"Win and the world wins with you" . . . so the cliche goes . . . "Lose and you lose alone."

Not if it's in the Olympics.

On the night of February 18, 1994, as he toed the starting line in the Olympic speedskating oval in Hamar, Norway, Dan Jansen knew better than anyone just how public defeat could be.

He'd made a career of it. Over the course of not quite four Olympiads, beginning with Sarajevo in 1984, extending through Calgary in 1988 and Albertville in 1992, and finally cruising into the 1994 Winter Games in Norway, he had consistently placed in what is politely known as "the field." Seven races he'd entered during the decade, and seven times he'd come up empty handed.

Of course, lots of people don't medal in the Olympics, even people who keep returning and trying. That's not news all by itself. But it *was* news when Jansen didn't medal. For two significant reasons:

First, for ten full years he had otherwise ruled the sprints—the 500- and 1,000-meter distances that are speedskating's show-stopping events. In these shorter races, the powerfully-built Jansen was a perennial champion. Coming into the 1994 Olympic Games, he had more than fifty World Cup medals to his credit, including a nice assortment of trophies from world championships and a succession of world records.

Second, ever since The Fall in the Calgary Games he had become a cause celebre for anyone with a heart. As something worthy to root for, Dan Jansen ranked up there with the whales and the rain forests. If not an Olympic champion, he had become, through all his very public trials, a most sympathetic figure.

The Fall came in Calgary only hours after Jansen's sister, Jane, died of leukemia. Dan, twenty-two, and Jane, twenty-seven, who was lying in a hospital bed in their hometown of West Allis, Wisconsin, had spoken on the phone earlier in the day. During the course of their brief conversation, Jane indicated she wanted her younger brother to go ahead and race. In fact, that's what she preferred. Then she died. And Dan raced.

Or tried to. He'd won both the 500 and 1,000 at the world sprint championship just prior to the Calgary Games, blowing away the field in the process, and he had already paid his Olympic dues with a fourth place finish as a hotshot eighteen-year-old four years prior in Sarajevo, so there was little question he was the man to beat. But when the odds-on favorite stuck his blade into the ice of the starting line on that fateful Valentine's Day, the first day of Olympic competition in Calgary, he was carrying the added weight of a heavy heart.

Much of America—eager to settle in and watch the Olympics and by now thoroughly briefed about Jane's death—watched what happened next. It did not take long. Barely a hundred meters into the race, looking like anything but himself, Jansen over-rotated onto his left ankle entering the first turn. His skate blade gave way. The world's fastest skater didn't stop sliding on his back and side until he ran into the padded infield wall.

After that, the world adopted him.

Four years later, when Jansen, still the fastest man on skates, arrived in Albertville, so did the world's largest fan club. If anything, his credentials were even better than at Calgary. Just three weeks earlier, he had lowered the world record for 500 meters to 36.41. Olympic vindication, surely, was about to be his. But in his first race, the 500, he hesitated coming around the far turn, as if anticipating a fall, and finished in a pedestrian 37.46, more than a second off his world best. He placed fourth. Three days later, in the 1,000, he faded even further, finishing twenty-sixth.

"Maybe," said a shaken Jansen, "it is not meant to be."

Two years later, in Lillehammer, he said the same thing—and this time, people agreed with him.

It was the 500, again, that reached up and grabbed him. Who could say why? Buoyed by cards, letters, and telegrams of encouragement from around the world and racing on Valentine's Day, the six-year anniversary of The Fall, the stage was set yet again. Just weeks before, Jansen had become the first skater ever to crack the thirty-five-second barrier. Once more, he was the man to beat.

But then, seemingly for no reason, he slipped on the third turn—a turn where, he said afterward, "I never slip." He beat himself. He finished in eighth place.

As disappointing as his other Olympic finishes had been, this one carried along with it the added burden of lost hope. At age thirty, these would undoubtedly be Jansen's last Olympic Games, and although he still had the 1,000 left to race, it was not considered his best event. Maybe if he had won the 500, but now . . .

Four nights later, as Jansen took to the Olympic ice one final time, the world watched between its fingers, afraid to take a close look at its hero's last gasp. From all past indications, it was going to be painful.

This time, however, Dan Jansen skated like, well, like Dan Jansen.

He didn't just win. He won in world record time, his 1:12.43 holding off Russia's Igor Zhelezovsky, the world record holder coming in and the prerace favorite.

He had saved the best for last, and as the reality of what he'd done—finally—sunk in, Jansen instinctively moved to the stands, where he kissed his wife, Robin, and took their nine-month-old daughter into his arms. As the crowd rose in a thunderous tribute, together they skated a victory lap, Jansen and the little girl, whose name was Jane.

Remember when Magic Johnson played his first NBA Game and after the Lakers won it at the buzzer, he jumped into the arms of the perpetually ticked-off Kareem Abdul-Jabbar and gave him a bear hug? Kareem supposedly told him, "Take it easy, there are eighty-one more of these." But Magic never did take it easy, thank goodness.

Magic Johnson

February 4, 1996

S ome weeks, things just go your way. Like with Magic Johnson, whose week included the following:

* You sign a contract to play NBA basketball again for $2.5 million for forty games.

* The Lakers buy back your five percent of the team (for roughly $20 Million).

* Your wife says Okay.

* So does everyone in the league, including the Lakers' forwards, whose jobs you're challenging.

* The lone exception is Vernon "Mad Max" Maxwell, who, the day after he says "I've got a wife and kids to think about," is sentenced to ninety days in jail on a marijuana charge.

* The Great Western Forum sells out—again.

* And, oh, yes, a team of doctors and scientists in Washington announce the discovery of an HIV treatment breakthrough that just might prolong your life for, well, life.

"God's been blessing me," Magic said as he ended his fifty-five-month leave-of-absence, coming back the way he went out, saying the right things, walking the walk *and* talking the talk. Sometimes good things do happen to good people.

Some people might say Magic paid the price for his questionable lifestyle choices and bought what he got. Maybe he did. But has anyone gone on to handle a tragedy, not to mention a most public humiliation, any better? Has anyone taken his medicine as well as Magic Johnson?

That's what makes his return to basketball so heartwarming. The way he acted while he was gone. The way he took a punch.

It was a gut punch. Think about it. One day you're one of the two greatest basketball players in the world, and you're the one who also got the personality. The next day they tell you that you have the HIV virus, which is another way of saying the jury has come back and they have given you the death penalty. You may win a few stays of execution, but in the meantime, make no mistake, you're residing on death row.

Who can even begin to fathom the distance between those two days?

So Magic retired, to deal with it, and if the world thought they'd seen him shine before, if they thought that night in Philadelphia when Jabbar was injured and the title was at stake and Magic played the pivot and had 42 points, 15 rebounds, and 7 assists, if they thought that was vintage Magic, well, that was just tuning the strings.

The part I liked most about Magic Johnson's "retirement" is that he did not brood. He talked openly about his disease and how he got it. He visited hospitals and clinics. He cheered up kids. He did benefits. He supported charities. He helped the community with business ventures (such as the Magic Johnson Cinemas he opened in South Central L.A.), and he continued to play a lot of ball.

Magic Johnson was a champion sick person. He was actually even better in adversity than he was in prosperity. We should all play a tragedy so well. He was given a death sentence, and did he walk around like life had done him wrong? Did he turn his smile upside down? Did he wear a chip on his shoulder and whine (a la Greg Louganis)?

Did he do what has become so fashionable in the '90s: become a Victim—and blame it on Race?

He did not. Didn't even come close. He had the money. He could have become a recluse who played golf and hid on a private beach the rest of his life, shunning the public, sulking as he awaited the inevitable. He could have done a Marlon Brando, but with a reason.

Because he did not, he has provided even more inspiration as an HIV carrier than he did as the most engaging player the game of basketball has ever seen.

One of my most enduring memories of the Barcelona Olympics came during the Opening Ceremonies, when the largest cheer, hands down, came when Magic Johnson walked into the Olympic Stadium. This was a year after he'd retired from the NBA, a year into his HIV sentence. Walking ahead of him were, among others, Michael Jordan and Charles Barkley, his Dream Team teammates. But the reception they got was tennis-crowd level compared to what Magic got. There was Magic, walking into an arena filled to capacity, eight thousand miles from home, and as he lifted his arms high above his head he did what he does best. He smiled.

Thousands upon thousands of Spaniards, of Frenchmen, of Russians, of Chinese, of Japanese, of Englishmen, of Americans, of *humans* rose en masse, lifted by that smile.

The smile of a dead man.

Gee, I'm glad he's back.

*So I wouldn't have to watch Greg Norman commit golf seppuku in the final round of
the Masters, I turned my TV off early, and I hadn't done that since
the last ten minutes of Sleeping with the Enemy. If Greg Norman ever does win the
Masters, it will be the biggest story in the history of golf. But that's
like saying, if England ever gets back the Colonies, it will be the biggest story in the
history of Great Britain.*

Greg Norman

The one and only week I ever spent with Greg Norman was in August about twelve years ago, when he was Arnold Palmer's partner in the Showdown at Jeremy Ranch. Norman rented the condo next door to mine, and at night he'd stand out on his deck, grill steaks, and go on about the scenery.

"I'd like to buy this place," said Norman. This was before he'd won very much on the American tour so he didn't mean, the whole mountain, just unit No. 5 of the Jeremy Ranch condominiums.

He might have just been trying to be nice, or he might have meant it, I don't know; but either way, he was an excellent neighbor, if only for a week. A kind of Crocodile Dundee come to life, and ever since, even if he did eventually settle in Florida instead of Park City, I've pulled for him during his golf career. I had no idea it was going to be such hard work.

I wanted to turn the TV off last Sunday as Norman made the turn at the Masters and suddenly looked like a train wreck in slow motion. But I didn't because I thought maybe he'd chip in or make a hole-in-one, and I sure didn't want to miss that. Stranger things have happened—usually *to* Norman, true, not *for* him. But maybe this was the day the law of averages would even the score. Maybe this was the day the holes would move to wherever he hit his ball.

I thought this even though I knew full well that when the wheels, as they say, come off in a round of golf, the auto club does not respond. It's harder to turn a golf round around than a lava flow.

But, still, I watched, screaming, "Just stand up and hit the ball!" as Norman continued to approach each shot like a man going to the gallows, and in no rush to get there.

I've always felt that it would be good if everyone reporting about, or watching, sports would be required to participate in some kind of a competitive situation at least once a year. It could be anything, a competitive 5K run, say, or a bowling tournament, a county rec basketball league, a golf tournament, whatever.

The point of it would be to make sure that those who write about it, or talk about it, or *see* it, could relate to how it feels to deal with winning and/or coming up short. If that were the case, then when somebody did "a Greg Norman" we could better appreciate the depths of the agony. And we'd probably be more sympathetic.

We could empathize even more with how Greg Norman felt after hitting his tee shot into the lake on No. 16.

How it felt to blow ten shots in less than sixteen holes, in full view of a live crowd of 50,000 and a worldwide television audience of countless millions.

And then have an inkling what kind of character it took to keep a grip and just keep on going.

How much self-control it must have taken after he hit that last water ball to not chuck his Cobras in the lake, give the Italian salute to the gallery, take a B.I.P. (Ball in Pocket), and walk off the course, which is what I probably would have done.

On those final three holes, when he was a dead man walking, let it be recorded that Greg Norman did not A) blame the weather, B) blame the crowd, C) curse at anybody, not even himself, D) refuse to talk about it, E) disappear, F) announce his retirement, or G) kill himself.

Even though he had to have wanted to.

When the collapse was complete, he gave Nick Faldo, his lifelong nemesis, a hug when he sure didn't have to, or want to, and he even managed to joke with reporters afterward. On the outside he was a regular "No worries, mate," just waiting for the billy to boil.

Sure, you might say that bringing up Norman's comportment in light of what happened might be a little like the old joke, "Other than that, Mrs.

Lincoln, how did you like the play?" But his was certainly not the first collapse in broad daylight in an athletic venue, and thousands of others have handled the post mortem a lot worse.

He didn't get the trophy, he didn't get the monkey off his throat, and he didn't get to shake the niche he shares in history with General George Custer. But he *did* win the sportsmanship trophy. Give him that. In my worst nightmare, I wouldn't want to go through a public execution at the Masters like he went through. But if I did, I'd like to be able to handle it even a tenth as well.

And I'd still like to have him living next door.

Commentaries

I came up with the Benson Poll/Educated Guess the first year I became a full-time columnist. The inaugural BP/EG, which ran on 2 February 1980, was, like most columns, motivated by the stark fear that accompanies an approaching deadline when you have absolutely no idea what you're going to write. I went to the student union buildings at both Utah and BYU, back when they each had a "cafeteria" (instead of a Taco Bell). Just like that, a tradition was born. This was one easy column. I did it every year just before Utah played BYU in basketball (usually the first game) for fifteen straight years. One year I'd go to the dorms, the next year the barber shops, the next year the law schools, and so on. I've included three samples, which follow. The poll, by the way, was right thirteen times in fifteen years, highlighted by the 1993 edition, which also happened to peg the point spread (Utah by 1) to perfection. Who says students aren't smart?

Benson Poll/ Educated Guess

Not that anybody's been holding their breath for these results, since this is the first annual and all that, but only slightly more than twenty-four hours remain before the game—I mean THE game—and if you were wondering how many points to give or ask for, or if you're just looking for some kind of yardstick by which to gauge the favorite, here it is:

The first and maybe annual-but-probably-not Benson Poll on who will win between the University of Utah and Brigham Young University. In this case, the contest is basketball, although somebody is bound to throw ideology and church-and-state into it.

This isn't George Gallup or even Lou Harris, but it's the best we've got.

What I did was dodge Wednesday's snowstorm to make an appearance at the University of Utah cafeteria just prior to noon and at the BYU cafeteria just after noon, gauging moods of the students during the same basic time periods.

Not that it matters, and this is drifting from the subject, but I couldn't help noticing: the enchiladas at BYU looked to be the tastiest lunch item; barbers are still a lot busier in Provo than Salt Lake; and when pressed to reveal their majors, Utah students were generally slower to reply, usually saying something like, "Oh, put down accounting."

There were several constants—I believe that to be a reputable polling term—incorporated into this survey, among them: 1) talking to twenty-five students at each school, selected randomly with maybe a slight bias toward better-looking coeds, 2) practicing no discrimination with regard to race, creed, or people from Idaho, 3) restricting participation to only self-proclaimed basketball fans, 4) trying hard to avoid psych majors, and 5) asking two basic questions: A) What will the point spread be? and B) Why?

Easy, huh? Well, it was. I guess the most astonishing fact was that at BYU I was rejected four times by students who couldn't care less what's going on at the Marriott Center, and at Utah, where apathy is supposed to be more pronounced on account of the school's "Commuter U." reputation, I only found two students not interested in something as life-and-death as BYU-Utah basketball.

You can check out the adjoining box score to see how everything turned out. It's right there in black and white: even the Ute students are making the Utes underdogs. Sixteen of twenty-five Utah students wouldn't bet their garbage on the home team. And at BYU, even two guys with mustaches didn't favor Utah, where it was 25-zip in overwhelming support of the royal blue and white.

Jay Ford, a Utah political science major from Sandy, Utah, insightfully said, "Well, in big games like this it comes down to the better team," while Steve Sherwood, an art major from Salt Lake, added, "BYU will be running, and that can be bad."

There was plenty of talk among the Utes about home floor advantage, prompting Bonnie Tenney, a health major from Salt Lake, to pick the Utes by ten and explain: "I just like our men better . . . you want my phone number?"

At the Y., they also talked about Utah's homecourt edge. "It's at the U., which is why it won't be worse," said Mark Brady, a recreation major from Tennessee.

Denise Kelly, a BYU theater major from California, said "The Y. will win by eighteen because I have faith."

So there you have it.

The students say BYU by ten.

Call it an educated guess.

THE BENSON POLL

Based on face-to-face interviews with twenty-five students each at BYU and the University of Utah.

	Utah will win	BYU will win
U. of U. students	9	16
BYU students	0	25
Total students	9	41
U. of U. females	5	4
U. of U. males	4	12
BYU females	0	11
BYU males	0	14
In-state students	6	14
Out-of-state students	3	27

Utah predicted point spread: BYU by 7.4

BYU predicted point spread: BYU by 12.6

Combined predicted point spread: BYU by 10.0

February 2, 1989

Despite the fact that a thousand or so tickets still remained for tonight's BYU-Utah basketball game, the Benson Poll/Educated Guess nonetheless enters into its ninth proud year. Rumors that collegiate hoops apathy had spread to the highly renowned poll have as much foundation as speculation that Jim Valvano is going to the Clippers or that Mike Tyson is going back to Robyn.

It takes more than empty seats and a pair of mediocre teams to knock the poll out of business. There's tradition involved; there's also the not insignificant fact that, after another successful pick last year, the BP/EG is—ahem—8–1 lifetime in picking the winner of each season's first BYU-Utah encounter.

Besides, rarely has there been a game offering more of a challenge to the basketball-studious students at the respective rival institutions than tonight's game. The two squads are a lot alike. If one of these teams got sick and couldn't make it to work one morning, the other one could take its place. Utah is 12–10, BYU is 9–8. Neither one has a center. Both are led by a guy named Smith. And both got beaten at home by Air Force.

In a year where there is no clear-cut favorite, extra study and additional deliberation are required. And so it seemed appropriate to take the poll at the law schools of each institution.

Unlike other walks of student life at the rival campuses—which can be quite, as you might imagine, different—the law schools are surprisingly similar.

The law students at Utah and BYU, the poll discovered, look, act, and move very much the same. These are not people with deep suntans and a frat party they're trying to forget from last night. These are not loiterers. This is serious school. Law students look like they're in the midst of a three-year race, which is what they are, the object being not to finish 150th in your class and have to do bankruptcies the rest of your life.

The main non-law topic at the University of Utah law school wasn't the BYU-Utah game. It was just WHICH study carrel did Ted Bundy sit in? Bundy attended the U. of U. law school in the '70s. He didn't graduate but allegedly got good grades in criminal law.

Rumor has it he sat in a carrel very near the fig tree on the mezzanine level of the library.

"Nobody knows for sure, although sometimes I think I see images pop up, here, where I'm sitting," said first-year student Derek Dahlstrom, who then added, "Let's see. I'd say, Utah by four."

There were five votes for a BYU win at Utah, although Brad Cahoon's wasn't one of them. Cahoon was a linebacker on the BYU football team before making his blitz move to the U. law school. "Utah by whatever the spread is," said Brad, who also observed that in the wake of last November's BYU-Utah football game, "It's been a long winter around here."

At the BYU law school, the atmosphere was somewhat more tense, even, than usual. Grades were coming out the next day.

It took Dave Tuckett, Bill Jeffs, and Frank Dibiase a while to come up with their personal point spreads. They acted like their answers were going to be graded.

They deliberated and debated this particular case study of Utah vs. BYU and then, just as a higher court might have done, split their vote, 2–1—in favor of the Cougars.

No one at BYU could come up with anyone like Ted Bundy in that school's history, although Jill Munden, a second year student from Washington, D. C., did say, "I don't know, I think we may have some current candidates." Then she said she was of course just joking and allowed that "BYU will win by one."

Several BYU law students liked Utah's home court advantage in tonight's game, and because they knew no judge was going to change this venue, went with the Utes. That, as it turned out, was the vote that swung the verdict, and it gave Utah a two-point edge.

First-year student Steve Hodge wasn't one of the Ute backers, however. "BYU by six," he said, loyally, briefly lifting his head out of page 685 of a book on contracts. Then he added, "I didn't even know there was a game."

No problem there. The Benson Poll got what it went after—yet another educated guess. And, it should be noted, at a more than reasonable price. In a year or two, getting an opinion out of these same people will cost at least $95 an hour.

Who will win tonight's game?

THE BENSON POLL

Based on face-to-face interviews with twenty-five students each at BYU and the University of Utah.

	Utah will win	BYU will win
BYU men	41	2
BYU women	3	6
BYU total	7	18
Utah men	11	4
Utah women	9	1
Utah total	20	5
Grand total	27	23

Utah predicted point spread: Utah by 4
BYU predicted point spread: BYU by 2
Combined predicted spread: Utah by 2.

January 8, 1993

Dispensing up front with any false modesty, the Benson Poll/Educated Guess enters yet another year as smug as ever. Make that *more* smug than ever. The world's most amazingly accurate poll is coming off its best year yet, having not only correctly predicted the winner of last year's BYU-Utah basketball game—which happened to be the Utes—but also having called the exact point spread—which happened to be one point.

Buoyed by such precision, the poll returned this week to the campuses of both Utah and BYU with renewed determination to accomplish the poll's annual purpose—to allow the students at the respective institutions of higher learning to predict the Big Game's winner.

This year the poll hit the students were they live. Some of them anyway. It went to the dorms.

For those of you who are ex-college students and wonder if dorm life has changed much since the old days, it hasn't. Chiefly this is because the dorms themselves have not changed. They are still the same seven-foot by ten-foot rooms they used to be, only with more names in the guest register and more initials carved into the door frames and computer desks.

The dorms remain, as always, inhabited by a collection of freshmen, athletes on scholarships, and the occasional budding socialist reading *Das Kapital* in his room by candlelight.

Collectively, the dorm-dwellers say Utah will prevail tonight . . . by three.

They said this while going to or coming from their accommodations midday Thursday at the U. of U.'s Austin Hall and at V Hall in BYU's Deseret Towers. Most respondents were well aware of the upcoming game—when you live in the center of things you tend to know what's going on—and did not have to be prodded for an opinion.

Jay Link was a typical Austin Hall respondent. He paused halfway through downing a quart of whole milk and predicted, "Utah by six." Link, a 6-foot-8, 289-pound, eighteen-year-old from Boise who is on a football scholarship, just moved into his room on Monday. "They're really pretty small," he said, then shrugged and added, "but you're not in them much."

Heidi Hofmann, a sophomore from Salt Lake City, said she "fears BYU will win" although she wasn't sure why, nor was she sure why, as a sophomore, she's still in the dorms. "I pledged a sorority," she said. "I'll be moving out soon. I don't even know my neighbors."

The only Austin Hall resident with absolutely no opinion—or, for that matter, any clue as to what he was being asked—was Yun Ho, a freshman from Korea who was playing the *Aliens* video game in the lounge and whose English did not extend beyond a blank stare. Since Ho said he is not on an athletic scholarship and has never heard of Rick Majerus, the only possible explanation is that he must have gotten admitted to the U. because he knows a foreign language.

The atmosphere at BYU's V Hall—the V stands for "V"—was different than at Austin Hall primarily because at V Hall you could actually walk freely down the residence halls. At Utah, you needed a special key and DEA clearance to get into the halls. At BYU, you need to meet dress standards.

Not that there aren't restrictions in the BYU dorms. Women, for instance, are not allowed in the men's dorm rooms except for rare hours no one has yet been able to decipher. Men are, however, allowed to be in the women's dorm rooms anytime between 8:00 A.M. and 11:00 P.M.

Rebecca Leavitt, a freshman from Madera, California, and a resident of Heritage Halls located next door to the all-male Deseret Towers, explained why the men have more liberal visiting privileges. "There are kitchens in the girls' dorms," she said. "The men are only allowed in the kitchens, not in the bedrooms."

Rebecca picked the Cougars to win tonight, but her friend from V Hall, Rob Hastings, from the Big Island of Hawaii—and, of course, a freshman—said, "Utah will win." He was one of four BYU men who sided with the Utes, a situation that effectively swung the overall favorite tag to the Utes.

Paul Jeppesen, a fourth-floor resident of V Hall, did not agree. He said the recent Utah-BYU football game, which saw Utah win on the strength of a last-second 55-yard field goal, would give the Cougars added impetus. "I pick the Y," he said. "The score will be, oh, low, 62–59."

So that's that. Another year, another Educated Guess. Stay tuned tonight. If the Utes win by three, by next year we will be completely insufferable.

Who will win the BYU-Utah basketball game?

THE BENSON POLL

Poll based on face-to-face interviews with twenty-five students each at BYU and the University of Utah.

	BYU will win	**Utah will win**
BYU men	9	4
BYU women	10	2
BYU total	19	6
Utah men	0	12
Utah women	2	11
Utah total	2	23
Grand total	21	29

BYU predicted point spread: BYU by 1
Utah predicted point spread: Utah by 4
Combined average point spread: Utah by 3

*In 1988, Canadian sprinter Ben Johnson became "Ban" Johnson when positive drug
tests at the Seoul Olympics cost him the world record and gold medal
he'd won earlier in the week and earned him a two-year suspension from competitive
track & field. In those same Olympic Games, Florence Griffith-Joyner,
just like Johnson, set a women's 100-meter world record that made everyone else look like
plow horses. Flo-Jo was even faster than Johnson: she never got caught.*

Flo-Jo

So here we are, sliding into another track season, ready to see how many
more records Florence Griffith Joyner can smash; to see if America's most
phenomenal athlete of this decade, relatively speaking, can have a really good
day and beat Carl Lewis and then take on something more her size, like a
cheetah.

But by now it's starting to sink in. Flo-Jo won't have the track world to
kick around anymore. She will not be exercising the female prerogative. She
will not change her mind. What she said in February will stand. She's through.
She's broken her last tape. She's a retiree. She's going to try to get by on the $4
million or so, per year, that she figures to make on windfall endorsements from
her merely incredible season of 1988.

It was a meteoric rise. Before 1988, the only people who knew Florence
Griffith Joyner from Florence Henderson were those who subscribe to *Track &
Field News*. Hers had been a rather nondescript career, with a silver medal
from the 1984 Los Angeles Olympics as her crown jewel.

Then came the U.S. Olympic Trials last July, and there came Flo-Jo, who
wasn't known as Flo-Jo until then.

She had these long funky fingernails, and these funky running outfits,
and every time she ran she was breaking records. She wiped .27 of a second
off Evelyn Ashford's 100-meter world record, from 10.76 to 10.49, which was
roughly the equivalent of what the gasoline engine did to the steam engine.

When she ran, people's mouths dropped. Somebody figured out that she could beat the national champion in about a third of the countries around the world—the national MALE champion. Somebody else figured out that she would have beaten O.J. Simpson for the 1966 NCAA 100-yard-dash title.

She had every woman in the world chasing her. If she ran, she won. She set world records at 100- and 200-meters, and she won three gold medals in Seoul. She was named Athlete of the Year by most of the organizations that name Athletes of the Year, including the Jesse Owens Foundation, the USOC, The Athletics Congress, and the AAU.

Then, at the prime-time age of twenty-eight, she quit.

She explained that it was more grueling than she thought, picking up all those awards and eating all that banquet food, not to mention taking care of all the endorsement deals. She said she had to choose one or the other, and she'd choose the spoils.

She said it with a straight face, as if no other active athlete in the world has to juggle business with business; as if the Michael Jordans and Orel Herschisers and Steffi Grafs don't have a few irons in the fire too; as if that isn't why agents were invented.

While she was saying what she was saying, others were saying other things. In Toronto, Charlie Francis, Ben Johnson's coach, was suggesting to a Canadian commission investigating drug abuse that his guy wasn't the only steroid user in 1988.

To illustrate his point, he showed a chart of the incredible rise in the women's 100- and 200-meter records, although he didn't mention Flo-Jo by name.

In Philadelphia, Carl Lewis told a group of students at the University of Pennsylvania that he knew, "from some very reliable sources," that Flo-Jo used male-hormone steroids in 1988.

And in Washington, D.C., at a steroid-investigation meeting of the Senate Judiciary Committee, before- and after-pictures from a West German track magazine were presented as evidence of the kind of dramatic steroid-induced changes that can occur in a human body. The pictures, with the head cropped off, were of Ms. Joyner's body, taken in 1985 and 1988. No one on the committee believed they were of the same person, or that the second photo was a woman.

Griffith Joyner has denied any and all charges.

It's true. She passed the drug tests in Seoul, the same tests Ben Johnson flunked. She must be considered innocent until proven guilty.

But, still, she's going a long way out of her way to duck another race. She's avoiding the one true and acid test: The Do-It-Again test. Do it again in 1989, when drug-testing, by both urine and now blood samples, will be more strict than ever.

What she's doing is largely unprecedented. Athletes who have great moments, or seasons, always return. Did Cassius Clay retire after he decked Sonny Liston? Did Roger Bannister call it a career after his sub-four-minute mile? Did John Stockton quit after his all-time assists season last year? The only ones who do this are race horses and mountain climbers.

Everybody else should have to do it again. Or, should WANT to do it again. Flo-Jo won every hand they dealt her, and now she's leaving early, as a winner. You don't have to have played many poker games to know that that's not going out like a man—even if you came in like one.

In the summer of 1989, I helped Jim Fassel write some articles about coaching football for a book. One day we met at the Marie Callender's Restaurant on Foothill Drive for lunch. There had been rumors that Fassel—whose Utes, with Scott Mitchell at quarterback, had finished the 1988 season by beating BYU 57–28—was being considered for other jobs. I asked him about that, and he said it was true, he had been approached, but he wasn't interested in leaving Utah because, in his opinion, the Utes had something a lot of other places just didn't have. That something was loyalty. He said he had met with then-University of Utah president Chase Peterson earlier in the summer and been assured the administration was solidly behind him in his long-range goals for the program. Fassel should have asked for their definition of "long-range." Six months later, after a 4–8 season, Peterson and the Utes fired him.

Jim Fassel's Firing

November 29, 1989

For the fifth time in the past seventeen years, the University of Utah had a coaching change in its football program Tuesday. The Utes change coaches the way some people change their oil. Their idea of stability is when the driver of the moving van takes his lunch break.

They make jobs like mercenary soldiering or serving as premier of Nicaragua look secure. There are more ex-Ute coaches out there than ex-husbands of Zsa Zsa. This year, they even had one of them—Tom Lovat (R.I.P., 1974–76, now a line coach at Wyoming)—come back and beat them.

It hasn't always been like this. In the forty-eight years before 1973, the Utes had just five coaches, and one of them, Mike Giddings, lasted only two seasons because he liked to water down the field when visiting teams with shifty running backs came to town.

But in the wake of Jim Fassel's unexpected firing yesterday, there is no such convenient hook to hang his dismissal upon. To anyone's knowledge, Fassel didn't water down the artificial grass in Rice Stadium.

Fassel's sins were more of omission than commission. What he omitted was large numbers in the win column. At 25–33, after five years, he didn't have a record to stand on.

So he's history, and the Utes are back to square one. A nationwide search—another one—is under way to replace him. There's got to be someone out there who hasn't applied before.

Some way, some day, somebody's going to pay off.

Fassel's inability to win consistently doesn't provide the coach with a terrific platform to suggest he shouldn't have been fired. Indeed, since his opening season of 8–4, his record was just 17–29 in the four years since—average records of roughly 4–7 each season. On that count, the Utah administration's swift move Tuesday was well-founded.

Still, a bile-like taste lingers from the whole affair. This is because of repeated administration indications—from University President Chase Peterson on down—that the Utes had entered into their own kinder, gentler era in athletics. They weren't in business for the quick fix or for merely the won-lost record. They wanted class coaches to build and run class programs, and if these coaches were to hang themselves, well, it was going to be with a very long rope.

That was Fassel's understanding. He never got the impression he had a gun at his back. He wasn't afraid to pick up the telephone. He was assured that what had happened with his predecessor, Chuck Stobart, who was released after a 16–17–1, three-year record accented by abject dullness, was a thing of the past.

Fassel bought a house. He got charge accounts at local stores. When he purchased items like carpets and microwave ovens that had guarantees for more than two years, he saved the receipts.

Last year, after a 6–5 record that included a season-ending victory over BYU, he went so far as to turn down job overtures from other schools, among them Stanford University. He was here for the long haul. They were in it together, he and the Utes. They were family. They liked him and he liked them.

Tuesday's firing hit him like a cold shower.

One minute he's thinking he's working for the Mother Teresa Orphanage, for the most humane people alive, for people who would tell him if there were any problems. The next minute he's feeling like Charlie Brown after Lucy has jerked the football.

In an interview this past summer, Fassel discussed why he had not been inclined to enthusiastically hustle any job offers last winter when his stock—after his team had beaten BYU and his passing offense had rated out as No. 1 in the country—was at an all-time high.

"I am working for the best president and the best administration I know of," he said. "There is loyalty here. That's a rare thing in this business."

Rarer than he knew.

The Utes can't be criticized for firing a coach who went 4–8 this season and was well below .500 after five years, or for firing a coach who had his share of discipline problems, including drug scandals the past two seasons. No big-time program in America can be criticized for trying to improve its won-lost record.

But shouldn't they have let him see the boom coming before it was lowered? Shouldn't he have been told he was on thin ice? Shouldn't he have been informed that behind the choir-boy smile was a bottom-line mentality: win or you're outta here faster than the next Amtrak?

Fassel said Tuesday he was stunned. Small wonder. Brokenhearted cowboys in country songs don't get blindsided worse than this. When the season was all said and done, the school with the second-worst defense in America finally was credited with sacking somebody—its coach.

I think this column raises a good point: If the Indians and Redskins ever do change their names, will Utah and Indiana have to change theirs?

Note the third to last paragraph. Four years after this column was written, political correctness did indeed hunt down the Washington Bullets and transform them into Wizards.

Nicknames

After several years of relative calm, the controversy over the use of American Indian nicknames and mascots for sports teams has heated up again. The on-field success of the Atlanta Braves and the Washington Redskins has been the main reason. If the Braves (and the "Tomahawk Chop") hadn't made it to the World Series, and the Redskins hadn't made it to the Super Bowl, the protests might not have gotten to the point where even some newspapers—*The Oregonian* in Portland, for example—are now refusing to print Indian nicknames, an editorial policy that changes the following sentence: "The Cleveland Indians lost 15–1 today to the New York Yankees" to read: "The baseball team from Cleveland lost 15–1 today to the New York Yankees."

Even if Cleveland should win a baseball game, the term "Indians" will not see the light of print in *The Oregonian*—a point that pleases the American Coalition against Indian Nicknames but certainly perplexes the Cleveland Indians baseball team, who keep wondering what Louis Sockalexis would make of all this if he were still playing center field.

In 1897, 1898, and 1899, Sockalexis played for the professional baseball team in Cleveland, known then as the "Spiders." Originally, the Cleveland team was known as the "Forest Cities," but their nickname was changed to "Spiders" in 1889 because there were, according to Cleveland baseball lore, a lot of tall, spindly guys on the club, and because "Forest Cities" was rightly regarded as the most ridiculous nickname in the league.

The nickname was changed again, in 1903, to the Cleveland "Naps," after Nap LaJoie, the team's star player. Around the turn of the century, baseball owners tended to name their teams after their star players instead of giving them pay raises.

But by 1915 a local newspaper, thinking it was strange to call the team the "Naps" when Nap was no longer playing, sponsored a contest for a new nickname. (The paper, presumably, was the *Cleveland Plain Dealer*, which, for reasons known only to itself, did not sponsor a contest for a new nickname of its own.)

The winner was the "Indians." The fan who suggested the winning nickname said that Cleveland should be proud for having fielded the first full-blooded American Indian to play professional baseball, namely Louis Sockalexis, a Penobscot Indian from Maine, who played the outfield and whose best year was 1897 when he hit .328.

Sockalexis had no problem with that. And the Penobscot Tribe had no problem with that either.

If an entire state could be named after a tribe (namely, Utah, after the "Utes") in 1896, then why not a baseball team after an Indian? Such was the feeling of the day. (Question: Will *The Oregonian* next stop printing the names "Utah" and "Indiana," and if so, what will it use instead?)

Similarly, there wasn't any outcry in 1932 when the new professional football team in Boston adopted "Braves" for its nickname, since the team would be playing its games at "Braves Field."

The next year, when a new field, called "Fenway Park," was finished and the team moved there, the owner, George Preston Marshall, sensibly changed the nickname to Redskins," so as not to confuse fans who otherwise might have gone to the wrong stadium. Then too, how would it be to play for the "Fenways?"

Four years later, in 1937, the franchise moved to Washington, D.C., and kept the nickname "Redskins," which met with little opposition until the 1970s, when public awareness hit a different plateau and some people began thinking "Redskins" has a negative connotation.

Although, for whatever reason, no such opposition resulted—and has yet to result—over other race- or lifestyle-oriented nicknames such as "Yankees," "Vikings," "Angels," "Hoosiers," "Rebels," and "Astros." Or over industry-oriented nicknames such as "Pistons," "Spurs," "SuperSonics," "Brewers," "Aggies," and "49ers."

Or, for that matter, over animal-oriented nicknames such as "Lions,"

"Tigers," "Bears," "Cougars," "Wildcats," "Wolfpack," "Bayou Bengals," "Bison," "Seahawks," and "Longhorns."

Neither has there been public outcry over "Nicknames That Don't Fit." There are no lawsuits on the docket against the Los Angeles "Lakers," even though they were originally named after Minnesota's 10,014 lakes; or the Los Angeles "Clippers," named for San Diego's sailing ships; or the Utah "Jazz," although Al Hirt reportedly still winces whenever he hears that oxymoron.

Or for "Names That Make No Discernible Sense," such as the "Hoyas," "Green Wave," "Tar Heels," and "Orangemen" (a protest movement waiting to happen—as soon as the Orangemen realize who they are).

If all of the above are causes whose time of political correctness has not yet come—whose uprisings are on the way—some franchises could be headed for particular danger. The Notre Dame "Fightin' Irish," for one, the Washington "Bullets" for another, and what about the Florida "Gators?"

With time, the Stanford Cardinal may become the role model for all sports franchises. Stanford used to be the "Indians" but bowed to criticism and changed, and now no one's sure what they are—a color, a bird, or a person who reports to the Vatican. And whatever it is, it's apparently only one.

Which could be Cleveland's answer, and Washington's, and Atlanta's too. Keep the nickname. But drop the *s*.

When 7-foot-6 Shawn Bradley decided, after much pondering, to forego his sophomore year of college eligibility in favor of turning professional, he stiffed a BYU program eagerly awaiting his return and turned his back on the award-winning maple bars in the Cougareat, all in favor of a Philadelphia 76ers team that would go 25–57.

Shawn
Bradley

More than a week has passed, and Shawn Bradley's decision to turn pro from Down Under makes less sense than ever. The 7-foot-6 center from Emery County is about to jump from the Australia mission field to the NBA. When he passes the international dateline, he'll skip three years of college life, just like that.

A lot of people, including his agent, have reasoned that it's a good move, putting a college education on hold in favor of a $30 or $40 million contract, and on the surface it's hard to argue with that logic. The problem is, Bradley is mortgaging his present at the expense of his future.

For a wide range of reasons, including:

READINESS: Coming home from a Mormon mission in June and immediately reporting to an NBA rookie camp or summer league team is enough to make even a Marine blanch. Bradley is bringing a whole new dimension to the term "transition game." It is safe to say he has not been running wind sprints on the way to door approaches. He has not been running the beaches of Sydney or Melbourne with kangaroos. If he's like most missionaries, the most physical activity he has done consistently over the last two years is lose his hair.

GAME MATURITY: The nagging question ever since Bradley's freshman year at BYU, and before that at Emery County High, is why this 7-foot-6 giant has not dominated any of the leagues he's played in. He has won championships and drawn crowds, true, but he has not dominated in the manner of, say, a Kareem Abdul-Jabbar. Mainly he has been taller than everybody else, not better. The early returns inspire comparisons closer to Ralph Sampson than Bill Russell. A tall guy who can shoot a jump shot. If anybody could use at least another year working on his game, instead of getting paid an armored car every night to match that game against the best talent in the world, it's Bradley.

BEING A KID: What's so distasteful about hanging around a campus for a year while being fawned over and glorified and getting all your books, tuition, and room and board paid for? At nights you could loll around your apartment eating pizza with your buddies instead of ordering room service by yourself in a hotel in Cleveland. All of a sudden Bradley is going to be in lockstep with eleven teammates who are older, have different interests, have already gotten their carefree college days out of their system, have never been to Castle Dale, Utah, and will look at you very strangely when you say "flip" and "fudge."

PROVING SOMETHING: The word is that it would be hard in college ball for a 7-foot-6 marked man like Bradley; that the triple teams and the zone defenses for his second season would begin to resemble Beirut at night. But that's not a reason to run, that's a reason to stay and take the same test that Lew Alcindor passed, and Bill Walton, and Wilt Chamberlain, and Bill Russell, and Patrick Ewing, to name several other high profile big men who had to live with packed-in college zones. Besides, if Bradley has a terrific sophomore year he'll be in the $50 million range instead of the $40 million range. One more good year of college might be worth an additional $10 million.

THIS DOESN'T LOOK GOOD: What's a Mormon missionary doing hiring an agent and making future business decisions while he's in the middle of his mission? How did he contact David Falk? Tracting? This isn't a religious issue, it's an issue of focusing on what you're doing while you're doing it. If Charles Barkley, say, were to hold a news conference this weekend and announce he's been agonizing over joining the Peace Corps, and he's going to sign on as soon as this season is over, what kind of reflection would that be on his commitment to take care of the business at hand—of the Phoenix Suns trying to rule the NBA? If his coach, Paul Westphal, were agonizing with him, as Bradley's mission leaders apparently were with him, what kind of reflection would it be on Westphal's focus?

LAST BUT NOT AT ALL LEAST, LOYALTY: If you've led BYU along

for two years . . . if Roger Reid thought you were coming back . . . if you said, "I'm going to take BYU further than it's ever been" when you first arrived on campus . . . if you never told them, "Maybe you guys ought to shop around for another center," then don't pull the rug out from under a program you signed on with in good faith and is counting on you to return for at least one more year and take it to the promised land or at least the Final Four.

The money will always be there if you're good. Salary caps were invented to loophole. If you get hurt and can't play, why would you want the money anyway? Why would you want to be paid for doing nothing? And if you're not that good, why, especially, would you want the money? As Jon Koncak might say, "Flip, who needs it?"

Nothing, including advanced calculus, makes less sense to me than major college football's refusal to decide a national champion on the field. When Nebraska and Penn State both finished the 1994 season undefeated, the unfairness was particularly glaring, giving voice to yet another in a long line of mocking, satirical, sneering, sarcastic commentaries on the subject. At least the polls are good for something.

The Football
Polls

January 8, 1995

O nce again, the college football bowl season has managed to finish off the year with all the finality of an L.A. jury trial. The University of Nebraska is the disputed mythical national champion, by order of the polls, and so stimulating is the surrounding controversy that sports everywhere are looking into changing their season-ending formats, so they too can have spirited offseason debates.

Among the possibilities:

* At Wimbledon, once the draw has been reduced to the round of thirty-two, they can switch to a format that calls for the field to pair off and play sixteen matches, after which members of the All England Lawn Tennis Association will, over the traditional strawberries and cream, vote to elect the winner by secret ballot.

* In track & field, the IAAF will be able to dispense with an actual world championship and instead conduct a poll of international track & field writers to determine the winners in all the various events it oversees.

* At the Masters, they can avoid the possibility of any further uncouth television commentators by mailing a list of the qualifying contestants to the season ticket patrons, who know best who ought to be the winner anyway, and who will send in their votes. If they'd had this system in place earlier, one of

golf's greatest injustices would have never happened and Bobby Jones would have won the tournament he founded at least once. And Arnold Palmer would have won at least fifteen Masters in a row.

* In major league baseball, it's dawning on them that if they conducted a season the way college football conducts a season then their worries about nagging things such as work stoppages will be over. Midseason strikes will be no problem—not with the World Series winner to be annually decided by a vote of panels of sports writers and coaches. This will also eliminate the unsettling possibility of ever having to actually play baseball in late October in Montreal.

* In college basketball, they're beginning to realize that all this time they've had it backwards. The selection committee is supposed to go into the hotel room in Kansas City AFTER the games have been played, where they are to select the champion, not seed the field.

* In the Olympic Games, they'll be able to change the entire format to one that ensures those countries with bigger TV markets get the prime time slots. If you're a boxer from Cuba, for instance, your country's reputation for boxing excellence alone will earn you a spot in a final day match, even if you have only a mediocre record coming into the Games—such as, say, 6–5–1. And the final day of the basketball competition will ALWAYS feature a matchup between the representative from the United States and the representative from Russia. To ward off protests from countries that might feel left out, the Olympics will invoke the grandaddy-of-them-all clause and hold a parade before the game.

* In World Cup soccer, all first round and final round matches—since the first round and final round will be one and the same—can be played in the world's great resort towns, more or less simultaneously, to be followed by worldwide championship polling. No more will penalty kick shootouts be needed to decide the winner. No more will crowd control and English hooligans be a problem.

Think of it, the face of sports around the globe changed to look just like Division I college football in America. No more actual championship games. Only "exhibitions" between the top contenders, to be followed by polling, to of course be followed by "discussions."

Every sports fan could have the potential to feel like the people in Pennsylvania are now feeling—fans with a 12–0 Penn State football team on their hands that won all its games almost without changing its pulse rate and yet is still considered second best.

Just as every sports fan could have the potential of feeling like the people in Nebraska, wondering how they got so lucky that they didn't have to play Penn State for the title.

And every sports fan, too, could have the potential of feeling like Notre Dame fans, whose allegiance gives them a lifetime pass to ride on the bowl/poll roller coaster that last year cost them a national title even though they beat the team that ended up No. 1 (Florida State) and yet this year got them into one of the season's biggest bowl games after many of the teams that beat them (Michigan, Boston College, and BYU, to name three) had already played in lesser bowls for much less money.

The whole world could get caught up in a system that makes less money than it could, adds an extra month of practice time for the teams involved, still gets coaches fired, grants unto sports writers incredible power, and gives everyone something to argue about. It's sports the college football way. It's never over, period.

One time when our hockey writer, Linda Hamilton, had a conflict, I covered my first hockey game. I didn't know a blue line from a Zamboni, and I still have to think about it, but when I went in the locker room after the game to interview the team's best player, Doug Palazzari, it was like I'd just walked onto the set of Cheers. I've honestly never met a hockey player I couldn't like.

Hockey Players

April 23, 1995

I am not a huge fan of big league hockey. I am not even a *semi*-huge fan. When the NHL highlights come on ESPN, I am off in search of a snack low in cholesterol. Well, low in bad cholesterol. I don't know why they spell Smith with a y and an *e*. I have no desire to drink from the Stanley Cup.

I'm sure it's mainly because I was born too far south of Winnipeg, and I wouldn't know your basic hockey household name if it slapped me up the side of the boards, eh? I was not grounded in hockey the way someone who lives north of Edmonton and plugs in his car's radiator every night is. Nobody said "Hey you, Hoser" when I was growing up in Sandy. Nobody I knew wanted to be the next Gordie Howe.

But, still, as a sports writer I've observed a lot of hockey and a lot of hockey players, and when it comes to team sports, there isn't a group of players I respect more. The events of the latest NHL season being yet more reason for that.

But wait a minute, you might be saying, isn't this the year hockey wasted half a season bogged down in contract negotiations? Which is true. But once the season finally got started have you noticed it's been as if nothing ever happened? It's been hockey as usual. No hard feelings. No whining, moaning, pouting, or sulking. No just going through the motions. No lawsuits.

Hockey players are like that. They get over things fast. Game misconducts, for instance. Ask any sports writer who's ever interviewed a hockey player who leads the league in penalty minutes, shaves only on a full moon, hasn't had his own teeth since he was nine, and is known as "Doctor Death," and they'll give you the same assessment following the interview.

"Nice guy."

I've talked to hockey players after games who have just been in more fights in one night than Billy Martin in his lifetime, and it's been like talking to Father Flanagan.

Ask a basketball player after a game about a technical foul he was assessed, and he'll tell you he didn't deserve it and he's thinking about suing the league. Baseball players remember brushback pitches thrown at their *fathers.* Hockey players don't even bother to write down license numbers.

As nearly as I can tell, hockey players are in such perennial good moods because they don't just *like* playing hockey they *really like* playing hockey. They are easily the happiest individuals in team sports. In the contentedness rankings, the major professional team sports line up like this:

Very content—Hockey

Mostly content—Basketball

Sort of content—Football

No comment—Baseball

Hockey is the one and only sport where you can find career minor leaguers wearing pleasant, albeit toothless, expressions. Minor league baseball players come in two categories: the ones angry because they just got sent down and the ones angry because they didn't get called up. It's not like that in hockey. When the Golden Eagles were in Salt Lake they always had guys on the roster whose resumes included approximately twelve minutes in the NHL—eight years ago. And every time you saw them they'd wonder if you wanted to come over to the condo that night and watch an NHL game with about half the team gathered around the TV. Most baseball players, and quite a few basketball and football players, have a rule that the only games they'll watch are ones they're playing in.

Actually, basketball sometimes runs close to hockey in the contented player department—as long as they don't compare contracts—and that's undoubtedly also due to the game's fun factor. Playing basketball is a lot of fun, just as playing hockey is a lot of fun. In football the fun quotient is on a sliding scale, starting with quarterback and ending with cornerback, but practices aren't much fun for anybody, and there are a lot more practices than there are games.

Baseball is the worst. Baseball players have fun ragging on each other during batting practice and while taking infield, but it's downhill from there. Plus they have too much time to stand and think during games. Thinking is what works baseball players into such foul moods.

Think about the two-sport guys of the past couple of decades who have had a choice between baseball and something else. How many have stuck with baseball exclusively? Bo Jackson and Deion Sanders couldn't resist going back to football, and Danny Ainge bolted for basketball, as has Michael Jordan.

Very little tempts hockey players besides hockey, except a little golf in the summertime on account of A) it's warm, and B) there's something satisfying about hitting a stationary puck.

The truth is, as soon as the lockout ended this year, the NHL's players swarmed back like Boy Scouts who'd been locked out of their tent. They've played their hearts out ever since.

For some reason, I don't think baseball players—who begin their own delayed-start season this Wednesday—will come back like that. Baseball players are more like Brett Butler, now of the Mets, who had to have at least $2 million or he was gone. Without at least that much money, he would have committed himself to retirement. And Brett Butler is one of the mellow ones.

Your average hockey player, he might hold out for $2 million, but he'd let you choose the lifetime you wanted to pay him.

I remember writing this on a Delta DC-10, flying back from Budapest after Salt Lake won the 2002 Olympic bid. After so many years of so many people worrying about whether Salt Lake could be successful, I decided to follow it up by worrying if everyone would keep worrying.

Olympic Behavior

W hew! The Olympics are coming. One less thing. The Budapest game plan—act hungry in Hungary—couldn't have worked any better. The bid committee did a masterful, straight-A job.

So now the Salt Lake Games can begin, and the bidding can end, and isn't that a relief? As recruiting trips go, it was a long one. More than thirty years to land one Olympics. We made more home visits than some mailmen. We made so many phone calls, MCI exempted us from "Friends and Family." If the NCAA had jurisdiction, the whole state would be on the death penalty forever. We couldn't be in bowl games or on TV until 3002.

I don't know about you, but I'm glad the bidding phase is over. All those years worrying whether we'd ever become Innsbruck West. Some worrying we would, some worrying we wouldn't. Well, there's no sense in worrying any more. As Sally Field once said, "You like me! You like me!" Unless we do a Denver, the Games are ours, and even Denver wishes it hadn't done a Denver.

All that's left is to sit back and enjoy the inevitable. Not everyone will, of course. Some people will begrudge the progress, others will moan about bidding in the first place, and still others will sweat out how we're going to look on two billion television sets—and none of it will change the fact that neither the Olympics nor the mountains are going anywhere else.

There's been enough Olympic angst the past thirty years, and the past eight especially, to last at least a lifetime. Bidding takes its toll. Another couple of years and Salt Lake City could have had a permanent tic, like Sweden. It could have been sister cities with Ostersund, the Perennial Bidder.

But as it turned out, you couldn't buy better advertising than the IOC's overwhelming endorsement of Salt Lake's winter preparedness. It isn't every city that goes head-on with the Matterhorn and a country that doubles as a meat locker and still wins in the first round. The moral is, all things come to a city that waits thirty years.

The official Olympic designation should effectively put an end to all the bid-generated anxiety of the past. Beginning immediately, Salt Lake's motto should change from "You'd Be Paranoid, Too, If Everyone Was after You" to "Be Nice To Me, and You Might Make the Short List for Figure Skating."

Other things we should do:

* No more whining about the ski jumps, luge run, bobsled run, and ice sheets we bought with public money for the bargain basement price of $59 million, tax included.

* Knight Tom Welch, Dave Johnson, and Frank Joklik.

* Quit maintaining luge is conducive to world peace.

* Never, ever again use the word *infrastructure.*

* Let the IOC delegates return to their castles, palaces, and villas with gratitude and thanks, and give someone else the opportunity to buy them streudel and cordon bleu.

* Organize a telethon for Ostersund.

* And come up with a real catchy Olympic tune. A theme of the Games of Salt Lake. Lillehammer had two of them, and if you ask my opinion, I think the songs were the secret to their resounding success and Norway's enduring reputation as keeper of the flame.

Beyond that, it's time to relax, to lighten up. Time for the bid committee to turn into an organizing committee and get some sleep. Time to stop accepting collect calls. Time to stop worrying. We should be able to finish the speed-skating oval in six and one-half years. We can even make snow, if it comes to that.

I've personally attended the past three Olympic Winter Games, in Calgary, Albertville, and Lillehammer, and trust me, it is not a rocket launching. Mostly what you need is gravity. We cannot foul this up very badly, even if we try.

We can go back to being American and boring, if we want to—the two things that made the bid committee blanch. The two things they feared more than sinister plots coming out of Quebec. We can even go back to admitting the Valley was settled by Brigham Young instead of Butch Cassidy (as Friday's IOC bid presentation inferred).

The votes are in. The verdict is cast in stone. Go ahead, exhale. What, we don't worry. The Olympics are coming. If we can't deal with that, that's our problem.

Nothing better illustrates the fickleness of modern-day professional sports than the way franchises move around. I just hope I'm still around when the Dodgers move back to New York.

Moving
Franchises

July 16, 1995

I t's been a tough summer in L.A. Football fans in the City of Angels are ticked off, to say the least. On the very same day the moving vans rolled up to the back door of Anaheim Stadium to move the Rams' belongings to St. Louis, Al Davis officially announced that the Raiders would be moving back to Oakland.

Just like that, the second-largest city in America lost two NFL teams, and the citizens, already rocked by mudslides, bankruptcies, sinkholes, Hugh Grant, and the occasional earthquake, waxed apoplectic. How could this happen? How could they be treated so shabbily? They hung Georgia Frontiere, the owner of the Rams, and Davis in effigy. They revoked their charge cards at Spago's. They told the police that next time they saw the villains on the freeways, ticket them for going fifty-six.

In the midst of all this wailing and hand-wringing, a letter to the editor found its way to the *Los Angeles Times*. It had a Brooklyn postmark.

"Hey, L.A.," it read, "how does it feel?"

So there you go. Yet another example of what goes around comes around. Especially when it comes to professional sports franchises. You can appear as immovable as Gibraltar. You can have rockband-like support. You can go to Super Bowls and World Series and the NBA Finals. And then you can leave.

It took nearly forty years, but Los Angeles finally was, indeed, able to relate to how New York felt those dark days in '57 when the Dodgers left

Brooklyn for L.A., and the Giants left the Polo Grounds for San Francisco. The sports may be different, but the parallels are the same. Two franchises from the same city representing America's most popular sport both doing a Bekins. One is from the suburbs, the other from downtown. The only difference is that in '57, New York was still left with the Yankees (which it got from Boston). Los Angeles will have to wait for another team—which it will probably get from Cincinnati or Tampa Bay or some other city that has a franchise interested in making a move.

Franchises move. That's what they do. The odds of an NFL, NBA, or MLB franchise staying in the same place for anyone's lifetime are about the same as George Foreman staying retired.

Of the eighty-three franchises currently existing in the NFL, NBA, and MLB, a full third of them—twenty-eight in all—have moved at least once, and that includes all the recent expansion franchises that haven't been around long enough to go anywhere.

Rare is the franchise that opens its doors for business at one address and stays there.

In American sports history, it's a phenomenon that has happened just seven times. Leading this short parade are the Chicago Cubs, who started out as an original National League baseball franchise in 1876. Four original American League teams—Cleveland, Detroit, Boston, and Chicago—are in the same city they were in in 1901, the year the A.L. began.

In the NBA, only the Boston Celtics and the New York Knicks are 1946–47 originals.

In the NFL, not a single franchise is where it was when the league began in 1920. Green Bay, which joined the league in 1921, comes the closest.

Go ahead. Name a major American city. It's either been raided or it's raided someplace else. Even Chicago, with its deep pan originals in the Cubs and the White Sox, isn't unscathed. The football Bears came from Decatur, and the original Chicago NFL franchise—the Cardinals—left for St. Louis (where they stayed for a half-century or so before moving to Phoenix). The NBA Bulls date back only to 1966, an expansion makeup for the NBA-original Chicago Stags who went out of business in 1950.

Some towns get whiplash from all the comings and goings. How about Kansas City? The baseball A's came from Philadelphia on their way to Oakland. The football Chiefs came from Dallas. The only original is the baseball Royals, an expansion franchise. There once was an NBA team, the Kings, but that was a gypsy franchise that began in Rochester, moved to Cincinnati, moved to Kansas City-Omaha, moved to Kansas City outright, and then left for Sacramento.

Sometimes, the bigger the city the worse. New York has lost the Dodgers, the Giants, and the basketball Nets with nothing in return. Washington, D.C. lost the baseball Senators to Minnesota and is still waiting for a replacement, although it did get the football Redskins from Boston.

Atlanta is a good example of patience—not to mention the benevolence of Milwaukee. The basketball Hawks are there after four moves—from Tri-Cities to Milwaukee to St. Louis to Atlanta—and the baseball Braves got there by way of Boston and Milwaukee.

Oakland is another example of patience. This is a city with three franchises—the A's, Warriors, and now, again, the Raiders—that have all been somebody else's.

But it is Los Angeles that leads the leagues in cherry picking. Only the baseball Angels are an L.A. original, and they're in Anaheim. The Dodgers came from Brooklyn, the Lakers from Minneapolis, and the Clippers from San Diego. Even the Rams and the Raiders—from Cleveland and Oakland, respectively—came from somewhere else.

Now the Rams have inched back toward their midwest roots and the Raiders have decided you *can* go home again . . . and back in Brooklyn, they've got to be wondering why on earth they paved over Ebbetts Field.

I'm not saying the world isn't full of "nice guys" and "jerks," I'm just saying that sports writers are probably the last people you want to pass that judgment.

Nice Guys

The single most difficult thing about being a sports writer is the psycho-analysis that many link inexorably with the profession. The style of journalism brought to an art form level by Frank Deford—and lowered to a notch somewhere below that by Dave Kindred—that delves into the human psyche, defines behavior, and attaches labels, has always left me confused. Confused because no one is the same two days in a row, let alone two seasons in a row.

As a sports writer you get asked all the time questions such as, "What's Karl Malone like? Is he a nice guy or is he a jerk?" "Is John Stockton a good guy?" "What's Rick Majerus really like?" And so on. Difficult questions, unless you've walked in their moccasins, as the saying goes. I don't even know how Karl Malone manages to *always* have a two-day's growth of beard, let alone anything definitive about his personality profile. Although I can say this: in the locker room after a game, he is generally in a better mood after a win than after a loss.

I bring all this up because I went to the movies the other night and saw *Cobb,* the story about baseball legend Ty Cobb, and a movie that portrays the lifetime .367 hitter as a person with two sides: one dark, the other darker. Tommy Lee Jones does a terrific job playing Cobb as he abuses virtually every-one and everything in his path, including, but not limited to, cars, buildings, deer, night clubs, women, minorities, alcohol, sports writers, his family, and last but not least, himself.

First, Pete Rose breaks Cobb's all-time hits record, and now this.

The credibility for *Cobb* comes from Al Stump, the real life sports writer who accompanied Cobb on a ten-month journey in 1960 while writing his biography. At the end of that journey Cobb died, and Stump dutifully wrote the "authorized" Ty Cobb biography, *My Life in Baseball*, which was published in 1961.

It wasn't until later that Stump wrote another, more personal view of Ty Cobb, first in articles for *True* and *Sport* magazines, and, just lately, in a 434-page revised book version of the original entitled *Cobb: A Biography.*

It is this book that inspired the movie.

Even if he did make him a pile of money in royalties, twice, Al Stump does not think Ty Cobb was a nice guy.

If they had adhered to the tenet that if you can't say something good about someone then don't say anything at all, the movie would be three seconds long.

Certainly Stump's isn't the only evidence that Cobb was a bad boy who went through life with spikes high, and sharpened. Cobb-bashing has been in vogue for decades and got mainstream movie treatment most recently in *Field of Dreams,* when Shoeless Joe Jackson said Cobb wasn't welcome on Kevin Costner's Iowa ballfield because "we couldn't stand the ——— when he was alive, so we told him to stick it."

Cameo tweaks are one thing, but the part that bothers me about a full length movie like *Cobb* is its definitiveness. Its lack of equal time. Its tendency to characterize a person as bad, not just the things he did.

That also obviously bothered a man named Harold Schefski of Long Beach, California, who wrote a letter to the editor of the *Los Angeles Times* not long after the movie premier of *Cobb.*

"In August of 1956, when I was a nine-year-old boy in the San Francisco Bay Area, my friends found Ty Cobb's phone number listed in the Atherton phone book," writes Schefski. "We dialed the number and found the voice on the line kind and receptive. Mr. Cobb invited us to his house, greeted us at the door, and gave us a tour. He then wrote out detailed autographs for all four of us and presented them, along with miniature bats with his name inscribed. As he said good-by to us two hours after our arrival, he kissed the little girl and gave the boys a handshake.

"While the recent film and Al Stump's biography may be well researched and the rumors about Mr. Cobb's racism, misogyny, and repressed anger over his mother's shooting of his father may have merit, wouldn't it be better to adhere to Leo Tolstoy's maxim about all men, namely that they are like rivers, deep in some areas, shallow in others? Undoubtedly, I met Ty Cobb on one of his deeper days."

Echoing a similar sentiment, and even more credibility, was Jim Cobb, Ty Cobb's son, who was interviewed this week on National Public Radio and said he wouldn't see the movie because it "distorted" his father's life. An enduring memory of Jim Cobb's is when he returned from World War II and his father met him at the pier with a box of donuts and a bottle of cold milk— "because he knew that's what I liked."

Al Stump's enduring memories are darker than that—memories collected while spending ten months with a man who had stomach cancer, was going blind, and who was staring into a light at the end of the tunnel that really was a train. When the egocentric Cobb told Stump in 1960 that he would "only hit .290 against today's pitchers. Why? Because I'm seventy-four years old, that's why," he could have added that he was far from his prime in more ways than that.

Was Ty Cobb a nice guy? Was Ty Cobb a jerk? As with most of us, I'm sure it depended on what day you met him, and where.

This column was historical for me in that it was the first time I used the internet to dig up facts for a column. I typed in the key words "Albert Belle," and there, at my fingertips, was all the information I needed, and more. The invention of the computer is the greatest thing to ever happen to sports writers. Even those who still type with just their index fingers.

Them and Us

Baseball came down with its biggest abuse-of-sportscaster fine in history this week when acting commissioner, Bud Selig, assessed Cleveland Indian Albert Belle $50,000 for an obscenity-laced tirade he directed at NBC reporter Hannah Storm in the Indians' dugout last fall prior to Game 3 of the World Series.

Thus Belle becomes the first baseball player in history to be fined for both corking his bat and not corking his mouth.

In accepting his fine and delivering a heartfelt apology—by way of the Indians' P.R. department—Belle moved away from his original defense, which was that he thought Hannah Storm was in reality another woman sportscaster, Leslie Visser, with whom he has a personal feud—to distinguish between that feud and the general feud he has with anybody else who might have anything to do with the media.

The incident provided a small glimpse into the grimy underworld of sports reporting, a place where a reporter must have razor sharp reflexes, 360-degree peripheral vision, thick skin, thin ears, and a good tape recorder.

There is a public perception that reporters and athletes get along in locker rooms the same way they do in beer ads, but of course nothing could be further from the truth. It's an E.R. in there. As adversarial as Johnnie Cochran and Marcia Clark on a bad day. A real chess game. On the one hand you've got all these people who want to talk and, on other hand, all these people who don't want to.

This paradox is only magnified when the stakes rise, a la a World Series,

Super Bowl, Final Four, salary dispute, etc. It's a fact of life any sports reporter learns early. The bigger the story, the harder. By way of example, I remember during the NBA playoffs a few years ago, trying to reach former BYU center Greg Kite who was playing for the Boston Celtics. I called the Celtics and, after asking for Kite, got this response:

"We're in the middle of the playoffs!"

"What a coincidence," I said. "That's why I want to talk to him."

But it was a waste of perfectly good sarcasm. They'd already hung up.

Kite, always a nice guy, would have talked to me, I'm sure, but not because he would have particularly wanted to.

No athlete really wants to talk to reporters, except runners, and by that I mean distance runners. Sprinters are the same as center fielders or power forwards. But distance runners will talk forever about—and this is the bad part—distance running.

Oh, and hockey players. A hockey guy will talk about hockey anytime, anywhere. Hockey players love their sport, and they love to talk about it. Ask them how they lost their teeth, they'll smile and cheerily tell you all about it. It will be a hot day in Edmonton the day a hockey player does an Albert Belle.

For the most part, though, sports reporters and sports figures manage to co-exist peaceably enough. Reporters are tolerated in locker rooms and dugouts and allowed to do their job, as long as they know their place. I wasn't there for the Belle-Storm incident, but probably what happened was that Storm, who works for television, didn't assume the position of deference (sometimes called "the quavering newspaper position") favored by the people who are getting dressed in front of you.

TV people sometimes think *they* own the place. I think it's a salary commensurate thing. I remember a Jazz playoff game a couple of years ago. I had a great press row seat, two rows off the floor. Next to my seat was Hannah Storm's. An hour before the game she came by to check it out. There was no television monitor directly in front of her seat. She screamed for Kim Turner, the Jazz's P.R. director. If she didn't have a monitor, she explained, the world was going to end, AND SHE WOULDN'T BE ABLE TO SEE IT. The monitors were quickly rearranged so one was directly in front of her seat. But by then Storm had left—and she never returned. She never sat in that seat the entire game.

Last fall, when the Indians were down two games to zero to the Braves in the Series, and the pressure was in the red zone, and Belle didn't want to see any reporters in the dugout, it was probably not the best time for his ego and Hannah's ego to meet.

It certainly wasn't Belle's first brush with conflict, or his last. Later that same month he chased down some kids trick-or-treating at his house on Halloween. In his truck. He's being sued for $850,000 in damages in that case, which is still pending, and in which he is reportedly sticking to his original excuse in the dugout incident.

He thought it was Leslie Visser.

Every once in a while, somebody comes along and does something so indefensible, so inane, so witless, so stupid . . . that he's a columnist's dream.

To Stand or Not to Stand

March 24, 1996

T hank you, Mahmoud Abdul-Rauf, for that civics clinic you recently staged for all of us. Yours was $31,707 well spent. What's one night's pay when you were able to help so many people make so many points? The government would have taken half of it anyway, right?

You reminded us yet again that in this country of ours you can still say any darned thing you want and no one is going to pull you out of your bed in the middle of the night. What Alexander Hamilton said still goes: What you say may not be agreed with, but we'll defend to the death your right to say it.

You stood up and said the flag—our flag, your flag—is "a symbol of oppression, of tyranny" and you weren't going to stand at attention when it was raised and some local Kenny G or a barbershop quartet or a nine-year-old-sure-to-be-the-next-Reba did the national anthem. You wouldn't stand if it were Whitney Houston herself, the deliverer of maybe the greatest national anthem ever rendered, prior to Super Bowl XXV in Tampa—as the Gulf War raged and 90,000 people stood en masse and fought back tears. If you'd been there, you'd have just sat there.

You also cited religious conviction, saying the Koran, the Muslim holy book, tells you that nothing must come between you and Allah.

No sooner did you make your stand than all kinds of people, from the American Civil Liberties Union to the NBA Player's Union to Constitutional scholars, were defending your right to say it. Others chose to remain neutral. Like, for instance, the Jazz's Chris Morris, who said, "I can't agree or disagree.

I'm not him, and I'm not into his head." In this country you can still be a "Don't Know."

And still others, and this group included most Muslims who've ever read the Koran and most Americans who've ever drawn breath, chose to exercise their right to disagree with what you said.

In the indefensible position category, you took your place in history somewhere just behind Marie ("Let them eat cake") Antoinette.

Tyrannical? Oppressive? America?

It was like calling Julia Roberts ugly. Like calling Dikembe Mutombo short. No sooner was your view made public than necks swiveled in places like Sarajevo, Beirut, Chechnya, even Belfast. If America is oppressive and tyrannical, where's the hope for any of us?

America, where rights of personal freedom are held so highly that you can walk out of a courtroom even if you did it, even if everybody knows you did it, even if the cocaine is piled high in front of you and those are your fingerprints—but they didn't first read you your rights. America, where if there's any error, if will be made on the side of freedom.

America, where, if we've got anything to say about it, it's the oppressors who get oppressed. There are Americans who are oppressors, sure, Americans who see color, who exploit and suppress—but not America. Not the Constitution. Not the Bill of Rights. "The right to life, liberty, and the pursuit of happiness." That's not just an advertising slogan. That's what the flag is a symbol of.

America, the nation that went in and rescued Kuwait, the nation that has a national debt in the trillions and still sends foreign aid like it's candy, that sends troops to Somalia and Haiti and Bosnia to make peace, not war. America, a country that keeps telling Israel and Palestine to shake hands.

America, a country that keeps trying to get it right, that learns from its past, that's more free now than it was two hundred years ago, and hopes to be even freer two hundred years from now.

America, where Quakers worship next door to Hare Krishnas.

People said, "Hey Mahmoud, why don't you go to Arabia and change your name to Chris Jackson for religious reasons." Try that over there and they'd throw you in the Mecca jail. Or, while you're there in the cradle of Islam, pose as a woman for a while. See what it's like when they won't let you drive, vote, dress how you prefer, show your face in public, or marry who you want. Or, pose as a Christian, and see what it's like to be put in a cell for celebrating Christmas.

So, whether you meant to or not, you provided a service *this week*, reawakening in many of us the reasons why we *do* choose to stand during the national anthem.

And in the final analysis, you also reinforced that basic civics lesson everybody had to learn in junior high: In America, the definition of freedom means you can do whatever you wish, as long as it doesn't encroach on the freedom of others. That contract you signed to play in the NBA, the one that pays you $31,707 a game, also bound you to assume a "dignified posture" during the playing of the national anthem.

You were stuck. They'd already read you your rights.

We will uncover the mystery of the Sphinx before we uncover the depths of the
internal BYU power plays that conspired to
fire BYU basketball coach, Roger Reid, a week before Christmas.

Roger Reid's Firing

December 26, 1996

S o now BYU, the school that once didn't play in the Fiesta Bowl because it was scheduled on the Sabbath Day, is also the school that fired the head of a crippled program a week before Christmas.

Who do they bring in for spin on this one, Dick Morris?

I know this sounds harsh, but the fact is, Roger Reid, the beleaguered chief of a basketball program that lost its star player to white collar crime this summer and its star recruit to Duke this fall, was fired as BYU's head coach last Tuesday, eight days before Christmas.

Reid is the fourth BYU basketball coach in twenty-four years to be fired, and every one of them had a winning record. Talk about a tough employer. BYU keeps this up, Kathie Lee Gifford will be organizing pickets.

BYU has become the Lucy of college basketball. Just when a coach gets rolling, he pulls into his parking space only to discover they moved the arena.

Let's see, Glenn Potter got fired for not being Stan Watts; Frank Arnold got fired because he thought he *was* Stan Watts; Ladell Andersen got fired because his lucky jacket from Mr. Mac's wore out; and Roger Reid got fired because he told star recruit Grant Burgess that nine million Mormons were going to be extremely ticked off.

At least I think that's why all of them were fired. At BYU, it's hard to tell because they never use the "F" word and when they hold a press conference— always to announce the NEW coach—instead of explaining why the old coach "stepped down," they praise the guy they've jettisoned as though he's just made Eagle Scout.

For example, at last week's Tiny Tim Memorial press conference announcing Tony Ingle's appointment as interim basketball coach, BYU athletic director, Rondo Fehlberg, said Roger Reid left "an unparalleled legacy of integrity and success" and that "he has been an example of all that's good about BYU and intercollegiate athletics."

That's the guy he just fired.

The motto at BYU: If you can't say something good about someone . . . he must still be on the payroll.

Or just how often over the past seven years have you heard the administration at BYU talk about Roger Reid the way he was talked about last Tuesday?

Last month, when Reid's comment to Burgess, the California high school phenom, became public—and it was Burgess, not Reid, who turned a private comment into a sound bite on the ten o'clock news—Fehlberg was the one who led the cries of consternation. The BYU administration cleared out and let ol' Rog go one on nine million.

The irony is that Roger was right. Well, maybe not about all nine million Mormons pouting. But certainly about the portion of that nine million who care about BYU basketball. If the coach's point was that the fans would stay away in droves if BYU didn't field a star-studded, winning team, it was a point well taken when all of 3,418 people came to the consolation game of the Cougar Classic to watch a team burrowing its way to a 1–6 start.

In a weird kind of way, Roger Reid prophesied his own doom. He *needed* Burgess and he knew it—especially in the wake of Bryon Ruffner's troubles with the law. Christian school or not, they're not going to keep you around at BYU unless you win and fill the seats.

Sure, he could have been more diplomatic with his words, even if they were off the record, but everyone can't be LaVell Edwards. BYU certainly had to know what it was getting when it hired Reid seven seasons ago. It was getting Mormondom's answer to Bobby Knight. He might not throw the chair, but he'd sure like to. This is a man with average skills who made it all the way to triple-A baseball because compared to him, Pete Rose looked like a transient sleeping under the freeway. (Personal aside: I remember playing golf once with Roger Reid, and he got upset with himself because a couple of the guys we were playing with had better scores. And the thing was, Reid didn't play golf!)

He has the coaching gene all right. Give him competitiveness or give him nothing at all. He used that coaching gene to overachieve for BYU for seven years plus seven games. He even beat Rick Majerus, eight games to seven. No way Roger Reid would have ever quit a fourth of the way into the season, even with the ship leaning, eight freshmen on board, and road trips to Albuquerque, Fresno, and Salt Lake looming like the black death. In athletics it's the one thing you don't do. You don't quit. They'd have had to hogtie him, throw him over the side, turn the sails into the wind, and rush off like a thief in the night, to get rid of him. Which, come to think of it, is just what BYU did.

The way a columnist's mind works is, first, you see something in the newspaper or on SportsCenter; second, you get an idea; and third, you write about it. Sometimes what you end up writing is a complete tangent, which was the case for me with the Walt Sweeney lawsuit. It gave me a chance to write about drugs in sports, and when I started, I swear I had no idea that's where I would end up.

Walt Sweeney
and the NFL

January 28, 1997

Now that Super Bowl XXXI is over and all those $2.4 million-per-minute TV advertisements are in the books, the National Football League can turn to other issues, one of which is what to do about Walt Sweeney.

Sweeney is the former San Diego Charger defensive end who sued the league for addicting him to drugs during his lengthy playing career—and who last week was awarded $1.8 million in damages.

The NFL's response, predictably, is to appeal. The league's position is that Sweeney addicted himself to drugs. Even if pills and shots were made available to him during his playing career, the league contends he was the one who chose to abuse them.

First, is it a frivolous lawsuit? Yes. Next thing you know, Muhammad Ali will be suing the World Boxing Council for his getting Parkinson's disease, the estates of Jimi Hendrix and Jim Morrison will be suing record companies and concert promoters for creating drug-infested environments, and kids will be suing their parents for their genetic makeup. And they'll all cite the Walt Sweeney case as precedent. It's the '90s; it's always someone else's fault.

But in spite of being a frivolous lawsuit, the Walt Sweeney case raises an important point—that the National Football League is really no better than rock concerts or dimly lit boxing gyms when it comes to stemming the insidious flow of drugs and other harmful things.

In the war on drugs, the NFL is at best Switzerland.

While it may be true that the league does not officially condone substance abuse, it doesn't work very hard at discouraging it, either. Or when was the last time you heard of a player being ejected for anything other than hardcore drug addiction? When was the last time you heard of a player being suspended for steroid use, or addiction to pain-killers? (When Brett Favre's addiction, to use one celebrated case-in-point, reached the breaking point last summer, he essentially turned himself in.)

Year-in, year-out, the Walt Sweeneys come and go, popping pills, drinking twenty cups of coffee on game day morning, shooting up cortisone at halftime, tossing back the percocets, and injecting human growth hormone or other non-detectable steroids that put on muscle, weight, and agitation—and the unofficial stance, "live and let live," remains.

The proof that substance abuse abounds in the NFL is on every roster, even in the AFC, where it hasn't done much good. Teams are filled with 300-pound linemen, with seriously injured players who make miraculous recoveries every Sunday—and sometimes in the space of a twenty-minute halftime—with players whose rap sheets include the kind of assault crimes associated with substance-produced rage.

It doesn't take a medical school diploma to know that lasagna isn't the only entree in the pre-game meal; that the league, overall, is about as "natural" as a Thanksgiving turkey. Twenty years ago, you couldn't find a 300-pound football player. Today, if you're not 300 pounds or close to it, the NFL has a name for you: punter. True, the human species keeps getting bigger, but at the NFL rate, everybody on earth would be shopping at the Big and Tall shop by the turn of the century. And asking if you want to make something of it.

Walt Sweeney's is just one testimony among thousands that the abuse is thriving. That the implosion, as they say, is from within. That pretty soon they'll be remembering Refrigerator Perry as "Tiny."

Instead of appealing Sweeney's case, the NFL should thank him for the epiphany and do what it should have done fifty years ago—get tough on the unnatural. Starting now, no shots of any kind should be allowed during games, and neither should the taking of any pain-killing drugs stronger than aspirin. Players who get concussions should be required to sit out three weeks, minimum. Anyone gaining more than twenty pounds in an offseason should be required to take extensive tests for steroid detection. And if you're caught with drugs in your system, you're out of the league—for at least a year.

Not only would there be an extensive trickle-down effect to compel college and high school players to live a similar no-drugs life, but the league could return to the days when quarterbacks lasted entire seasons and offensive linemen stopped having liver problems at age fifty.

On top of all that, almost overnight, it would be a better game, one that stresses skill more than brawn and natural toughness more than drug-induced hysteria.

Out of messy lawsuits come silver linings. Looked at in the right light, Walt Sweeney did the NFL a favor. And for a mere $1.8 million, or about the cost of a forty-five-second commercial spot in Super Bowl XXXII.

After Mike Tyson bit a chunk off Evander Holyfield's ear, the image that stuck in my
mind, oddly enough, was of a shaking, shrunken Muhammad Ali
trying to light the Olympic torch eleven months earlier at the Atlanta Olympic Games.
After that I started thinking about any number of former
heavyweight champions in some sort of decline or another. In the end, they all fall down.
My prediction: One day we'll look at prize-fighting the way
we now look at the days when people could smoke anywhere they wanted and cars
weren't required to have seatbelts.

Tyson's Bite

July 7, 1997

As Exhibit A in the case against pugilism, the People call Jerry Quarry. Mr. Quarry is fifty-two years old and lives with his sister, who does just about everything for him since he's in third-stage dementia and can't even remember the poundings he once took from Muhammad Ali and Joe Frazier, let alone how to make breakfast. They called Jerry Quarry the "Great White Hope" until a CAT-scan performed when he was thirty-seven revealed early tell-tale signs of brain damage. When he returned to the ring for a "comeback" at the age of forty-four, they didn't know quite what to call him, but at least his decision to return to the ring saved the cost of another CAT-scan to verify that his condition was getting worse.

As Exhibit B in the case against pugilism, the People call James "Buster" Douglas.

Mr. Douglas is thirty-four years old and in the midst of a comeback after briefly ruling the heavyweight boxing world in 1990 and then retiring to prove once and for all that you really can have too much of a good thing. With the millions Douglas got for beating Mike Tyson—back when the Tyson myth was alive—and then losing with all the effort of a snail against Evander Holyfield, Douglas retired to Florida where he spent his money on a huge house and virtually every video movie ever made—and then proceeded to watch all of them, eating himself into a diabetic coma in the process. When he emerged from the coma, at 350 pounds, he decided nobody could beat him up any worse than those videos, so he put the gloves back on.

As Exhibit C, the People call Riddick Bowe.

Mr. Bowe, twenty-nine, the only man to ever hold all four boxing organization heavyweight titles at the same time—although even he never actually got them straight—retired recently from boxing to become a school crossing guard; this following a three-day stay at a Marine boot camp in Parris Island, South Carolina, where Bowe quit in disgust because he couldn't get used to the spartan lifestyle and having to take orders all the time.

As Exhibit D, the People call Oliver McCall.

Mr. McCall was fined $250,000 and suspended from boxing for a year after refusing to defend himself against British heavyweight Lennox Lewis in a title bout in Las Vegas this past February. An emotional McCall, who just six weeks before the bout had been fined for tipping over a Christmas tree in a hotel lobby in Tennessee and then spitting on a police car, finally left the ring in tears, looking disoriented and confused. Later, McCall said it was an act, like Ali's rope-a-dope. He wanted Lewis to think he was nuts. Lewis said he had a point, because it worked.

As Exhibit E, the People call Ray Mercer.

Mr. Mercer, once an Olympic gold medalist and a longtime heavyweight contender, was recently charged by police for throwing a terrific hook at someone's jaw . . . his girl friend's.

As Exhibit F, the People call Tommy Morrison.

Mr. Morrison reluctantly retired last year as a heavyweight contender when he discovered he had contracted the H.I.V. virus, only to un-retire for one last fight seven months later in Tokyo. His first chosen opponent, Anthony Cook, had to cancel, however, when authorities in Oklahoma recognized Cook as a man wanted on rape charges. Morrison finally fought a man named Marcus Rhode, who said he liked living life on the edge—but still hoped he wouldn't cut Tommy.

As Exhibit G, the People call Muhammad Ali.

You may have seen Mr. Ali last summer at the Centennial Olympic Games in Atlanta. As two billion people watched, it took him two tries to ignite the Olympic torch, on account of the Parkinson's disease that severely restricts his movements. Ali once had the moves of a poet, now he couldn't fight his way out of a convent, though he could probably still take Jerry Quarry.

Finally, as Exhibit H, the People call "Iron" Mike Tyson.

In Las Vegas last weekend, Mr. Tyson thought he was at the all-you-can-eat Big Kitchen buffet when in fact he was into the third round of his championship fight with Evander "The Real Meal" Holyfield. Amazingly, in a span of less than nine minutes, Tyson was able all by himself to epitomize the erratic behavior of nearly all of the above named exhibits.

Boxing takes big, tough men and turns them into . . . this. What the American Medical Association, the Canadian, British, and Australian medical associations, and the American Neurological Association have all called for—the outright ban of prize-fighting—makes a lot of sense. When you look at the evidence.

Magazine Length Articles

Jack Gardner, 1994
Alma Richards, 1996

Few men in history have done more for the sport of basketball, or shown more loyalty, or seen more games, than Jack Gardner. It was a shame he never got to shake Dr. Naismith's hand, and vice versa.

Jack Gardner

R eprinted from *NCAA Official Final Four Program*
He was twenty-nine years old in 1939, when he went to the railroad station in San Francisco and booked passage to Chicago. Not being clairvoyant, the man selling him the ticket didn't guess he was going to the Final Four. Jack Gardner, not being clairvoyant either, didn't guess he was on his way to the first of fifty-five Final Fours in a row.

Who's to know when traditions begin? Who was to know that when Jack Gardner, basketball coach, newly hired to take over the program at Kansas State, kissed his wife and told her not to wait up, that he was going on a business trip, and he got on that train in San Francisco and got off in Chicago, he was starting a pilgrimmage that would, with time, become a rite of spring not just for him, but for an entire sporting nation?

Don't say no one's seen it all. He has. The Final Four knows Jack. He's never, not once, missed a championship final. Wilt's Kansas team losing in overtime to North Carolina in 1957? Saw it. Bill Russell's back-to-back championships in '55 and '56? Saw them. Bill Walton's near perfect night in 1973? Saw it. Villanova shooting 78.6 percent to beat Georgetown and Patrick Ewing in 1984? Saw it. Adolph Rupp and Kentucky beating Kansas State 68–58 in 1951? Saw it AND coached in it.

He was there the night John Wooden retired with the net around his neck. He was there the night Bill Bradley scored 56 points. He was there the night Georgetown threw the ball and the championship into James Worthy's Carolina hands. He was there the night Louisville sent West Virginia's Jerry West to the line twenty times. He was there the night Al McGuire cried. He was there the night Jim Valvano hugged. He was there the night St. Joseph's and Utah combined to score 247 points in four overtimes. Even if at the end he wished he wasn't. He coached in that game, too, and more than thirty years later he'll still tell you that the definition of a bad night is having your Utes score 120 points, the second highest total in the history of the Final Four, and somehow wind up losing anyway—by SEVEN.

Through a World War, a Korean War, a Vietnam War, and a Persian Gulf War, through the end of a Depression, through eleven presidents of the United States, through twenty-nine heavyweight champions, through the setting up and the tearing down of the Berlin Wall, through the invention of television, through Beatniks, Hippies, and Earth People, through obscurity, through prime time, Jack Gardner's viewing habits in late March have yet to change. Being at the Final Four in person is mandatory. How else do you know for absolutely certain that one season is over and the next one is beginning?

How else, for that matter, do you keep track of the fraternity, of the brethren, of the men who made Sansabelt what it is today? Nike cruises in the summer don't come close to comparing. Swallows go to Capistrano. Coaches go to the Convention/slash/Final Four. Like Muslims to Mecca, they go, renewing friendships, sharing secrets, analyzing, staying up late, working the lobby, looking for jobs, looking for better jobs, looking for games, critiquing, dissecting, reviewing, wishing, genuflecting, watching the best.

Even in 1939, he knew all of the above. Somehow he knew. The way he knew uptempo basketball was the only way he could ever coach and be happy. He just knew.

* * * * *

In '39 he was a rocket on the rise. For four years as the head coach at Modesto Junior College in Modesto, California, he had taken the Pirates to unaccustomed heights. Letters from James Naismith lay on his desk. The good doctor was out of coaching by then and working on the faculty at the University of Kansas. But he hadn't forgotten his creation. Jack Gardner, who played for Sam Barry at USC, Class of '32, and then coached high school ball in the Los Angeles area before moving on to Modesto, had gone to Japan in 1935 to put on basketball clinics in the Land of the Rising Sun. Dr. Naismith wanted to know how it had gone. Could they defend the basket? Could they run the weave? Were they at all enthusiastic?

Coach Gardner wrote back. Answered yes, yes, and yes, and, since he had just accepted the coaching position being vacated at Kansas State, said he would be pleased to report to Dr. Naismith in person that fall. How far could Lawrence be from Manhattan, anyway? Before he could find out, fate interceded. In November of 1939, Dr. Naismith passed away. "The closest I came to seeing him was in his coffin," remembers Gardner, still reverently. The new coach at K-State went to the funeral and, as best he could, paid his respects to the man who had invented basketball.

He's been paying them ever since. As a college coach—first at Kansas State, then at Utah; as a scout and consultant—for the Utah Jazz since their relocation to Salt Lake City in 1979 until now; as an international ambassador with the Partners of the America's—since his retirement as an active college coach in 1971. And as a Final Four fixture.

That first national championship in 1939—won in Patten Gymnasium on the Universty of Northwestern campus in Evanston, Illinois—hooked him on more levels than one. Yes, he was able to see the best as the Tall Firs of Oregon dismantled Ohio State 46–33 in a clinic of a final (to this day Gardner remembers the names of Oregon's starting five . . . "There was Laddie Gale, Bob Hardy, Slim Wintermute, Bob Annet, and Wally Johansen," he said a month ago via telephone from Palm Springs, where he now spends his winters. "I forget things now. Sometimes I can't remember somebody's name who I met yesterday. But I've always kept those names in my mind").

Yes, he was able to fraternize with the college coaches whose club he was about to join.

Yes, he was able to talk coaching until the last bar in the hotel closed down.

But the clincher, the setting of the hook as it were, was the realization that not only did he want to keep coming back and back, he wanted to bring a TEAM with him.

In twenty-eight seasons he did it four times. No coach has ever taken two schools to the big dance twice each. Except him. Kansas State in 1948 and 1951. The University of Utah in 1961 and 1966. Three decades. Four trips. There might have been more if the tournament had always been open to sixty-four teams; if UCLA hadn't been so good out West for so long; if in 1960, his 26-and-3 Utes hadn't decided a regular season victory over John Havlicek, Jerry Lucas, and the rest of the top-ranked Ohio State Buckeyes was good enough and flamed out—against an unheralded Oregon team—in one of those second-round upsets that have since made the tournament so terrific for television ratings.

But four Final Fours was great. Four was enough to be thankful for.

"I remember going to all the tournaments," says Jack. "But it's those four I remember the best."

He never did win it all. In '48 Baylor beat Kansas State in the semifinals. In '51 Kentucky prevailed in the title game over the best team Gardner ever assembled at Kansas State. Ernie Barrett was the Wildcats' ace. He went wild in a 24-point semifinal win over Oklahoma A&M, the 1945 and 1946 national champions, coached by Henry Iba. But Barrett hurt his shoulder while burying the Oklahomans and could barely lift his arm in the final. Kentucky came back from a 29–27 halftime deficit and won by ten, 68–58. (For the past several years, Gardner and Barrett have watched the Final Fours together in person. Gardner gets the seats; Barrett is his guest, and during breaks in the action you can still see them shaking their heads over what went wrong in '51.)

In '61, Cincinnati—without the Big O—beat Gardner and Utah in the semis and then won its first of two straight titles. (It was in the third-place game that St. Joseph's and Utah staged their four-overtime, 127–120 marathon, setting records for points and overtimes that still stand, and delaying the start of the nationally televised final between Cincinnati and Ohio State for a full hour—another record.)

In '66, Texas Western knocked off Gardner and Utah in the semis, 85–78, and the next night, with five black starters, the Miners made color barrier history with their 72–65 win over Kentucky in the final.

It took Gardner a while to get over that setback. To this day he calls himself "an All-American chump" for what he did at the start of that season. But how was he to know? Don Haskins, now a thirty-two-year coaching legend but in '66 only a thirty-five-year-old coach just settling in at Texas Western (now UTEP), called Gardner in Salt Lake City and asked him if he could come to his fall practices and learn how to run the break. He said he had a bunch of raw recruits, most of them city kids with playground experience, and he thought they could maybe go someplace if they learned how to run together. Who better to teach him than the master of the running game?

Gardner had never forgotten how coaches such as Howard Hobson at Oregon and Harold Olsen at Ohio State, and his own college coach, Sam

Barry, had helped him when he was getting started. He said yes. Haskins spent a week in Salt Lake in October of 1965, taking notes the whole time.

"Turned out to be the best scouting report he could have ever gotten," says Gardner.

* * * * *

After more than half-a-century, the memories parade constantly in his mind. They take a number. Especially in Palm Springs in the winter, when the games are going nonstop on cable and the travel agent calls and says Mr. Gardner's reservations are set for New Orleans for the end of March . . . must be going to the Final Four.

He remembers friends, players, games, gossip, discussions—often quite lively—over rules changes, referees, restaurants, hotels. The Muehlbach Hotel in Kansas City, especially, where, except for the war years, he stayed for each of the nine Final Fours held in the Municipal Auditorium. During the war he stayed on the base. But the base was the Olathe Naval Air Station, located just outside Kansas City. How was that for a stroke of luck? It wasn't exactly breaching national security to take a furlough long enough to drive into town and watch Stanford and Jim Pollard beat Dartmouth 53–38 for the 1942 title.

He remembers when Madison Square Garden held court in New York City as the center of basketball's universe—hosting seven tournament finals from 1943 through 1950. He remembers Ned Irish hosting every coach in town at Mamma Leone's Restaurant. He remembers the first TV cameras showing up in 1946. He remembers rivals such as the late Henry Iba who became cherished friends. He remembers the advent of the Dome Era in the '80s.

But before that he remembers the 1979 Final Four. That one was held in Salt Lake City at The House That Jack Built. That was the year the Final Four came to him. During his eighteen years at Utah he had poured his heart and soul—and whatever fund-raising skills he could muster—into seeing to it that the 15,000-seat Special Events Center (now the Jon M. Hunstman Center) would become just maybe the best basketball arena in the world. The arena became a reality in 1970. He spent his last two seasons coaching there. Then he campaigned for Salt Lake City to get the 1979 Final Four, which arrived on the shoulders of Larry Bird and Magic Johnson. Their great moment was Jack Gardner's great moment as well.

For sheer player magnificence, however, he'll pass over Magic and Bird and take Bill Walton in 1973. "The best individual performance I've ever seen," he says of Walton's 44-point, 21-of-22 shooting performance that led UCLA over Memphis State for the national crown, 87–66.

And for runnerup best individual? He'll take Jerry Chambers of Utah in 1966. So what if Chambers played for him and he might be accused of bias? And so what if the Utes took fourth place in that Final Four, losing to Texas Western and Duke? Nobody stopped Chambers. He scored 70 points and pulled down 35 rebounds in the two games—the most prolific Final Four performance in history, if you don't count Bill Bradley's 87-point, 24-rebound rampage in 1965. Chambers was awarded the Most Outstanding Player Trophy, the one and only player from a fourth place team to be so honored.

Others fall into place in the highlight film of the mind. How about Danny Manning in 1988, asks Gardner, who personally saw Kansas overcome the odds and Oklahoma, in that order? How about Bill Russell in 1955 and 1956—even if those were his prints all over the scene as Utah fell both years to Russell's San Francisco Dons in the West Regional?

For sheer artistry, who could forget Cincinnati's Oscar Robertson in 1959 and 1960—or the irony that his school didn't win its two national championships until 1961 and 1962? And speaking of 1960, how about that Lucas-Havlicek Ohio State team?

There were the Tall Firs in 1939. There was Michael Jordan, a freshman no less, hitting the baseline jumper that would prove to be the game-winner for North Carolina in 1982. ("But I have to admit, I didn't know then he'd be the player he has become," says Gardner.) There was Louisville's Darrell Griffith in 1980, a college player without peer, who could dunk the ball even though he couldn't palm it. After that Final Four, which also included seven-footer Joe Barry Carroll of Purdue, Gardner, now in the employ of the Jazz, made his way back to Utah's draft headquarters. He said take Griffith. The Jazz took Griffith, who became the NBA's 1981 Rookie of the Year. That was Gardner's original claim to scouting fame . . . a few years later he came up with an encore when he discovered for the Jazz a player who didn't make the Final Four—John Stockton.

And who could remember fifty-four Final Fours without remembering UCLA and John Wooden? Thirteen Final Fours in fourteen years from 1962 through 1975. Ten championships. Lew Alcindor and Bill Walton. Walt Hazzard and Gail Goodrich. Kenny Washington and David Meyer.

They found themselves on the telephone last January—Gardner and

Wooden. They're good friends. They have a lot to talk about. They could keep a long distance company in business just remembering where they've been, what they've seen, and debating the nuances of the fullcourt press. For years, they would meet at the Final Four and catch up. But since Wooden, slowed by the death of his wife, Nell, and by declining health, stopped being a fixture at the finals, their relationship has been picked up by the telephone. "We were in the same class in college. Different schools of course (Gardner at USC, Wooden at Purdue) but still the same class. We keep in touch," says Gardner.

"Last time we talked I asked him, 'John, of all the games you've seen and played in, what was the most memorable?'

"He said it was the first national championship he won with UCLA, in 1964. He'd gone (to the Final Four) before, in 1962, but they didn't make the finals. In '64 they won it. They beat Duke. UCLA that year was the best pressing team I'd ever seen. John said it was his shortest team and that made it even better. He said because it was the first one it was the most exciting. He said the second most exciting title was the last one, in 1975, when he wasn't supposed to win. They'd already lost three games that season when they got there. For them that was a lot."

"Naming my favorite Final Four coach is an easy one," says Gardner. "John Wooden. He wins that one hands down."

*　*　*　*　*

The old coach's mind swims as he talks. If his brain were a videocam he could sell a million copies. So much to remember. So much to savor.

"I enjoy the associations so much," he says. "I enjoy the coaches. The old ones, the new ones. That's what I'm interested in now. Even more than the games. The dinners, the convention, I still catch some of the sessions."

And by now his seats are the very best. Seniority has its privileges. Ernie Barrett is a lucky man.

"I've never really come close to missing one," he says. "I've never wanted to miss one. The closest I came was two years ago when Marion, my wife, was in the hospital. She had an infection. She was there for three months. But she insisted that I go and I did.

"Oh, it's changed over the years," he says of the tournament. "I've seen it change. I've seen it grow. Unless it's the Super Bowl, I don't know of anything that's grown greater. The traditions that have built up, the media coverage. It's all grown to such a magnitude. My gosh, last year when I went to Minneapolis they took me over to Williams Arena, where we played Kentucky for the championship in 1951, and they made such a big deal over it.

"It wasn't like that in the beginning. It was nothing like it is now. It was just this small fraternity. I remember the first one. There was hardly anybody there."

But he was there. And as much as any of them, that's the one that stands out. The one at Northwestern, in Patten Gymnasium, on March 27, 1939. An estimated 5,500 people sprawled out in the gym, and he was one of them. Ohio State versus Oregon for the national title. The Tall Firs of Oregon won. He can still remember their names . . .

I never got to interview Alma Richards, the only native Utahn to win a gold medal in the first hundred years of the modern Olympic Games, in person. He died before I got the chance. In preparation for a chapter in a book I wrote with Doug Robinson called Trials & Triumphs, *and for this magazine article, I researched his story via the archives at the Brigham Young University library. I think the The Alma Richards Story has everything: the old West, passion, royalty, romance, poetry, spirituality, a gold medal, and Jim Thorpe. All it lacks is popcorn. It ought to be a movie.*

Alma Richards

R eprinted from *Brigham Young Magazine*

It is a story that, once you've heard it, you'll think either James Thurber wrote it or Metro Goldwyn Mayer made it up. It is equal parts *Rocky, The Natural,* and *Chariots of Fire.* It includes maybe the greatest football coach there ever was, maybe the greatest athlete there ever was, and maybe the greatest poem that was ever written. It stretches from the jackrabbit flats of southern Utah to the King's palace in Stockholm, Sweden, to ticker tape parades in New York City and Provo, Utah. And the value of an education figures in there too. If it weren't for school, Alma Richards would never have known he could jump so high . . . and go so far.

Named after, in this order, a prominent Book of Mormon prophet and the fourth President of the Mormon Church, Alma Wilford Richards was born on 20 February 1890, to Mormon pioneer parents sent by Brigham Young to help settle the southern Utah outpost of Parowan. Of ten children, Alma was the ninth. He liked everything about high plains country living if you don't count going to school. He dropped out in the eighth grade, when, at fourteen, he was already about as big as he'd ever get—6-foot-2, over 200 pounds. Few men in those days were bigger. He worked the land and in his father's store (Parowan Mercantile & Cooperative) and, whenever he could, he would saddle up his horse and just ride.

One night when he was eighteen, he found himself far from home when a downpour hit. He made it to Lund, a small railroad town, where he gave in to the rain, seeking more shelter than he could get sleeping under his horse. Because of the storm, the available rooms were at a premium, and he ended up sharing a bunk with a man on his way to California who'd come all the way from Michigan. The man's name was Professor Thomas Trueblood, a Native American and a lecturer with a traveling Indian exposition commissioned by Michigan State University.

The conditions were more conducive to talking than sleeping that night, and so they talked through much of it, the boy and the professor. Alma found himself telling Dr. Trueblood about his hopes and dreams—how he wanted to be as free as the breeze. He longed to travel the world and see it all. The professor told him he could do as he wished, but only if he first got his education. It was learning, he said, that would open the door to such freedom.

By the time the rain stopped and the sun came up, Alma had made up his mind: His days as a dropout were history. He kicked his horse and didn't stop until he got to Beaver, Utah, where he enrolled in the Murdock Academy, a private school, grades nine through twelve. He moved in with his sister and her husband, who had a home near the school. When you have nine brothers and sisters and almost all of them are older, it can come in handy.

On his way to becoming "an educated man," one of the Murdock teachers asked Alma, the biggest kid in the school, if he'd like to join the track team. Alma didn't know how to answer. He knew nothing about athletics. All he'd ever raced were jackrabbits.

The teacher suggested he at least give it a try.

There have been worse suggestions.

The shot put, the discus, the sprints, the distance runs, the pole vault. You name it, he entered it. In the end, he didn't just join the track team. He *was* the track team. Three months later, when the state finals were held in Salt Lake City, Alma Richards, all by himself, scored enough points to win the Utah state team championship for his school. Improbably, little Murdock Academy unseated Salt Lake High, the perennial powerhouse, 32 points to 22, and took the first-place trophy back home to Beaver.

By itself, not a bad story to tell the grandkids. But, heck, that was just the warmup.

The next year, Alma transferred to the Brigham Young High School in Provo. At the turn of the century, the students of B.Y. High and Brigham

Young University co-mingled on the same campus. So it was that, once again, as was his wont, Alma caught the eye of a coach and an educator. This time it was a man named Eugene L. Roberts, whom everyone called "Timpanogos." Roberts coached the track team at Brigham Young. One day, after observing Alma's jumping ability in a pickup game of basketball, Timpanogos Roberts pulled young Richards aside.

"See that bar," he said.

"Jump over it."

Still wearing his basketball uniform, Alma watched a few others go over the bar and then, with no further warmup, ran toward the high jump pit and cleanly cleared the bar.

Timpanogos Roberts went pale.

The bar was set at 5'-11".

The school record was 6'-2".

The world record was 6'-7".

The coach, not realizing the twenty-one-year-old in front of him was still in high school, stammered out a question Alma had heard before.

"Like to join the track team?"

Roberts had coached thousands of athletes and never seen anyone so natural. With a little coaching, he told Alma, he could have him jumping with the best in the world; he could get him ready for the Olympic Games.

Said Alma, "The what?"

And so life took another dramatic turn for Alma Richards, as he and Roberts went to work. Through the fall and winter they studied form and technique. Daily they'd meet and train. The Olympics, Roberts explained, were to be held late the next summer in Stockholm, Sweden. Flush from the resounding success of the previous Olympic Games, held in London in 1908, the world was taking considerable interest in the pending Stockholm Games. The United States now had a full-fledged official Olympic committee, and the dates and times for any number of trials that would be held to select the official U.S. team had been posted at schools and athletic clubs around the country. For his protégé, Roberts targeted the high jump trials scheduled in Chicago in May.

But if the athletic community was enthused about the new Olympic movement—the first Olympic Games of the "modern" era had been held just sixteen years earlier, in 1896 in Athens—the world at large wasn't yet so enamored of either its success or commercial value. That's what Roberts found as he made the rounds of the businesses and philanthropists in Provo, trying to raise money so he and Alma could book passage to the meet in Chicago. Benefactors were few and far between. In six months all the coach could raise, thanks mostly to a $150 donation from the BYU administration, was enough for *one* passage. One of them wouldn't be able to go.

At the Provo station in early May of 1912, Roberts put Alma on the train. He gave him some last second advice, wished him luck, and, for good measure, gave him a rolled-up copy of Rudyard Kipling's poem *If,* the coach's personal favorite.

"Read it," he told him. "It will bring you inspiration."

Little was Alma able to realize at that time how literally much of that poem would apply to him:

Especially the part about *"If you can make a heap of all your winnings, and risk it on one turn of pitch and toss"* . . .

. . . And the part about *"If you can walk with kings nor lose the common touch"* . . .

. . . And the part about *"If you can fill each unforgiving minute with sixty seconds worth of distance run . . ."*

He got to Chicago late in the afternoon the day before the meet. Taking Roberts's advice, he went straight to the track at Northwestern University and took a few practice jumps. He easily cleared the bar at six feet, finishing with a jump of 6'-2". Fortunately, as he did so, a man was watching from the far end of the field. That man was Amos Alonzo Stagg, the football coach at the University of Chicago and one of the most powerful men in sports in the country. Coach Stagg was a member of the Olympic selection committee.

At the next day's competition, Alma was the most anonymous contestant there. No one knew who he was or where he came from. Since he wasn't a college student yet, he had never actually competed anywhere but in Utah and so he had no real credentials. Undaunted by his lack of notoriety, however, he jumped as well as he ever had and, with a jump of 6'-3", wound up winning the high jump competition.

But politics and the Olympics have always been fast friends, and it was no different in 1911 than now. When the results of the Chicago meet were sent to the selection committee in New York, Alma Richards was not assigned to the U.S. team because no one had heard of him. He was dismissed as a "one-meet wonder," a "fluke." Well-known (and well-connected) jumpers from other "trials" held in California (at Stanford) and on the East Coast (at

Harvard) were named to the United States' high-jump team. The high school kid from Utah was out of luck.

Or so it seemed. Until Amos Alonzo Stagg cleared his throat.

Apparently, Stagg arrived late in New York for the official "selections," because he didn't contribute his input until the high jump team had already been selected. When he scanned the list and noticed that "Richards" was not on it, he asked why. His fellow selectors told him. To which Stagg said, "I saw this kid jump with my own eyes. I saw him jump six feet in his sweats!"

A spirited debate ensued.

Stagg won.

They put A. Richards on the "supplemental" Olympic team. He would be sailing to Stockholm after all.

Instead of going west to Provo, Alma went east to New York, where he boarded the USS *Finland,* bound for Sweden with the rest of the U.S. team.

He was not, however, the toast of the boat.

Rustling jackrabbits in Parowan was one thing; sailing on an ocean-liner with the cream of America's athletes was another. Rube, bumpkin, hayseed, hick. Name your turn-of-the-century rural insult, that's what they called Alma. The name didn't help either, and neither did the case of red-eye he developed as they crossed the ocean. He found a floppy felt hat, which he constantly wore to keep the sun out.

When the ship finally docked in Stockholm, Alma was not at all unhappy to get off.

He was one of a crowd of American high-jumpers when the competition began a couple of days later in Stockholm's sparkling new jewel of an Olympic stadium. These were the good old days of stockpiling the field, and the U.S. entered eleven athletes in a total field of fifty-seven high jumpers, representing twenty countries. Among the Americans was George Horine, a Stanford University student and current world record-holder at 6'-7", and Jim Thorpe, a Sac and Fox Indian from Oklahoma and star of the U.S. team who was also, beyond the high jump, entered in the Olympic pentathlon and decathlon competitions.

Young Alma Richards, still wearing that floppy felt hat, was just along for the ride.

And he looked it as the competition began. At the opening height he missed twice before a successful third, and final, try. At the next two heights, same thing.

But, at that, he was still alive while others weren't so fortunate. By the time the bar got to 6'-1", the only Americans remaining were Horine, Thorpe, Egon Erickson, and Richards.

They were joined by one German, Hans Liesche, who was striking fear into them all. At every height, the lanky German had cleared the bar with ease on his opening try. No American could say the same.

When the bar was moved to 6'-2", Liesche did it again.

Only two Americans managed to finally clear the height on their third and final tries.

Horine . . .

. . . and Richards.

Now it was a battle among three men for the three medals as the bar was set a quarter inch above 6'-3". Again, Liesche cleared on his first jump. Again, Horine and Richards missed on theirs.

On their second tries, the Americans missed again.

Horine, the world champion and premeet favorite, tried one more time—and missed.

If Richards missed, the gold medal was Liesche's.

He did not.

Now there were just the two of them.

By this time, an amazing transformation had taken place among Richards's teammates. They had become mesmerized by the country bumpkin who had been the butt of all their shipboard jokes, but who was now battling the German head-to-head for the gold medal. They all assembled to the side of the high jump pit to root for him. It was Horine and Jim Thorpe who led the cheering. Now they were not making fun of the guy in the floppy hat. They were his most ardent supporters.

The bar was raised to an even 6'-4".

Richards was to jump first.

But before he did, he walked to a spot on the infield grass. There, in full view of the soldout stadium crowd of 24,000, he took off his hat and kneeled on the ground. He said a prayer.

As he recounted in his memoirs, this is what he said:

"God, give me strength. And if it's right that I should win, give me the strength to do my best to set a good example all the days of my life."

As soon as he said "Amen," he put his "lucky" hat back on, walked to the end of the runway and, without hesitation, raced for the bar.

He cleared it by what Thorpe and Horine would later agree was "a good two inches."

After that, Leische never had a chance.

For the first time all day, he missed on his opening attempt. He also missed on his second try. And then, as he composed himself for his third and final attempt, he was distracted by the conclusion of the 800-meter run. Looking over at the finish line, he watched as his countryman, Hans Braun, the prerace favorite, was passed at the tape by three Americans, led by Tad Meredith, an unknown teenager.

Leische's third try was his worst.

The medals ceremony was held shortly thereafer, where they gave Horine the bronze medal and Liesche the silver. The King of Sweden himself, Gustav V, draped the gold medal around Richards's neck, after which he invited Alma to his palace. He told him his son, the prince, was an aspiring high jumper and that he'd appreciate it if Alma could give the lad some pointers.

As Alma spent his time at the palace in the ensuing days, Jim Thorpe managed to avenge being shut out of the high jump medals by winning both the pentathlon and decathlon, whereupon King Gustav made his famous "You, sir, are the finest athlete in the world" declaration. When they finally doused the flame and the USS *Constitution* set return sail for the States, Richards and Thorpe could compare king stories.

Upon landing in New York, the U.S. team, which won a resounding sixty-one medals in Stockholm, including twenty-three gold, was feted in a ticker tape parade down New York's Fifth Avenue. For Richards, that was a forerunner to the parade he'd get when he finally pulled into Provo about a week later, on 22 August 1912. As he emerged from the train, more than a thousand people rushed to congratulate him. After many speeches and a heart-felt salute by Alma to Timpanogos Roberts, in which he dedicated his gold medal to his coach, there was a parade from the station to the B.Y. campus, where his final year awaited Alma . . . of high school.

He graduated from the Brigham Young prep school with honors and accepted a power company scholarship to attend Cornell University in New York. The Olympics did wonders for his self-confidence, and where he was once just a marginal student, his aptitude and attitude now were boundless. He thrived at Cornell, in the classroom and on the track. He was the national AAU high jump champion in 1913 and later, as he expanded his repertoire, he became a decathlete as well. At the national AAU championships of 1915, held in conjunction with the World's Fair in San Francisco, he became the national decathlon champion, finishing some 500 points ahead of a man by the name of Avery Brundage, who would later head the International Olympic Committee. He never did compete against Jim Thorpe in the decathlon, because Thorpe had become a professional football player after the Stockholm Olympics and was ineligible for amateur track competitions. But at the San Francisco meet, Richards's 10-event points total in his first major decathlon was only slightly less than what Thorpe had scored in Stockholm.

He was far and away the United States' best decathlete entering the 1916 Olympic Games, not to mention its best high jumper. That he would win two gold medals was a distinct possibility. But those Games were never held, cancelled in favor of World War I. It was one of the ironies of Alma Richards's life that he got to the Olympic Games when he hardly knew what they were, and didn't get there when he had them squarely in his sights. After Stockholm, he would never return to an Olympic arena, and neither would Hans Liesche. On the date when they should have had their "rematch" in the 1916 Olympic Games, which had been scheduled for Berlin, they instead were each wearing the uniform of the army of their respective countries, on opposite sides of the fight.

Alma did manage to enter the American Expeditionary Force Track and Field Championships in Paris while he was a soldier, where, at the age of twenty-nine, he won the high jump and standing broad jump, finished second in the triple jump, and took third in the broad jump. His personal total of fourteen points was four points higher than anyone in the meet, and when he came to the winner's podium for his fourth medal, General George Pershing himself said, "Whose medal are you after this time?" When Lieutenant Richards said, "Mine, Sir," the General saluted. "Good to see old-timers still making good," he said.

After graduating with honors from Cornell, Alma attended graduate school at Stanford before enrolling in law school at the University of Southern California. He got his law degree and, as high jumpers do, he passed the bar. But he chose not to practice law. Instead he went into teaching. He got a job as a science teacher in Los Angeles at Venice High School, where he remained for thirty-two years until he retired. To those who knew him, his choice of vocation came as no surprise. If it hadn't been for teachers, he always said, he'd never have found his way.

He was named Utah's track and field athlete of the century and was inducted into the national Helms Foundation Hall of Fame. After his death in 1963 he again returned, according to his wishes, home to Parowan, where he was buried.

Except for Kresimir Cosic, who played on Yugoslavia's gold-medal winning basketball team in 1980, Alma Wilford Richards remains the only student from Brigham Young to win a gold medal in the Olympic Games—and even if it was Brigham Young *High School,* nobody's quibbling. He got a late start, was all, but he made up ground fast.

Side Trips

Biking to L.A., 1977
Di and Charles, 1981
Nanci Griffith, 1990

Bicycle touring has become much more popular since my twin brother and I embarked on our odyssey to the ocean, but you still don't see many bike trips between Utah and Southern California. Maybe it has something to do with the heat, the lack of towns, the monotonous landscape, the constant headwinds, and the fact that Nevada is involved.

Biking to L.A.

POP'S OASIS, Nevada—Seated here in front of a blackjack table at five in the morning in a last-chance casino on the Nevada-California border, the old guy looked, by anybody's standards, a little bit strange.

But who was I to be saying anyone else might be playing a couple of cards short of a full deck?

At the time, my brother, Dee, and I were approximately equidistant between Utah and the Pacific Ocean, at the midpoint in a six hundred-mile bicycle tour—an expedition I will deny undertaking in certain psychiatric circles—and we were somewhat anxious about the Baker Grade we would be negotiating as soon as we threw a couple of six packs of soda pop in our saddlebags.

"It's forty miles and pretty near straight up," said the old gambler. "I've had a '66 Valiant for years, and she's never made it all the way to the top."

Anyway, it had sounded like a good idea—back during the dead of winter when my twin brother, who I figured to be somewhere on the black side of the sanity ledger, suggested, "buying ourselves a couple of 10-speeds and cycling to L.A."

We bought two Azuki Imperials, equipped them with touring accessories (except for maybe a couple of riders), and warmed up by pedaling along Salt Lake's foothills. Once we made a loop from Dee's place on Yale Ave., around the Capitol, around the U., past Hogle Zoo, and back home—a whopping fifteen-miler.

Getting to the ocean would be candy.

We picked an April morning to start, driving by car past the congestion of the Wasatch Front, and setting off somewhere south of Nephi.

Once underway, we had eighty-five miles between ourselves and Beaver—our first night's destination.

That first day, except for a miscalculation that resulted in having no water for forty-five miles, was not bad. We got into Beaver in time for a couple of T-bone steaks, an extra piece of pie, and a soft bed at the TraveLodge.

After that it was all uphill.

Now I'm not scientifically prepared to argue why the law of gravity does not apply to a biker traveling from Utah to sea level, or why the wind blows due south every day across the desert from noon on, but if some graduate student wants to research an interesting phenomenon, he could bike it himself.

Simply said, the uphills exceeded the downhills, and the afternoons would have been great for sailing.

Still, we forged on, encouraged in the face of that second morning's fifty-five mile jaunt from Beaver to Cedar City by a car radio playing the theme from *Rocky*, creating a moment that could be called the emotional high of the trip.

Cedar City to St. George, despite a 2,000 foot drop in elevation, was somehow hilly—and windy. Arriving in St. George, we figured we had logged 112 miles from Beaver, and while attacking a hamburger steak, decided that was plenty for one day.

At that point we pulled off perhaps the sanest move of the trip. A highway patrolman had warned us not to ride the freeway between St. George and Mesquite, Nevada—a thirty-mile stretch of narrow road whose only redeeming biking features would have been spectacular scenery, a totally downhill grade, and the constant thrill of maybe hooking onto an 18-wheeler's front bumper if he didn't see you while rounding a curve.

We hitched a ride.

In exchange for a promise of full coverage of Dixie College football and basketball for the next twenty-seven years, Roland Lee, a good friend and the public relations director at the college, loaded us into his station wagon and ferried us to Mesquite.

Mesquite to Las Vegas was a pleasant eighty-mile stretch. We spent mid-day in Vegas scarfing down 49-cent shrimp cocktails and shopping in a drug-store for suntan lotion to combat the 95-degree sun.

An afternoon nap on the Hacienda Hotel lawn, however, nearly proved our undoing. We were directly under the path of Salt Lake-bound airliners, and next to a sign advertising Waylon Jennings and Jessi Colter that night at the Aladdin. Being country music fans and still three hundred miles from the ocean, the temptations to abort were great.

But Pop's Oasis was only twenty-eight miles away.

We arrived at dusk. We left at dawn.

And that brings us back to the Baker Grade, which proved as long and steep as advertised, but not bad during an early Mohave Desert morning when the wind was still down. Twenty miles of downgrade into Baker, California, nearly made up for the uphill miles.

After Baker came fifty miles to Barstow, and a better appreciation of why Henry Fonda stopped there in *The Grapes of Wrath*. San Bernardino County is bigger than three of the Eastern states, and by the time you hit Barstow, you're sure there will just be more of the same.

From Barstow we traveled through Victorville, past a couple of hungry-looking Doberman pinschers, and over Cajon Pass into San Bernardino—the downgrade on the other side of the pass easily winning best-stretch-of-the-trip award, and fastest, too, except for the half-mile we were neck and neck with the aforementioned Dobermans.

We stayed with friends in Anaheim, and after a night at Anaheim Stadium, putting away an American League record number of hot dogs, found the ocean the next day at Huntington Beach. Getting to the Pacific hadn't been candy.

We flew home, the bikes going free. As the Western Airlines agent put it, "If you rode them down, we'll fly them home. I'm just happy you guys came to your senses."

Well, I thought we had. But it's my brother I'm starting to worry about. Somehow he found my unlisted phone number the other day and called. "If I can get ahold of a 24-foot sailboat," he asked, "what would you think of L.A. to Honolulu?"

By a coincidence, I happened to spend a week in London just prior to the wedding of Prince Charles and Lady Diana Spencer, so I filed this report for our Lifestyle section. The excitement over a then-unknown Diana was already overwhelming. It was the first and only time I got to "advance" a royal wedding.

Di and Charles

LONDON—It was 10:30 P.M.—or "half-ten" in the vernacular of the Queen—when the pretty girl in her late teens boarded the underground train at the Charing Cross tube stop.

She was dressed in pure fashion of the day—black cotton pants, tapered at the ankles; a white satin blouse frilled at the top and buttoned to the neck; and atop it all she wore a haircut with a vague part on the lefthand side and flowing bangs across the forehead, sweeping back to a stylish trim at the bottom of the neck, not unlike the Beatles hairdo of the mid '60s.

In the dim light of the subway, she could have passed for Lady Diana Spencer, easy.

There is nothing so fashionable in all of England these days as to have some connection, even if it's merely the same hair style, with Lady Diana Spencer, the fiancée of His Royal Highness the Prince of Wales, better known outside the Commonwealth as Prince Charles. Their upcoming marriage, set for July 29 in London's St. Paul's Cathedral, has captivated the country, and the world, since the announcement of their engagement nearly six months ago.

It isn't every day that a future king selects his queen and not even every century when they both happen to happily be English. This hasn't occurred in England, in fact, for more than three hundred years. The blue-and-red, Union Jack-waving traditionalists could not be giddier. Very British this wedding. Very British, indeed.

There are congratulatory banners all over London: in shop windows, on billboards, on coasters atop bar tables in public houses, even in the grafitti on walls bordering vacant lots. The first thing a traveler sees upon alighting at Heathrow Airport is a welcome sign proclaiming this the year of the Royal Wedding.

The ultimate indication that this has caught the public's imagination is that it has been afforded full treatment in Great Britain's noblest and subtlest tradition: cynicism. The country that gave the world Benny Hill and Monty Python is having a field day with all the fuss over a wedding between monarchs who, quite frankly, still don't have the authority to give parking tickets on the mall in front of their rent-free palace.

Tongue-in-cheek souvenirs abound alongside official souvenirs. *Mad Magazine*-type guides to the Royal Wedding; bricks to throw at the telly when the coverage gets too boring, too insufferable, or both; an advertised get-away excursion to France.

For the most part, however, Great Britain is gushing over the happy event, especially since Prince Charles, who is thirty-two (nearly thirty-three), has finally found a suitable mate, and even more especially since the mate he has chosen has been declared more or less perfect, even if she does bite her fingernails and even if she is an inch taller than the Prince.

I spent eight days in London a week ago and to say the approaching Royal Wedding is a big deal would be bordering on serious understatement. There is simply no avoiding the subject.

It is impossible to spend a week in London and not know that Charles and Diana have been dating since August of 1980, that they both can trace their royalty to Henry VII, that consent was given by Queen Elizabeth and the Privy Council on March 27—a big deal, this, since Lady Diana would have had a miserable time of it with her in-laws without such consent—and that their wedding will be watched by 2,700 specially invited guests at St. Paul's and a television audience estimated at 500 million around the world. In America, there will be live coverage beginning at 5:00 A.M. on the East Coast and 3:00 A.M. here in Utah.

It is also fairly common knowledge that up until six months ago, Lady Diana—a name that has been shortened to "Lady Di" by uncouth commoners who don't know any better, says Diana's mother—was a kindergarten teacher, that she is twenty years old, that her older sister Sarah, twenty-six, used to date Prince Charles, and that her father is Earl Spencer with royal ties of his own.

It is Lady Di who has caught the media spotlight in Britain. Charles has been scrutinized closely over the years, especially since 1969, when he was crowned Prince of Wales, thereby ensuring that when his mother dies, he will be King of England. He is an old story.

Not the Lady Diana.

Her photograph is everywhere. On Thursday last week, when rioting and looting in Manchester was in high gear, there was Lady Di on the front page of *The Sun,* one of England's major morning tabloids, sharing headlines with "Rioters Besiege Police." The bride-to-be was pictured with her new solid gold watch, a birthday gift from the Prince. She wore it to a polo match in which Charles was playing. This earth-shattering news was declared a "Red-hot *Sun* Exclusive."

She is described variously as "demure," "lovely," "intriguing," "sophisticated," "madcap," "appealing," "aristocratic," "down-to-earth," "polite," "warm," "captivating," "tranquil," and—hold on to those bricks—"a shimmering flower" and "a rose without a thorn."

No less than five million visitors, according to the English Tourist Board, are expected to gather in London for the wedding, and it is projected they will spend in the neighborhood of 200 million pounds (about $400 million). You don't have to go far in London to find mementos that will ensure you shall always remember the historic day.

There are the usual souvenir trinkets—key chains, pennants, travel bags, badges, hair brushes, dog leads, wallets, that kind of thing—not to mention official souvenir programs and full-color posters. You can even order food and drink with a Royal Wedding twist. At the Sheraton Park Tower in London where I stayed, you could order the Royal Romance cocktail for one pound, five pence.

Then there's the big stuff. These are called royal commemorative pieces, and in Britain it is customary to collect such pieces whenever the opportunity arises. The country is filled with mugs and trays and clocks and goblets commemorating the coronation of kings and queens and royal marriages. It's a smart investment, too, since these collector's items theoretically increase in value, although most Britons would never think of parting with one.

You can buy a long case clock to remember the occasion for a mere $2,000, or commemorative pure silver goblets for $600 a pair, or maybe a couple of silver thimbles at $11 a pair. Bear in mind that production will be limited to only 100 long case clocks, 1,500 silver goblets, and 5,000 thimbles.

Anybody knows you need a once-in-a-lifetime gift for a once-in-a-lifetime occasion. That's how Britain is treating this latest Royal Wedding—even if the pretty teenager mentioned at the start of this story wasn't so condescending.

"Oh, this," she said of her royal-looking Lady-Di haircut. "I've had this style for ages."

She smiled, "Actually, I think it was *she* who copied me."

My favorite singer of all time is Nanci Griffith, a one-time kindergarten teacher from
Austin, Texas, who writes most of her own songs and who also
once wrote a novel. Prior to her performance scheduled for Salt Lake, I bribed the music
critics in the Today *Section to let me write the advance. Thus it*
was that I got to speak to my all-time favorite singer on the phone, and write about
the arts. I hope she read it.

Nanci
Griffith

S he has been written up in *Rolling Stone,* has been called the "Queen of
Folkabilly," is so popular in Ireland she could work both sides of the
rebellion, has done eight albums, and is working on her ninth, so you couldn't
say she isn't successful.

Still, when Nanci Griffith makes her third appearance in Salt Lake City
this Sunday at 7:30 P.M., it will be in the 1,917-seat Kingsbury Hall, an indication that her following leans more toward cult than mainstream. Which is
how it is when you carve your very own musical niche and don't budge from
it, even if it doesn't happen to land on any prominent radio frequencies.

If you were to draw a line between Woody Guthrie and Loretta Lynn,
somewhere close to the middle you would run into Nanci Griffith. She is a
blend of Greenwich Village, 16th Avenue and Congress Avenue in her native
Austin, Texas, and, as loyalties go, is as true to her music as your average Texan
is true to high school football.

She writes the majority of her material. Mostly her songs are about where
she and her relatives are from and about how people feel about life—and if
her music must be changed in order to make Bob Kingsley's top 40 countdown, she's content to let someone else—Kathy Mattea, for instance—convert it to the commercial level. That is precisely what happened with Mattea's
hits "Going, Gone" and "Love at the Five & Dime."

Now, as her Salt Lake appearance approaches, it has been announced that a Nanci Griffith song has been recorded as a single by Emmy Lou Harris and Willie Nelson. They've teamed on a duet called "Gulf Coast Highway," a house-by-the-road ballad about blackbirds and bluebonnets and life's changes that Griffith originally recorded two years ago with Mac McAnally on her *Little Love Affairs* album.

As she did with the Kathy Mattea remakes, Griffith is suffering no angst over this one. "I'm delighted to have them do it," she says. "I've always considered myself a songwriter first. That is a song close to my heart. They did it exactly like Mac McAnally and I did it on the album . . . and you could tell in Willie's voice he knew what a bluebonnet was."

You'd expect no less from another Texan, from Austin.

"When I was a little girl, that's how you got from Austin to New Orleans, where my cousins live," she says of the song and the two-lane Gulf Coast Highway (Highway 90) that winds through the bayous of southwestern Louisiana. "Then they built the interstate, so now most people go that way, by Route 66. Nobody goes by Highway 90, but it's still prettier."

As is often the case away from the mainstream.

Personal

Favorites

The Battle of Lake Victoria, 1984

East Meets West, 1988

Pioneer Park, 1992

The Los Angeles Games were my first Olympic experience and made quite an impact on me. Walking to my car from the Coliseum after the track meet one night, my column for that day already filed, I stopped in next door at the Sports Center to watch the fights just because I wanted to. Then I ran into this column, so I wrote it.

The Battle of Lake Victoria

LOS ANGELES—It is late at night in the Olympic Sports Arena when the two black fighters enter the ring and begin to box. Ryan O'Neal and Farrah Fawcett, seated across the way, smile for a TV camera, oblivious of what is going on in the ring. The journalist next to me in the nearly deserted press box is from Uganda, and his right leg is doing a couple hundred gyrations per minute, easy. "I feel much tenseness," he looks over and says.

They are a Ugandan and a Tanzanian up there on the canvas, Peter Okumu and Neva Mkadala by name, and while what's at stake obviously doesn't mean much here, where they're from it does. Roughly along the order of Yankees-Dodgers, Pepsi-Coke, Republicans-Democrats. Their countries are neighbors, separated by an invisible boundary that lies below the waters of Lake Victoria. And since the recent demise of the Ugandan madman, Idi Amin—an ouster perpetrated by Tanzanian forces—they're close once again.

But not so close they don't have strong feelings about who should do what to whom within the confines of the ring.

The Ugandan journalist isn't writing anything down; he just continues to jiggle his leg like a realtor anticipating a closing. It's a close bout, and he knows history is on the Tanzanian's side. The last time Mkadala met Okumu, he beat him in the 147-pound class of the Eastern Central African Championships.

That notwithstanding, these judges give it to the Ugandan, by a split decision, 3–2, and Okumu raises his hand in weary triumph. The crowd that wasn't paying attention now boos, strictly out of reflex.

The writer next to me jumps with happiness. "That's very good," he says and bounds off to interview his countryman for an account that will undoubtedly be read with expanded happiness in Entebbe the next morning over tea.

Nowhere are the Olympic Games more international than in the boxing ring. From the corners of the earth they come, and not necessarily from the corners dripping with riches. Mostly these 359 fighters chasing twelve gold medals have the eye of the tiger about them. From the barrios and ghettos and developing countries they've arrived, here to the land of Joe Louis and Sugar Ray and Ali, with thoughts in their heads of setting the world on its ear and then buying a sports car and a swimming pool.

One fighter, from a small country in South America younger than he is, cried in anguish after losing his opening bout. "I was told if I win the gold medal," he said through his tears, "it would mean a house with a swimming pool."

Mostly they're darkly colored, these fighters, which is not to say white people can't box, but that they don't. Not generally at any rate. Ryan O'Neal tells the TV announcer he did box once, and won the majority of his bouts. But he gave it up for the sweeter science of acting.

Back in the ring, a lumbering Italian named Bruno is peppering a fighter named Boco who is the pride of Benin but who is now obviously out of his league. With nowhere to hide, Boco takes his only option, clinching repeatedly and for as long as possible with the Italian, who mocks the tactic and looks more like Sylvester Stallone with every passing confident second.

The crowd likes Bruno, cheering his first-round TKO lustily, getting anxious now to see who they stayed around this late at night to watch, Mark Breland, pride of the 147-pounders, who is to meet a Puerto Rican five inches shorter and one hundred wins poorer.

Breland is black and from Brooklyn and, at twenty-one, is both a movie star and a champion boxer, the holder of 105 career wins. He already has his pool. He enters the arena like a mafia boss and the press box fills. A journalist from the *New York Times* takes the spot where the Ugandan once was. The *Times* writer, like Breland, is a pro. He takes up his task with his knee lying dead still and his pen fast at work, detailing the carnage. The bout is stopped early in the third round, the Puerto Rican's machismo finally spent since he has nothing even remotely resembling a jab. The journalist from New York leaves. He says nothing.

Before this thing is over, perhaps they'll meet, the journalists from New York and Entebbe and the 147-pounders from America and Uganda. I hope so. I don't think the kid from Uganda can take Breland, but a pool's at stake at the very least, and I'd like to see him have his shot.

The undercurrent when Ray Mercer stepped into the ring to face Hyun-man Baik was as intense as any I ever felt at a mere sporting event. The Korean crowd pulled hard for their countryman, but I'll never forget how that one-two combination of Mercer's deflated everything in the arena, Baik's face included. It's true, boxing is a barbaric endeavor, but, still, infinitely better than a war. I loved writing this column.

East Meets West

SEOUL—Given the somewhat strained feelings that have arisen during the run of the Seoul Olympic Games between the host country and the USA, it came as no surprise that every seat in the Chamshil Students Gymnasium was full at 10:00 A.M. Saturday morning.

Tickets to the first day of the boxing finals were an especially hot item, in no small measure due to the last gold-medal bout on the morning's six-fight card between, you guessed it, a Korean heavyweight, Hyun-man Baik of Seoul, and an American heavyweight, Ray Mercer of Jacksonville, Florida.

East was East and West was West and they were meeting in the ring.

The promoters of the world had to be tearing their hair out. They knew this fight shouldn't be held until they had six months of lead time to milk the media and build the tension, not to mention the gate. And it should be staged in Madison Square Garden or Caesar's Palace or Atlantic City or maybe Nairobi.

But if the Olympics are going professional, they're not going *that* professional.

Olympic rules stood: three, three-minute rounds, and no betting line in Vegas.

The purse: whatever a gold medal and a silver medal cost these days.

For whatever reasons, the South Koreans and Americans have had a rather tumultuous Olympics together. Early in the Games, the Koreans reacted negatively to NBC's TV coverage of a temper tantrum staged by a losing Korean—a boxer, no less—and that seemed to kick it off.

The NBC coverage—no more extensive or one-sided than, say, typical coverage of Bobby Knight throwing a chair—was seen around Korea, courtesy of the Armed Forces Network, and officials of the Seoul Olympic Organizing Committee were particularly distraught, sensing that the world's largest garden party they had been throwing had been tainted.

It escalated from there, with editorials and newscasts questioning the Americans' ability to behave properly. Film clips were shown of the U.S. team's rowdy behavior at the opening ceremonies. The term "Ugly American" was tossed around a lot.

Not that there should be any impression that things got even close to out-of-hand, or that the Americanization of South Korea perceptibly lessened. Korean spectators at the Olympic Stadium were still wearing sun-visors that said "Pizza Hut." Cute little Korean kids were still smiling and saying, "Hello." They continued to accept dollars, no problem, at the Reebok stores in It'aewon; and no one was rushing up to the DMZ to tell the 45,000 American troops stationed there that they could go on home now.

But, still, there was enough bad blood to turn the Chamshil Gymnasium, when it was time for Baik and Mercer to fight, into, by Korean standards, a raucous atmosphere.

"In the red corner, from the United States of America . . ." said the announcer, and there were boos all around.

Three large Americans, wearing caps that said "Nothing Runs Like a Deere," stood up amidst a sea of black hair and gave the thumbs-down sign.

This was better than any of the Rocky movies except maybe the first one. "In the blue corner, from the Republic of Korea . . ."

The place went berserk. Baik, who weighs 201 pounds and is therefore larger than 99.9 percent of his countrymen, did a kind of Hulk Hogan routine as his name was announced.

Then the American fans—who were in the minority but still well-represented—seized a break in the din and started chanting, "U.S.A.!" "U.S.A.!"

They were soon drowned out, first by chants of "Hyun-man Baik!" "Hyun-man Baik!" and then by a simpler chant of "Zwissha," "Zwissha," which, according to a Korean usher wearing an "I Speak English" badge, translated into American, means "Wow!" "Wow!"

Amid this commotion, the bout began. Both fighters rushed at each other, and the brawl was on. Few punches landed, emotion overruling the basics of pugilism. And it appeared that Baik, a southpaw, was confusing Mercer, a straightforward puncher noted more for winning fights with knockouts, not points.

The tension heightened as the round wore on and then, out of nowhere, came this long right arm, attached to Mercer, that hit Baik flush on the jaw.

A left soon followed.

Baik hit the canvas of his home arena, and when the referee asked him if he knew what country he was in, Baik didn't have an answer.

So the fight was stopped. Mercer went into a gold-medal high-five jive routine, the American fans waved their flags, the three guys in the "Nothing Runs Like a Deere" hats gave the thumbs-up sign, and the Korean fans quietly sat down.

The fight was over, that much was obvious. And the ending had been quite civilized. Everyone knew when to quit.

Prior to the remodeling that transformed Derks Field into Franklin Quest Field, there
was a brief movement, led by the mayor's office, to turn Pioneer Park,
a homeless harbor on the west side of Salt Lake City, into Pioneer Ballpark. It was that
movement that prompted this excursion to the park, and a visit with the regulars.

Pioneer Park

Basking under the summer sun yesterday at midday, Pioneer Park, by all outward appearances, seemed oblivious to the controversy surrounding its future. There were no picket lines for one side or the other; no public debates; no triple-A baseball teams lobbying for the dream of a ballpark Salt Lake mayor Deedee Corradini wants to build there—and no anti-ballpark protesters either.

There wasn't much going on at all. There were a few people brown-bagging lunch, as it were; a few others were napping; three guys without shirts were playing on the basketball court, shooting at a bent rim with a torn net. No one was using either of the tennis courts, which have no nets.

Tourism was not running rampant even though, as notable historic sites go, Pioneer Park could be considered a tourist's kind of place. There is a stone monument in the center of the park stating that the ten-acre square is officially "Pioneer Square" and marks the original spot of the "Old Fort" built by the Mormon Pioneers soon after they arrived in the Salt Lake Valley in 1847. "Soon after" could be considered an understatement since, as the plaque goes on to say, Brigham Young laid the foundation for the fort on August 10, 1847, only seventeen days after the pioneers arrived in the valley.

The early pioneers were worried about A) the winter, and B) the Indians. The Old Fort was to guard against the latter, an ironic enough beginning since it is Indians who now comprise something of a majority in unofficial Pioneer Park census counts.

A few park regulars were lying in the shade of trees yesterday next to the Union Pacific Railroad engine that was pulled onto the square years ago as an added attraction. More recently, a chain link fence was built around the engine. Attached to the fence, on the side that faces the sidewalk, is a kind of welcome-to-the-park sign that reads: "Beer and Alcoholic Beverages Prohibited."

The sign might also be considered ironic, since it is Pioneer Park that has become a refuge for consumers of beer and alcohol. Do your public drinking somewhere else in Salt Lake City and you're liable to get the "Public Intox" ticket, as it's known, which gives you a choice: either pay the police the $375 fine or spend the next six days in jail.

"This park is a place where Indians and black people, and white people, and everybody, can drink, hang out, and have a good time," said a man named Floyd who it appeared was trying to do just that yesterday afternoon. "These people don't want a ballpark here, but do you think they're going to say anything? If they put a baseball field here it will just push what's happening somewhere else. Maybe into, pardon my expression, the white man's area. Maybe Jordan Park (a dozen blocks to the southwest) will become Pioneer Park."

Floyd shrugged his shoulders. "Deedee's going to do what the —— she wants to do," he said. He looked around the park that Brigham Young built. His gaze fixed on the railroad engine.

"What I want to know is what they're going to do with that train?" he said, smiling. "It's got to be sixty tons. How they going to move that?"

The mayor hasn't said what she has in mind for the train, only that the deterioration of city-owned Derks Field suggests that a new baseball park be built somewhere else, and among the sites being considered is Pioneer Park, a place that already has grass and where the last family picnic, in the traditional sense, was held in roughly 1957, which was also about the last time a kid climbed around on the train and a real tourist read the plaque in the center of the square.

Restaurants and souvenir stands and hot dog vendors have not sprung up around the park, as might be the case around a more traditional city park. The only adjunct business is an Alcoholism Counseling and Recovery House across the street. The only new housing is a partially built apartment complex next to the Recovery House—a project stopped at the particle-board stage because the developer ran out of money.

The mayor looks at the half-done apartments and sees an Olympic ice-skating rink—the ideal next-door neighbor for the new ballpark. They could share parking. They could help create, along with the $66 million Delta Center just two blocks away, Salt Lake City's own Sports Corridor. What better use for public property than public use?

A park regular walked past, ignoring the train, ignoring questions about the future. "Can I have a quarter?" he asked. Presumably, it wasn't for the ballpark.

Life after Sports

This column, which appeared in the Deseret News *on Memorial Day, 1998, represented a kind of crossing of the Rubicon for me. For the first time, I was no longer officially a "sports writer" but a general interest columnist with a new address in the* Metro *section of the paper. I cannot lie. The shift of gears left me feeling vulnerable, suddenly facing a world without the familiar boundaries of sidelines and end lines and goalposts—and free press food—to provide a blanket of order.*

With time I would adjust, but it would be a while before I could get that old story out of my head about the two NBA players getting on the airplane at the start of a road trip and scanning the seats for any newspapers left behind by disembarking travelers. One player, so the story goes, bends over to pick up a copy of The Wall Street Journal, *while a teammate farther up the aisle shouts back, "Don't bother, somebody already got the sports."*

The Wall Street Journal, of course, doesn't have a sports section. And that's the point.

From Sports
to This

May 25, 1998

Subscribing to the theory that the best defense is a good offense, allow me to introduce Ernest Hemingway, George Plimpton, Oscar Madison, Craig Kilbourn, Kurt Vonnegut, and, of course, Ronald Reagan.

All of whom started out as sports writers and/or sportscasters, or they played one in a movie, and then moved on to other things, such as writing about the Spanish civil war, describing epic struggles landing marlin, fighting Archie Moore, dismantling the iron curtain, or hosting *Comedy Central.*

Sports writers don't die. They retire and write *Slaughterhouse Five.*

And though it's true that many sports writers never do steer their way out of the fraternity, with its endless supply of press box food, preferred parking, trips to the Masters, gifts of complimentary casual wear with logos, and constant access to millionaires who will gladly talk to you—providing the conversation begins with, "Nice game"—it is possible to voluntarily walk away from a life of sports writing if you want to. Look at Pat O'Brien.

∗ ∗ ∗ ∗ ∗

For over twenty years I wrote a newspaper sports column, regularly attending sporting events and thinking, *Wow! Not only do I get in free and sit in the expensive seats, but I get paid!*—a state of induced euphoria disrupted only by the rude awakening that after the game you can't go home until you write something acceptable about what you just saw.

All jobs have their downside. Ask Karl Malone. Ask Bill Clinton.

I spent the last four years avoiding those daily deadlines by writing books. I moved to California and collaborated on a number of book projects with a number of sports figures.

I wrote a book with LaVell Edwards; I wrote a book with Henry Marsh; I wrote a book with Peter Vidmar. I wrote two books on the Olympic Games. I liked my subjects. I got to know Rincon Point, County Line, Colorado Boulevard—places the Beach Boys sang about. I bought a surfboard and though I never did "hang ten," I did master the art of hanging my entire body off the board.

It was a good life. Pleasant working conditions, agreeable collaborators, no major earthquakes while I was there, only an occasional flood, and whenever I went to a sporting event, I left early.

I once left a Dodgers-Cubs game in the seventh inning with the score tied. Sailed out of the parking lot. Real happy.

I eventually busted loose from all-sports-all-the-time and wrote a book dealing with the sordid and practically unbelievable affair of Enid and Joe Waldholtz. This was new ground. Greed, ambition, power, and deceit. Athletes never got this carried away. I spent several months going back and forth between Washington, D.C., Salt Lake City, and Pittsburgh, scenes of the crime, and wrote a nonfiction novel I entitled *Blind Trust: The True Story of Enid Greene and Joe Waldholtz.*

The media panned *Blind Trust, and* Enid hated it. Her parents hated it. And I never heard from Joe, all of which I chose to take as a compliment and harbinger of good things to come. But the publishing business is a crap shoot, and it wasn't long before my initial high hopes for the book's commercial success sank into harsh reality.

After reading the manuscript and seriously considering playing the part of Enid in *Blind Trust—The movie,* Demi Moore (honest) reconsidered and went on to film *G.I. Jane.*

Then the distribution company representing the book went out of business just after Christmas (honest).

It was becoming apparent that *Blind Trust* was not going to supplant *Midnight in the Garden of Good and Evil* at the top of the true-crime bestsellers list.

My plans for the gated house at Rincon Point (south-west facing, in the direction of the Channel Islands, twenty paces from the blue Pacific—I had my eye on Kevin Costner's old place) had to be put on hold.

That's when the *Deseret News* called. They said they had a general column position open. They said Salt Lake was the most vibrant, exciting city in America. They said the world could be my press box. They said I could write about the Olympics if I wanted (my request). They said I could leave sports. I could do what Hemingway had done. They said they'd include health insurance.

I took the job.

It's your fault.

You should've bought more books.

In this column, I got to write about my high school, my sister, and the house I grew up in, all of which conspired to have an interesting confluence with Larry Miller and the Sandy Salt Palace. There are a lot of things I hadn't imagined would happen when I was growing up on my father's farm in Sandy. I never dreamed they'd film a movie in my house starring the Fonz, I never dreamed a version of the Salt Palace would move in one block away, and I would have bet the farm they'd never tear down Jordan High School and replace it with a 14-plex movie theater.

The
Neighborhood

S o just how much did Larry Miller, who once paid rent in the original Salt Palace, know in advance about the location of the new Salt Palace recommended to be built in Sandy, across the street, as it turns out, from Miller's new Jordan Commons development already under construction?

Calculated or just lucky? Who's to say? But with Miller, never bet against just lucky. This is a man who started out in the business world behind a parts counter, selling alternators.

Nearly twenty years ago, he went into major debt to open his first auto dealership in Murray, selling Toyotas, at a time when Toyotas weren't cool, and neither was Murray.

The Jazz weren't all that cool, for that matter, when Miller bought them from Sam Battistone for $18 million in 1985 and 1986.

How could Miller have known an NBA bull market was just around the corner and that within two years, the franchise would be worth $100 million? (Sam Battistone. Nice guy. But he went to the same buy-high-sell-low school of economics I graduated from. Sam's specialty was treating loans like income.)

Maybe Larry Miller, whose auto empire now spans six states, had no idea you'd be able to look down from the penthouse offices at his new Jordan

Commons development and see Salt Palace South, which is like moving into a new neighborhood and discovering Cindy Crawford will be living next door.

* * * * *

Besides housing business offices, Miller's new Sandy complex will be home to shops, restaurants, a 14-plex movie theater, and an IMAX theater, all of which could come in handy for any conventioneers in the area.

The complex is situated on the block where the old Jordan High School once stood. I have a close personal connection to the area, since I graduated from the old Jordan High and grew up just across the street, where my Grandfather Adolph settled after arriving from Sweden. (I *know* Adolph had no idea the Salt Palace might be coming.)

I personally like the thought that they'll be showing movies on the site of my old high school all day every day—just the same as Mr. Milne used to do in American History class.

The new Jordan High was finished two years ago, about a mile to the south, seriously numbering the days of the old Jordan High, which was built in 1914.

The old building went out proud, however. Just before the demolition team moved in, ABC did a television movie there. Perhaps you saw *Seige at Johnson High*. It was filmed on site, and it starred Henry Winkler, the Fonz, who played a bungling sheriff who rises to the occasion, and Rick Schroder, who played a disturbed high school student who takes his classmates hostage at rifle-point.

They filmed Schroder's down-and-out home life in the basement of the house across the street—the very house my dad built and that I grew up in. Schroder flips out in the basement—eerie, I think, since the same thing happened to my brother while we lived there.

* * * * *

I'm not terribly emotional over the changes in my old neighborhood. But my sister, Karen, is. She still lives there, in a house on the lot next to our old family house, with her husband, my brother-in-law, Joe.

Karen cried when the wrecking balls arrived to level the old Jordan High. She cried when Larry Miller announced plans for the 14-plex—and she likes movies. (Karen could out-cry Larry Miller, I'd bet on it.) To make herself feel better, she bought about a hundred throw rugs with a likeness of the old school on them and sent one to everybody in the family.

She and Joe aren't too sure about the new neighbors who are about to move in. For my sister and her husband, the good old days are when the kids used to drag race on the street outside their house and sneak out of third period and smoke cigarettes.

They've had several peace-making meetings with the Miller group, and Larry has been good to them. He sent Karen and Joe, and all the neighbors on 9270 South, gift certificates for an overnight stay at the Cottontree Inn and free lube jobs. Nice. But they were really looking to get free playoff tickets and Toyotas.

The Salt Palace on one side. My sister, Karen, on the other. As far as I'm concerned, Larry Miller lucked out twice.

Ever since I can remember, people have been coming up to me as though we're long-lost friends—and I don't have a clue who they are. Without even trying, I know my twin brother and I have managed to snub more people than we can imagine, or would care to know. But we have used our close resemblance to our advantage on numerous occasions. One of the most memorable was when I covered my first Olympics Games in 1984 in Los Angeles. Not long after arriving in L.A., I phoned my brother, who lived in Washington, D.C. at the time. I told him they'd given me a press credential that gave me access to every Olympic event, and since there was no way I could possibly get to all of them, he might as well come out and spell me off. There was only one other person on earth who could use my photo pass. Him. And he didn't have to write any columns.

Twins

I was at einstein bros. on Main Street, having just ordered a cinnamon-sugar bagel, when I noticed the two DEA agents sizing me up.

"How's it going?" they asked, innocent-like, as if we were good friends. I'd never seen them before in my life.

"Who are you guys with?" I asked, buying time.

"Drug Enforcement," they answered, like I should know, and I began searching my past for possible felonies.

* * * * *

So I have this problem.

Sometimes I am not me. Sometimes I am my brother.

My brother is a federal judge. Before that, he was a U.S. Attorney. Before that he worked for the Justice Department. He knows DEA agents, and FBI agents, and CIA agents, and federal marshalls, and federal prosecutors. He once shook hands with George Bush—when George Bush appointed him to the bench. He is on a first-name basis with Ron Yengich.

It's a good crowd to know. But it's a crowd he knows. I don't.

The problem is, we look alike. We are identical twins. If O.J. had been us, he could have cut those DNA odds in half.

We don't look *that* much alike, if you ask us. But to the world we are Hayley Mills in the *Parent Trap*. Especially if you don't see us together, which you usually don't, on account of our different professions.

You might have thought we'd wind up in twin professions, and we might have, if not for the fact that we went to college and picked majors using a method later made popular by Forrest Gump.

I wound up a writer because *journalism* came alphabetically after *economics*. My brother wound up in law because after graduating with a teaching certificate he made the mistake of actually showing up for his student teaching assignment at Hillcrest High School.

He didn't know much, but he knew he didn't want to teach high school. After Hillcrest, taking the LSAT looked fun. He sold his MG roadster and went to law school. Now he has a staff of clerks, a secretary named Charity (apt, I think), a courtroom on the second floor of the Frank E. Moss Courthouse—and associations with many people around town who think because they know him, they know me.

* * * * *

The duplicity has, on occasion, come in handy. One time, during college, my brother had a scheduling conflict with an intramural Ping-Pong tournament and a ballroom dance class. Being a twin, he was able to do both. I went to the first half of the dance class, and he played his Ping-Pong match. At intermission of the class we met in the bathroom and changed shirts. Back on the floor, his dance partner wondered why he was no longer mangling her feet.

It works both ways. These days, I sometimes go down to the courthouse and roam the halls just to enjoy the deference.

"Good morning, Your Honor," people will say. And, "How are you, Your Honor?" And "How about a cold beverage, Your Honor?" And, my personal favorite, "You're looking extra sharp today, Your Honor."

Still, for the most part, looking alike can be an aggravation.

I remember the time, several years ago, when my brother's first two daughters, Angie and Natalie, were very young, and I was accompanying them to Salt Lake on a flight from New York. During the flight, I got to know the flight attendant working our part of the cabin. I made a point of telling her that I was not married and that the little girls were my nieces.

At which point, Natalie, the two-year-old, looked up at me and said, "When are we going to get there, Daddy?"

I looked up at the flight attendant.

"Uh," I said, "their father is my identical twin brother."

She didn't buy it any more than those DEA agents had.

For a while, I was literally on the outside looking in as the second NBA Finals in city history dawned on Salt Lake City. Once we'd negotiated our transaction, our seats turned out to be way up there. It is absolutely true that when they lowered the Western Conference championship banner from the ceiling, it was at eye level.

Finals without a Pass

June 5, 1998

I got my first rejection notice just after four in the afternoon, three hours from the beginning of Game One of the NBA Finals.

The man in the "Beverly Hills Polo Club" T-shirt didn't say anything, just got a look of disdain on his face and turned away.

I had offered him $100 a piece for two upper bowl tickets.

I took his departure as an indication we did not have ourselves a deal.

* * * * *

A year ago, I was a card-carrying member of the the sports media, and it wasn't like this. When the Finals began, I walked through the front door of the Delta Center and let them buy me dinner. I had credentials. I had a good seat. I had free run of the arena. When Karl Malone gunned his Harley through the halls, I got to jump out of the way.

For Jazz-Bulls II, I was not so well-connected. I would not be covering the game. I felt like Sarah Ferguson after the divorce.

But some places you should just be. The opening of the NBA Finals in your home town is one of them.

I devised a simple plan. It consisted of, first, stopping at the ATM machine, and, second, buying scalpers' tickets.

I knew $100 for a seat, even a bad seat, was on the low end of the low end. But a hundred a seat was what I had.

* * * * *

There is a scalpers' corridor that flanks the Delta Center, running between South Temple and Pioneer Park. To get into a sold-out game, this is the gauntlet you must run.

Heads down, my son Eric—a U of U student who contributed exactly nothing to finance the venture—and I weaved through the masses. Our first loop produced nothing. Second loop, same thing.

Two hours before tipoff, we watched as the Bulls team bus arrived. About two hundred people had camped out, waiting for this event. In my former life of privilege, I couldn't understand these people. Now I could. Catching a glimpse was free.

We stood in line at the KSL Radio booth for a free beef shishkabob, compliments of the Utah Beef Council. In front of us in line was a ticket scalper who moments earlier had offered us two lower bowl seats for $650. Each.

* * * * *

An hour to tipoff, and prices are going UP! Tickets that were $200 are now $250. Good seats that were $500 are now $700. And rain clouds are brewing.

But not everyone is a bloodthirsty capitalist. A lady offers me two excellent seats, "seventeen rows behind the Bulls bench," for $400 each. Relatively speaking, a going-out-of-business type bargain.

"I just got divorced, and I don't want to sit by my ex," the woman explains.

Hopes rising, I offer her my $100 each.

"Geez," she says, "I don't dislike him that much."

To let the seller's market time pass, we accept a complimentary Haagen Dazs mango sherbet cone outside the Eyndham Hotel. Twenty minutes later, we are back on the street for one last push.

Salvation comes at 6:54 P.M., in the form of a man with so many tickets and so little time.

"I'll sell you these for $100 each . . . they're not bad," he says.

Tax was included.

* * * * *

The seats were on row 20. In the upper tier. Of the upper bowl.

We spent the game feeling sorry for the poor schmucks sitting in rows 21 and 22—the only rows higher than ours.

You may have seen us. Before the game, when they unfurled the Western Conference title banner from the rafters, we were directly behind it.

We were so high, we were surrounded by Bulls fans.

Three hours later, with Tim McGraw singing, "I like it, I love it, I want some more of it," we exited the Delta Center. We got a whole game, plus an overtime, plus a slice of history, for our money. And a Jazz win. As we stepped outside, it was raining. Scalpers' Corridor was empty. Game Two was forty-eight hours away. All in all, a triumphant evening.

I got more mail on this column than any column I ever wrote in sports. Why, I'm not sure. Must have something to do with religion.

The Baptists

ne 8, 1998

And a big Salt Lake City welcome to the Southern Baptists, here for your national convention. Excellent choice.

Expressing what I trust reflects the sentiment of the entire citizenry, let me say what a pleasure it is to have you here, and add that you have already made history—the first major convention ever to come to Salt Lake and not complain about the liquor laws.

Interesting that your stay coincides with the NBA Finals, meaning you've been sharing hotel space these past few days—smack in the middle of "witnessing weekend," as it's turned out—with members of the nation's sporting press.

Having been a sports writer in an earlier life, I am well aware of the contrast between the two groups. The sports media thinks Bourbon Street is on the conservative side.

I know it helped that the writers were coming back to their rooms when you were getting up.

But that guy with the purple and green hair commuting back and forth from Las Vegas was not a sports writer. That was Dennis Rodman, a.k.a. "The Worm," who belongs to a sect or a cult called the Chicago Bulls.

Witnessing alternately to Mormons, sports writers, and Dennis Rodman. By the time you get back home, you will sure have some stories to tell. Where might it have been tougher? Mecca? Baghdad? Vatican City?

* * * * *

In the wake of what happened at the big Southern Baptist convention last year in Dallas, everyone is especially interested in this year's activities, wondering if there will be any further bombshells along the lines of boycotting Disneyland.

Religious conventions aren't usually noted for grabbing front-page headlines, but you changed all that in Dallas when, after announcing the winners of the elections, and the new organ for the congregation in Augusta, Georgia, and all the other usual business, you cleared your throat and said, as meekly as possible, "Down with Disney."

The Disney Company's friendly attitude toward gays and lesbians, including giving the green light to ABC to produce *Ellen,* had, in your opinion, gone too far. By way of protest, nothing less than an outright boycott was deemed strong enough.

That was news!

To Disney, it meant fifteen million fewer customers. To the rest of us, it meant fifteen million fewer people in line to ride Indiana Jones, Temple of the Forbidden Eye.

Things for a Baptist to avoid: barrooms, brothels, betting parlors, Big Thunder Railroad.

So now we're wondering, what's next? Hawaii? The entire state of California? Wendover? Pearl Jam?

By the way, while you're here, you may want to visit Lagoon, our local amusement park. Lagoon does not, to anyone's knowledge, endorse the production of any TV sitcoms with alternate lifestyle themes, and it has a roller-coaster called Colossus that favors those who ride sober.

* * * * *

Being, for the most part, populated by Christians, no one around here will be surprised by any old-fashioned Southern Baptist missionary zeal.

"Spreading the word," and "adding to the fold" are as common to all Christianity as turning the other cheek and arguing about the trinity.

Each Christian church has its own approach to adding growth. The Catholic Church, with a membership of more than one billion, gets by fine primarily on birth-rate and inter-marrying alone, whereas organizations such as yours, with a membership of fifteen million-plus, as well as the predominant local church, the "Mormons," with ten million-plus, opt for the more aggressive approach of utilizing missionaries and toll-free 800 numbers.

According to preconvention scuttlebutt, it appears that one of the major objectives of this week's convention will be to launch a campaign ensuring that "every person in the world shall have the opportunity to hear the gospel of Christ by the year 2000," and that half a million people will be baptized Baptists in the millennial year.

Lofty goals, to be sure. Roger Williams would approve. But, still, it will be nice if the convention is able to come up with something even more dramatic—more newsworthy, more man-bites-dog. Some religious news to put Salt Lake on the map.

Index

Stanley, Bob, 50
Stant, Stanley, 178
Stern, Andrew, 102
Stern, David, 12–13, 22, 102–4, 129
Stobart, Chuck, 202
Stockton, John: drafting of, 12–13, 248; as NBA All-Star MVP, 21–23; on Dream Team 1992, 61–62; plays against Chicago in Finals, 65
Storm, Hannah, 225–27
Strange, Curtis, 84
Stuhlreher, (one of the Four Horsemen of Notre Dame), 147
Stump, Al, 222–23
Sumitomo Trust (bank), 19
Super Bowl: XIII, 77, 79; XX, 45–47; XXV, 228
Sweeney, Walt, 234–36

Tate, Richard, 167
Taylor, Jim, 59–60
Team USA 1992 (Olympic basketball), 61–63
Tenney, Bonnie, 192
Tesch, John, 180
Thompson, John, 52
Thorpe, Jim, 255–58
Throneberry, Marv, 152
Thurmond, Nate, 144
Tiger, Dick, 116
Tournament of Africa (basketball), 93
Trevino, Lee, 138
Triad Center, 19
Trueblood, Thomas, 252
Tucker, Della, 119
Tucker, George Jr. 119
Tucker, George, 119
Tucker, Karl, 119–21
Tucker, Monroe (Toby), 119–20
Tucker, Ray, 119–20
Tucker, Wayne, 119–20
Tuckett, Dave, 194
Tuckett, Glen, 120
Turner, Kim, 226
Tyson, Mike, 237–39

U. S. Open Golf Championship, 39, 141–42
UCLA, 154–56
Utah Jazz: draft Mailman, 12–14; host NBA Finals, 30–32; vs. Bulls 1997, 64–66; vs. Bulls 1998, 296–98; worth of, 96–98;

under Frank Layden, 105–7; come to Utah, 127–29; play Celtics, 143–45
Utah Stars (ABA), 123
Utah State Class 4-A games, 45
Utah, University of: football, 46, 174–76, 201–3; basketball, 191–97, 245–47

Valvano, Jim, 244
Vidmar, Peter, 288
Villanova University, 42–44, 243
Virginia Commonwealth, 43
Visser, Leslie, 225, 227

Walcott, Jersey Joe, 116
Waldholtz, Enid and Joe, 288
Walton, Bill, 208, 243, 248
Warhurst, Ron, 163
Washington Redskins, 204–6
Washington, Kenny, 248
Waterfield, Bob, 115
Watson, Tom, 138
Watts, Stan, 231
Weber State University, 85–87
Welch, Tom, 217
West High School, 45, 47
West, Jerry, 243
Westphal, Paul, 208
Whiddon, Derek, 176
Wilbur, Dwight, 43
Wilkens, Lenny, 62
Wilson, Mookie, 48, 50
Wilson, Ted, 128
Wimbledon, 138–40
Winkler, Henry, 291
Wintermute, Slim, 245
Witt, Katarina, 178
Wooden, John, 106, 243, 248–49
Wooden, Nell, 248
Woods, Tiger, 74
World Series of Golf, 74
World Series: 1984, 40–41; 1986, 48–50; 1989, 171–73
Worthy, James, 243

Yergensen, Chris, 174–76
Young, Steve, 28, 30, 99–101
Young-Sook, Yun, 55
Youngblood, Kendall, 87

Zale, Tony, 116
Zhelezovsky, Igor, 182